T0305100

Technical Progress and Economic Growth

Technical Progress and Economic Growth

An Empirical Case Study of Malaysia

Ranald J. Taylor

Economics Faculty Member, Murdoch Business School, and Research Fellow, Asia Research Centre, Murdoch University, Australia

Edward Elgar
Cheltenham, UK • Northampton, MA, USA

Published by
Edward Elgar Publishing Limited
Glensanda House
Montpellier Parade
Cheltenham
Glos GL50 1UA
UK

Edward Elgar Publishing, Inc.
William Pratt House
9 Dewey Court
Northampton
Massachusetts 01060
USA

A catalogue record for this book
is available from the British Library

Library of Congress Cataloguing in Publication Data

Taylor, Ranald J., 1962-
  Technical progress and economic growth : an empirical case study of Malaysia / Ranald J. Taylor.
     p. cm.
  Includes bibliographical references and index.
1. Malaysia—Economic conditions. 2. Malaysia—Economic policy. 3. Manufacturing industries—Malaysia. 4. Human capital—Malaysia. 5. Malaysia—Commerce. I. Title.
  HC445.5.T39 2007
  338.9595—dc22

                                                      2007029859

ISBN   978 1 84720 583 4

Printed and bound in Great Britain by MPG Books Ltd, Bodmin, Cornwall

Contents

Foreword

I am delighted to write a Foreword to Ranald Taylor's fine volume on technical progress and economic growth in which he uses Malaysia to illustrate his case study approach. The volume originated in Taylor's PhD dissertation of which I was an examiner. I was impressed then (and am even more so now) by his open-mindedness, seriousness of purpose and ability to adapt ideas and insights from many different, sometimes conflicting, approaches into relevant, useful and convincing structures of his own. It is pleasing to see how well he has absorbed the huge literature on his topic in order to produce carefully analysed narratives of modern Malaysian experience with regard to its development over a long historical period.

Taylor's book is political economy in the best sense. First of all, he emphasises how important the stability or instability of social and political structures are for understanding why growth takes off in the first place and then is or is not sustained. Secondly, he very early on escapes from a fundamental weakness of the early pioneers of modern growth theory, their failure to realize (or at least introduce in their models) that potential growth is ultimately bound up with the actual growth process now, because new ideas are embodied through investment in the stock of capital goods, with crucial implications for growth overall, and of productivity in the future. Thirdly, he is well aware of the interconnections between sections of the economy and their implications for the growth process, drawing on the insights of past giants of our profession, Adam Smith, Allyn Young, Nicholas Kaldor, Trevor Swan, for example, as well as on those of current leaders, Kenneth Arrow, Robert Solow, for example. Fourthly, he intermingles his careful empirical and historical work with his theoretical structures and conducts careful statistical analysis in order to get a feel on the orders of magnitude on the values of the key parameters in his theoretical specifications.

Finally, his narratives include evaluations of the effects of past policies and suggestions for future research culminating in further relevant policies. Altogether, Taylor's volume provides a role model for how serious research should be done on pressing vital, real-world problems especially those of developing countries.

G.C. Harcourt
Jesus College
Cambridge
January 2007

Preface

Studies on the growth of developing countries have not paralleled those of developed countries primarily because of the lack of reliable data and differences in institutional peculiarities. These factors in turn render the traditional analytical tools inappropriate for examining the economic growth of developing countries. The recent expansion of the endogenous growth paradigm has, to some extent, addressed this need for better tools for analysing the growth of developing countries. Unfortunately, these 'new' theories have grown largely independent of or in isolation from empirical findings. It is the purpose of this book to bridge the gap between theories and facts by using Malaysia as a case-study.

This case-study of Malaysia aims to test and explain economic growth, paying particular attention to the evolution of the production structure, productivity growth and technical progress. Since growth is a dynamic and complex process and is based on the interplay between exogenous elements (such as sociological and political factors) and endogenous elements (such as the evolution of productivity and technological progress), this book's analytical framework is drawn from a combination of historical, neoclassical and endogenous perspectives. In order to shed further light on the growth process, this book attempts to trace the whole growth path and not just the steady state, which most cross-sectional growth analyses tend to focus upon (Solow, 2000).

The examination of Malaysia's economic growth involves three stages. The first stage examines the importance of initial conditions in economic growth. A historical perspective will be utilized for this purpose because the counterfactual cannot be tested. There is also an emerging literature emphasizing the incorporation of historical facts into the growth analysis (Solow, 1994; Nelson, 1996; Crafts, 1997; Setterfield, 1998; Lucas, 2000). The second stage employs an endogenous framework based on Kaldor's technical progress function and growth propositions to trace the evolution of Malaysia's production structure and employment patterns with respect to output growth.

The final stage involves the evolution of technological progress as captured by total factor productivity (TFP) growth. Most of the TFP estimations on East Asian countries, including that on Malaysia, have been based on either the standard Cobb–Douglas production function or the growth accounting approach. The method presented in this book departs from them.

Here, human capital and international trade are allowed to impact upon the coefficient of the capital share of output. The logic is that the value of the coefficient of capital will be lowered due to improvement in labour quality brought about by learning-by-doing, and technological progress embodied in foreign equipment made possible through international trade. The results show that the coefficient of capital share declined and the coefficient of labour increased when compared to the standard production function. This is in turn translated into higher TFP. An important policy implication of these findings is that a weak R&D or knowledge base does not necessarily translate into lower economic growth as postulated by the recent expansion of the endogenous growth paradigm. Instead, the Malaysian experience has demonstrated that opening the economy up to the global communities could accelerate a country's TFP growth through learning-by-doing activities brought about by new technology embodied in new foreign capital equipment.

This book was made possible with the unfailing support and understanding of the people who are dearest to me, my family: Jeannette, our two children, Alanna and Saul, and my in-laws and parents. I am very grateful to Jeannette who provided useful comments on various drafts of this book. I would further like to add that it is only right to dedicate this book to Alanna and Saul. It is this younger generation that stands to gain most from the benefits of sustained prosperity once we see and act on the urgency of eradicating chronic poverty in developing countries.

I owe a special debt of gratitude to two remarkable economists: Ray Petridis and Geoff Harcourt. They provided me with wise, kind and tireless guidance on this book. I appreciate the meticulous care and monumental effort Ray put into reading innumerable drafts. It was Ray who rekindled my interests in economics. Geoff introduced me to the captivating works of Kaldor, Mirrlees and Salter; they played a crucial role in shaping my thoughts on growth analysis. It was also Geoff's works which taught me to appreciate the splendours of Keynesian economics. Through their enthusiasm and extensive intellectual and analytical capacities, my views on economics have been profoundly transformed.

The development of this book has also benefited from the helpful comments provided on some of the chapters from others. For that, I would like to thank Malcolm Tull, Paul Flatau and Phil Lewis. I alone am responsible for the shortcomings and views expressed in this book.

1. Introduction

Income disparities, and therefore living standards, between the developed and developing countries have widened considerably, yielding a ratio of 60:1 in the 1990s (United Nations, 1997). There is little sign that this trend will reverse in the near future. According to the World Bank (1997), only 26 out of 133 countries shared a per capita annual income above US$9400 in 1995. Per capita annual income for the poorest 56 countries was less than US$980, with Mozambique at the bottom of the scale at US$80. Even with the most optimistic estimates, the prospect for many developing countries is not encouraging. At best, based on a growth rate of per capita income of 2 to 3 per cent per annum, it will take more than 100 years for many developing countries to catch up with the current per capita income of the OECD countries. Are the benefits associated with high living standards found only in the advanced economies? Is there anything that the governments in developing countries can do to improve their citizens' living standards?

In the last 40 years of the last millennium, a small group of initially poor, economically and technologically backward countries in East Asia managed to break away from this persistent trend. Japan, Korea, Taiwan, Hong Kong and Singapore experienced a fourfold increase of per capita income over a 35-year period compared to the 80 years or more that it took the United Kingdom (UK), United States of America (US), France and Germany to achieve the same percentage increase (Nelson and Pack, 1999). In fact, the growth performance in these countries not only exceeded those with comparable income levels in 1960 but outperformed virtually all the countries in the world, with the exception of those countries that are rich with precious metals such as Botswana (World Bank, 1993; Nelson and Pack, 1999). The World Bank (1993) heralded the success of these countries as a miracle.

In terms of per capita income, Hong Kong, Singapore, Korea, Japan and Taiwan have joined the ranks of the developed economies, with Malaysia and Thailand following behind. These countries' annual growth averaged more than 8 per cent between 1979 and 1998 (Institute of South East Asian Studies, 1999). During the period 1980–95, Malaysia, Singapore and Thailand more than doubled their real income per person compared to the US with an increase of only 20 per cent, and even less when compared to other industrialized countries and many other regions of the world (Sarel, 1997). This led Rowan (1998, p. 1) to comment that 'their record of development is so exceptional, not only in comparison to other developing regions but in world history'. While the 1997 financial crisis may to some extent have discredited the Asian miracle, nevertheless the East Asia countries' leap from poverty and economic and technological backwardness over a period of less than 40 years has been something of a miracle (Nelson and Pack, 1999).

Why have only a small group of countries managed to develop and grow at such a rapid pace while most of the developing countries around the world have either stagnated or gone further backward? The last 30 years saw an upsurge in the literature that focused on explaining the growth experiences of these newly industrialized East Asia countries. The neoclassical growth framework became the most widely used method of analysing their growth performance. Technological progress or total factor productivity (TFP), a proxy for the Solow residuals, has been the key focus in analysing the growth process of East Asia. To a large extent, the huge desire to find the determinants of economic growth in this part of the world spearheaded the renewed interest in growth theory after it had 'tailed off as a research topic ... in the 1970s' (Solow, 2000, p. 97). The neoclassical growth model has not enjoyed this much recognition since its introduction in 1956.

A motive for many of these studies is that once they have found the key determinants in driving the East Asia growth miracle, they can then be applied to poor and technologically backward economies. Subsequently, it might lead to a narrowing of the 'development gap' over time, and with this comes the convergence of income, and hence, a less divided world. Some 30 years later (after vigorous debate in many books, journal articles, academic conferences and the popular press), the picture that has emerged is a world of even greater disparities. By 2000, the number of poor countries falling further backward had continued to increase at a rapid pace. The poor countries have become poorer while the rich countries have grown richer in a manner never before witnessed. Why is this so? Does this mean that the neoclassical model is no longer relevant in explaining growth? Or are the growth experiences of the East Asia countries so unique that few lessons can be drawn from them? Moreover, the benefits of globalization are thought to be more promising for alleviating poverty. Yet, in the new millennium, despite the fact that economic activities, social, cultural and political ideologies, and technological progress have been evolving on a global framework, the number of people living in abject poverty has continued to increase at a rapid rate. Does the reality of globalization fall short of its promises?

The initial aim of this book is to provide some pragmatic solutions to the alleviation of poverty. This is most important because poverty is not only the root to human misery; it has also on many occasions generated havoc in social, political and economic institutions. History continuously reminds us that poor people are more ready to seek alternative paradigms that offer some hope in which they can escape their miseries caused by poverty. The French Revolution, the Russian Revolution, and the Mao Revolution were all brought about by the poor masses embracing what were then new paradigms. As John Galbraith (1994, p. 260) rightfully pointed out:

> The modern advanced economy is peaceful partly because, as has been sufficiently noted, its more fortunate people have something to lose. The rich or the merely affluent, facing, along with the camel, the eye of that biblical needle, do not take readily to the risk from personal demise. The poor are more willing or have no choice.

There is also the view that largely attributes the recent Islamic terrorism with poverty. If we accept this view, and wish to find solutions which will bring an end to global Islamic terrorism, then solving the poverty problem should be our highest priority.

The objective of this book is to provide an alternative perspective to shed further light on the growth process. It employs a blend of historical, empirical and theoretical techniques of analysis. The justifications for integrating historical, neoclassical, Kaldorian and endogenous growth frameworks are discussed throughout the book.[1] In doing so, it hopes to provide some answers to one of the hardest and deepest questions: how do we get developing countries on the path to sustained growth?

The subject of economic growth is so complex and enormous that it is impossible to do more than make a few observations in a small book. In order to keep the book manageable, the focus will be on the evolution of production structures, technical progress and productivity growth. These are the areas associated with faster economic growth. This enquiry into the growth process takes the view that an economy is a dynamic system, in that economic growth starts with political stability (stage 1), evolution of the production structures (stage 2) and technological advancement (stage 3). Each of these stages is important, all the more so as they are interrelated. For instance, the disruptions to the evolution of the production structure (stage 2) brought about by political instability (stage 1) could hamper the rate and speed of the transition from an agricultural to modern industrial production structure. This in turn would profoundly impact upon stage 3 by slowing the accumulation and diffusion of new technology into the production process.

Neoclassical growth analysis and most of endogenous growth analysis often do not take into account initial conditions. Instead, they tend to concentrate on the construction of a market structure in order to enable technological progress to grow without bounds. This is a satisfactory approach in analysing advanced industrialized economies where political and social structures are taken for granted. The situation is, however, different in many developing economies where political, social and economic structures are either evolving in various development stages or are in constant turmoil. The significance of political factors, for instance, has been widely documented (Lipset, 1959; Friedman, 1962; Campos and Root, 1996; Barro,

1997, 1999). This does not imply that a causal relationship exists between political freedom and economic growth, as argued by Lipset (1959) and Friedman (1962), but rather that a stable environment is needed for resources to be allocated more efficiently.

A historical perspective will be utilized to analyse the impact of initial conditions on the growth process. According to Temple (1998, p. 11), 'Statistical research on growth seems rather cruder and less informative than historical case studies. Certainly it is important to remember that growth regressions will never offer a complete account of the growth process, and that historical analysis must have an important complementary role.' As Nelson (1996, p. 6) notes:

> Only a small portion of what empirical researchers have learned about economic growth, however, has been described in the form of 'numbers'. Put another way, the quantitative record of growth contained in gross national product statistics, time series of national labor and capital inputs, industry output and input series, numerical price indices, trade flows, and the like accounts for only a relatively small portion of what economists know empirically about growth. And while it is important that growth theories square with the quantitative record, that alone is not an adequate check of a theory. I would like to argue that economists doing formal growth theory had, for the most part, paid far too little attention to the qualitative historical record.

Furthermore, the strong divergence pattern between the developed and developing economies suggests that the explanation may lie elsewhere and is likely 'to be found in the writings of the economic historians, the social and political analysts, and even the "casual observers"' (Valdés, 1999, p. 73).

A CASE-STUDY APPROACH

Malaysia is taken as a case-study. Why a case-study approach? According to Solow (1994, p. 53) 'the best candidate for a research agenda (on economic growth) right now would be an attempt to extend a few workable hypotheses from the variegated mass of case studies'. An obvious limitation of grouping several countries together is that country-specific differences cannot be identified among the developing countries. For instance, initial conditions in the form of socio-economic characteristics could differ among developing countries, which could lead to substantial conceptual and statistical problems hindering cross-country investigations. Levin and Zervos (1993, p. 426) argued that:

> Statistically, entries are sometimes measured inconsistently and inaccurately, and almost without exception, a person with detailed knowledge of a country can quickly identify contradictions between readily available data and what actually

happened in that country. Even putting measurement difficulties aside, it is not clear that we should include vastly different countries in the same regression. Regression analysis presupposes that observations are drawn from a distinct population, but as argued by Arnold Harberger (1987), Thailand, the Dominican Republic, Zimbabwe, Greece, and Bolivia may have little in common that merits their being put in the same regression. Thus, the statistical basis upon which we draw inferences from cross-country analyses may be in doubt.

This view is supported by Crafts (1997), who argued that despite the recent expansion in empirical research based on international cross-sections, relatively little research had been done to examine the implications of endogenous growth utilizing time-series data. He stated that: 'Empirical growth economics has relied thus far rather heavily on regression analysis of international cross-sections drawn from the recent past. This has been useful but lacks the perspective that can be gained from a long-run vantage point which takes into account the changing socio-economic environment' (p. 68).

There are also problems of heterogeneity associated with parameters which vary across countries that could render the estimates inconsistent (Levine and Renelt, 1992; Quah, 1993, 1997). The primary aim of conducting a cross-country analysis is to provide generalizations about economic growth through averages. However, there is a high likelihood that average estimations may be inconsistent (even when the length of time series tends to infinity) due to parameter heterogeneity associated with the regressors. Quah (1993) pointed out that estimation of growth rates from a cross-section regression is inappropriate because growth performance differs widely across countries.

Similarly, Levine and Renelt (1992) indicated that cross-country regression of growth rates on a variety of determinants are sensitive to the choice of countries, the period covered, and the selection of variables for the regression analysis. Taking these limitations into consideration, it appears that the convergence postulate of the neoclassical growth framework may not be robust. In fact, empirical evidence (Maddison, 1982; Baumol, 1986; Barro and Sala-i-Martin 1991, 1992; Mankiw et al., 1992) of a convergence in per capita income between poorer economies and richer economies at a fairly uniform rate of around 2 per cent per year has been challenged by several authors (Romer, 1986; De Long, 1988; Grossman and Helpman, 1991; Quah, 1993, 1996a, 1996b; Pritchett, 1997; Durlauf and Johnson, 1995; Jones, 1997) based on the limitations indicated earlier. This view is also reinforced by Solow (2000, p. 124)[2] who argued that:

There has been an explosion of work on using international time series and cross-sections to test the implications of the standard growth model against data. The occasion for this style of empirical work is primarily the availability of valid data. Summers and Heston (1991) have produced, as best they can, comparable National Accounts for something like 120 different countries. These have been used to study the empirical correlates of growth rates and the facts of convergence and divergence among groups of national economies. One conclusion from all these cross-section studies is that most results are not very robust.

Perhaps Pack (1994, p. 66) is correct when he asserts that:

> Regardless of whether one is using a neoclassical or endogenous growth approach, it thus seems necessary to examine one country at a time, insofar as there is no identical international production function along which changes in capital exert their effect.

For this study, Malaysia is taken as a case-study for several reasons. First, although the characteristics and structure of the Malaysian economy may not be homogenous, it shares several characteristics with many developing economies. As Snodgrass (1980, p. 5) commented some two and a half decades ago: 'Malaysia, is, I think, a good case to study because it has much in common with a significant group of poor countries yet it is in some important respects a polar case, in which widespread problems and possibilities appear with particular vividness and urgency.' As with many developing countries, Malaysia was once a colony and accordingly inherited Western political and economic institutions. Malaysia also inherited complex social and political conditions which in many instances, particularly during the initial stages of economic development, had acted as barriers which slowed the pace of economic development. Together with the multiracial composition of its society and the uneven distribution of economic wealth among the different ethnic groups, Malaysia has experienced many racial conflicts in its modern economic development. This alone justifies the need to include initial conditions in the analysis of the economic growth of Malaysia.

Malaysia is experiencing rapid modernization of its production structure with manufacturing as the engine of economic growth. This modernization process has led to rapid output growth after political independence in 1957. During the period 1963–2005, real GDP growth averaged above 6 per cent per year. During the 1970s, per capita income in Malaysia grew at an annual rate of 7 per cent, and by the late 1980s, per capita income was above US$2 000, which placed Malaysia well above many developing economies during that period. By 1993, Malaysia's GDP per capita had risen to around US$3 000 compared to Thailand's US$1 780, Indonesia's US$635, the Philippines' US$692, China's US$490, India's US$290, and Vietnam's US$170 (Institute of Southeast Asian Studies, 1997; Malaysia, 1996). This figure increased to US$5 005, US$2 577, US$1 259, US$1 159, US$1 703, US$714 and US$612 for the respective countries in 2004 (Ministry of Finance, Malaysia, 2005).

Economic restructuring saw a decline in the agricultural sector as the main contributor to Malaysia's GDP, and by the early 1990s, the manufacturing sector had supplanted the agricultural sector.[3] Although Malaysia is still the world's largest exporter of tin, rubber and palm oil, as well as a significant producer of oil, natural gas and timber, it has now become one of the world's largest manufacturers of semiconductors, and a sizeable producer of electronic and electrical products and textiles. Since the mid-1980s, Malaysia's industrial sector has become the nation's engine of growth. In 1997, for example, export trade in manufactured goods and machinery, electronics and transport equipment accounted for 70.2 per cent of GDP (Ministry of Finance, Malaysia, 1998). At the same time, the manufacturing sector has become the dominant employment sector. The contribution to employment from the manufacturing sector was 7.4 per cent in 1957, 26.2 per cent in 1995 and 27.1 per cent in 1997 (Malaysia, 1996; Malaysia, 2001). As a result of the rapid economic development, the incidence of poverty declined significantly from 49 per cent in 1970 to less than 9 per cent in 1999 (Malaysia, 2001). By tracing Malaysia's modernization experience, we may be able to suggest reasons for the large disparity in income among different countries in the world, and understand why a large number of the world's populations are living in a state of chronic poverty.

The bulk of studies on economic development in East Asia have focused on Japan, Hong Kong, Korea, Singapore, China, Taiwan and Indonesia. Very little has been written about the economic development of Malaysia.[4] Most of the published works on Malaysia cover the period between the 1930s and the 1980s. This is the first attempt to provide a comprehensive economic analysis based on the integrations of various theoretical techniques to trace the growth experience of Malaysia. The inclusion of education (proxy for human capital) and openness (international trade) into the analysis of productivity and economic growth, based on a cointegration approach, is also a first for Malaysia.

Lastly, despite the fact that the Malaysian economy is based on a 'free market system' the state has played an active part in its economic development, particularly in the stabilization of initial conditions in the form of political instability and the deterioration in the terms of trade during the initial stages of development. Initial conditions can affect the development of capital and labour in several ways. Political instability may explain why capital does not flow from rich countries to poor countries as predicted by the neoclassical growth framework; it would be too risky for such investments in an unstable political climate. Political instability may also affect the accumulation of human capital which is crucial to long-run growth in the endogenous paradigm. A regime that constrains the flows of trade may also hinder foreign investments and the efficient allocation and distribution of resources. Thus, by using Malaysia as a case-study, an alternative perspective is provided for understanding the significance of the role of the state in achieving more rapid economic development.

Within the book, Chapters 2 and 3 provide the theoretical basis for the examination of economic growth for Malaysia from 1963 to 1998. Chapter 2 presents a brief overview of the neoclassical growth models, followed by a discussion of some of their limitations and a brief survey of total factor productivity (TFP) and economic growth in the East Asian economies. Chapter 3 provides a brief coverage of the new growth models that have arisen recently to augment the Solow growth model. Chapter 4 gives a background for economic analysis and an examination of the impact of initial conditions in the form of political instability and external trade. As the transition to a mature economy is often associated with the expansion of the manufacturing sector, Chapter 5 evaluates the role of the state in the development of the Malaysian industrial structure. Chapter 6 presents an overview of the Malaysian labour market and its role in economic development. The findings from Chapters 5 and 6 are utilized in Chapter 7 to trace Malaysia's growth experience based on Kaldor's three propositions of economic growth.

There has been a recent emphasis on the role of human capital development in the determination of economic growth. Accordingly, Chapter 8 focuses on the role of human capital in Malaysian economic development.

Since the mid-1980s, we have seen a growing protest against globalization and free trade largely because of the belief that these external forces will make many developing countries worse off. Yet the Malaysian experience of globalization suggests the contrary. Chapter 9 will analyse the benefits and impacts of globalization on the economic growth of Malaysia. Finally, Chapter 10 provides an integrative summary of the findings with reference to relevant theories, policy implications and some suggestions for further research.

NOTES

[1] The employment of this integrated approach may not fit comfortably with mainstream thinking, and it may even engender some disagreement. It needs to be emphasized that this approach aims to broaden our understanding of the growth process rather than to generate heated debate.

[2] From Robert M. Solow, *Growth Theory: An Exposition*, 2000 Oxford University Press, New York. By permission of Oxford University Press, Inc.

[3] Manufacturing has supplanted agriculture as the major contributor to Malaysia's GDP, accounting for 48.5 per cent in 1995 (Malaysia, 1996) and 55.5 per cent in 1997 (Malaysia, 1998).

[4] Hirschman (2001) remarked that Malaysia is 'below the level of popular consciousness'.

2. Technological progress and long-run economic growth

INTRODUCTION

Productivity isn't everything, but in the long run it is almost everything.

Krugman (1997, p. 11)

Our knowledge of economic history, of what production looked like 100 years ago, and of current events convinces us beyond any doubt that discovery, invention and innovation are of overwhelming importance in economic growth and that the economic goods that come from these activities are different in a fundamental way from ordinary objects. We could produce statistical evidence suggesting that all growth came from capital accumulation with no room for anything called technological change. But we would not believe it.

Romer (1993, p. 562)

The central proposition of the neoclassical and the endogenous growth models is that positive and long-run growth of output per capita hinges on technological progress. Solow (1956) and Swan (1956) postulated that without technological progress, economic growth would cease as a result of diminishing returns to factor inputs. When the economy finally arrives at its steady state growth path, output per worker is determined primarily by the rate of technological progress.[1]

Despite the mechanical rigour of the Solow–Swan growth model (Denison, 1962; Jorgenson and Griliches, 1967), the validity and applicability of the neoclassical growth accounting approach in explaining long-run economic growth has been criticized on many occasions. As early as the 1960s, intense criticisms were mounted from Cambridge (England), with Joan Robinson as the leading advocate, against the construction of capital in the growth accounting framework. More recently, the validity of the convergence hypothesis has been challenged. Past studies (De Long, 1988; Romer, 1994; Quah, 1993, 1996a, 1996b; Sala-i-Martin, 1996; United Nations, 1997) found no convergence of per capita income on a worldwide basis, and that poor countries were not catching up with the rich countries.

The early 1990s saw an expansion in the growth literature in utilizing the total factor productivity (TFP) approach to explain the divergence in per capita income between developed and developing countries, and the East

Asian growth 'miracle'. Several authors, such as Krugman (1994), Young (1994) and Kim and Lau (1995), argued that the growth phenomenon of East Asian economies was not sustainable because the high growth levels experienced by these countries derived from massive growth in inputs of capital and labour rather than technological progress. As such, there is no miracle. Instead, growth is the result of temporary transitional dynamics. If the Solow–Swan growth exposition is correct, growth for many East Asian countries will cease as soon as diminishing returns set in. These arguments, especially those of Kim and Lau (1994) and Krugman (1994), have been taken seriously by the decision-makers in Singapore[2] and Malaysia (Malaysia, 1996).

Despite conflicting views between different disciplines in interpreting the determinants of long-run economic growth,[3] there seems to be a consensus among them that technological progress is the underlying factor for long-run growth. In order to understand the logic and importance of technological progress as the engine of economic growth, it is necessary to start with the building blocks of the Solow–Swan growth framework.

THE SOLOW–SWAN GROWTH EXPOSITION

In aggregate terms, the production function of the Solow–Swan growth model can be written as:

$$Y_t = F\left(K_t, A_t, L_t\right) \qquad (2.1)$$

where Y is the aggregate level of output, K is capital stock, L is labour, A is the level of technology[4] and t is time.

This production function is constructed based on the following assumptions:

1. Labour force and technology grow at a constant rate, n and g respectively. Hence:

$$L_t = L_0(1 + n)^t \qquad (2.2)$$

$$A_t = A_0(1 + g)^t \qquad (2.3)$$

2. Marginal products are positive:

$$F_k, F_L > 0 \qquad (2.4)$$

3. Marginal productivities are diminishing:

$$F_{KK}, F_{LL} < 0 \qquad (2.5)$$

Although equation (2.4) states that each increment in capital or labour can generate additional flow of output, successive increments in capital or labour will decrease the flow of output as shown in equation (2.5).

4. There are constant returns to scale:

$$\pi Y_t = F(\pi K_t, \pi A_t L_t) \quad \pi > 0 \tag{2.6}$$

By setting $\pi = 1/AL$, equation (2.6) can be expressed in per capita format:

$$Y/AL = F(K/AL, 1) = f(K/AL) \tag{2.7}$$

where Y/AL is output per effective labour input and K/AL is capital per effective labour input.

5. A constant proportion of Y is assumed to be invested. The fraction of Y that is devoted to investment is s. One unit of Y devoted to investment yields one unit of new capital. Existing capital depreciates at a rate represented by δ. $\dot{K}$ is given by:

$$\dot{K_t} = dK/dt = sY_t - \delta K_t \tag{2.8}$$

DYNAMICS OF THE MODEL

In order to derive the relationship between output per effective worker and capital per effective worker, equation (2.8) is divided on both sides by AL. Hence:

$$\dot{K_t}/A_t L_t = sY_t/A_t L_t - \delta K_t/A_t L_t \tag{2.9}$$

Substituting expression $Y_t/A_t L_t$ with (2.7) gives:

$$\dot{K_t}/A_t L_t = sf(K_t/A_t L_t) - \delta(K_t/A_t L_t) \tag{2.10}$$

Writing $\dot{K_t}/A_t L_t$ as $\dot{k_t}$, $f(K_t/A_t L_t) = k_t$, and using equations (2.2) and (2.3) where the growth rates of labour and technology are n and g respectively, the expression $\delta(K_t/A_t L_t)$ will become $(\delta + n + g)k$. Equation (2.10) can then be rewritten as:

$$\dot{k_t} = sf(k_t) - (\delta + n + g) k_t \tag{2.11}$$

Equation (2.11) specifies the rates of change of capital stock per unit of effective labour. This exposition is depicted in Figure 2.1.

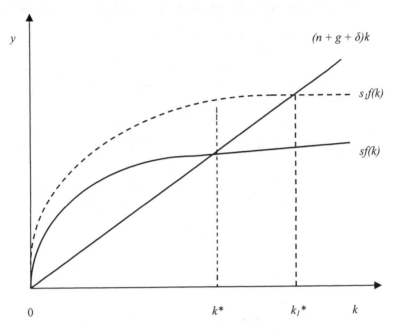

Figure 2.1   Dynamics of the Solow–Swan growth model

Figure 2.1 shows that capital to effective labour ratio increases when $sf(k)$ exceeds that of $(n + g + \delta)k$, and decreases if $sf(k)$ is below $(n + g + \delta)k$. This is based on the assumption that the marginal product of capital exceeds that of $(n + g + \delta)k$ when the capital to labour ratio is small. When the marginal product of capital declines below $(n + g + \delta)k$, the capital to labour ratio increases. As such, capital per worker rises when k is initially less then k^*, and falls when k exceeds k^*. At the steady state, k^*, the capital to effective labour ratio is constant. This implies that, regardless of the starting point, the economy will converge to the steady state path, where each variable in the model is growing at a constant rate. The shape of the $sf(k)$ curve therefore satisfies the Inada conditions.[5]

In the Solow–Swan model, the most important policy variable is the saving rate, s. The impact of s on growth of output per worker is reflected in a shift of the investment curve from the original $sf(k)$ curve to the new $s_1 f(k)$ curve. At this new level, $s_1 f(k)$ exceeds $(n + g + \delta) k$ as shown in Figure 2.1; k will continue to rise until it reaches the new constant value as represented by k_1^*. This implies that permanent increases in the saving rate will only have a temporary increase in the growth rate of output per worker. In short, a change in saving rate will only have a level effect but not a growth effect. Therefore, in the Solow–Swan model, only changes in the rate of technological progress have growth effects while other changes have level effects.

Although the Solow–Swan growth model is claimed to provide an ideal technique for empirical analyses (Kendrick, 1961, 1973; Denison, 1962, 1967, 1974; Jorgenson and Griliches, 1967), critics, particularly those associated with the Cambridge (England) school of thought tend to disagree with its assumptions of an aggregate production function and aggregate capital (Robinson, 1978). More recently, empirical evidence in the form of large disparities in per capita income between the developed and developing economies has highlighted the limitations of neoclassical growth expositions.

CAPITAL CONTROVERSY: THE CAMBRIDGE CRITICISMS OF THE AGGREGATE PRODUCTION FUNCTION

This section touches briefly on the main issues in the capital controversy. Additional analytical insights are provided as a result, and the analysis of economic growth is more complete. Although it can be argued that this is an unsatisfactory procedure as a large amount of information is omitted, it should be noted that this chapter is not an exploration of the critique of the theory of capital. A comprehensive account of the Cambridge Controversy can be found in Harcourt's (1972) *Some Cambridge Controversies in the Theory of Capital*. Nonetheless, this brief section is intended to highlight the difficulties associated with the construction and measurement of capital. Despite the capital controversy, empirical research based on the neoclassical model has continued apace.

The neoclassical growth model is an attempt to analyse economic growth systematically through the aggregation of economic behaviour that is governed by rigid assumptions for the determination of factor prices. However, once these assumptions are relaxed, it is difficult, if not impossible, for factor prices to be set in the neoclassical framework. Its limitation in determining factor prices led to the intense scrutiny of the capital controversy in the 1960s and 1970s (Harcourt, 1972; Elmslie and Milberg, 1996). According to Robinson (1978), these ambiguities with respect to the determination of factor prices can result in difficulties associated with the aggregation of capital stock.

The summation of the entire capital stock in the whole economy in the neoclassical production function framework also led to intense criticism. Hunt (1979, p. 400) stated that:

> While it is perfectly clear what we mean when we aggregate the amount of labor

employed (in order to ascertain its marginal productivity), it is by no means clear what we mean when we aggregate capital. If we say 100 labourers work for a week, the meaning is unambiguous. But what does it mean to say 100 capitals worked for one week? One hundred factories? Of various sizes? One hundred shovels? 50 factories and 25 shovels and 25 oil refining plants? This is obviously nonsensical. One piece of capital can be anything ranging from a screwdriver to a gigantic plant that employs tens of thousands of workers.

This view was shared by Granger (1997) who argued that the actual economy is a complicated system, partly as a result of the aggregation of millions of non-identical, non-independent decision-making units, such as households, corporations and government institutions.

With reference to the calculation of TFP based on the aggregate growth accounting approach, Scott (1993) commented on the validity of the residual which is assumed to be attributed to technical progress. Scott noted:

> the change in 'total factor productivity', as the residual is sometimes called, has been and continues to be calculated again and again. Yet, if I am right, there should be no residual and no change in TFP. Inputs are heterogeneous, as all will agree. How, then, should they be weighted in the above calculation? The answer has already been given: each must be multiplied by its marginal product. The mistakes that have been made are usually the results of failure to do this. (1993, p. 421)

It has been argued the aggregate production function is invalid except within the confines of a one-commodity world (Garegnani, 1970), or when the capital–labour ratios and technologies are equal in the production of all goods (Stiglitz, 1966). Salter (1966) attempted to depart from the ambiguities associated with the measurement of capital by distinguishing between *ex ante* and *ex post*, substitutability, and the heterogeneity of capital goods. Kaldor and Mirrlees avoided the difficulties of measuring the quantity of capital by taking obsolescence into account based on:

> the fact that the profitability of plant and equipment of any particular 'vintage' must continually diminish in time and it assumes that this continuing obsolescence is broadly foreseen by entrepreneurs who take it into account in framing their investment decision. The model also assumes that, irrespective of whether plant and equipment has a finite physical life-time or not, its operative life-time is determined by a complex of economic factors which govern the rate of obsolescence, and not by physical wear and tear. (1962, p. 174)

Hence, in the Kaldor and Mirrlees (1962) framework, it is irrelevant to measure the stock of capital (thereby avoiding the ambiguities associated with measuring the quantity of capital). Instead, 'it operates solely with the value of current gross investment (gross (fixed) capital expenditure per unit of time) and its rate of change in time' (Kaldor and Mirrlees, 1962, p. 174).

The marginal productivity theory (in determining factor shares) forms an essential part of the neoclassical growth model. This methodology has been continuously scrutinized, but the 'sharpest arrows in the quivers of the neo-Keynesian critics are the results of the double-switching debate' (Harcourt, 1972, p. 118). The concepts of reswitching and capital-reversing were first noted by Robinson (1953, 1956).[6] Sraffa published a systematic account of the reswitching and capital-reversing process in 1960.[7] Robinson (1953) indicated that aggregate capital stock is a heterogeneous group of capital goods that differs according to how long it takes labour and other types of capital to produce them. The longer the period of time required to construct each type of new capital, the higher are the interest costs as a proportion of total production costs. When the relative wage-rental cost of capital changes over time, profit-maximizing firms will invoke different techniques with different combinations of capital goods in order to minimize production costs. This implies the possibility of reswitching in that a given technique can be that of least cost at both high and low interest rates but not in between.

Another flaw in the neoclassical growth framework, according to the Cambridge school, is that ignoring time in the accounting framework meant that capital would be difficult to measure accurately. Robinson (1980) remarked that the neoclassical analysis of capital is a static one:

> there is no movement forward and upward or backward and downward, except the movement of the reader's eye along the curve ... if we are to introduce decisions into the model, we must introduce time. (p. 22)

Kaldor and Mirrlees (1962, p. 188) argued that a production function based on a single-value relationship between some measure of capital stock, K_t, labour, L_t, and output, Y_t, all at time does not exist because 'everything depends on past history, on how the collection of equipment goods which comprises K_t has been built up'. This concern over the time factor is shared by Carvalho who postulated that:

> 'Time' is a concept that is usually neglected even in methodological discussions. Neoclassical economics, particularly, has treated this problem in a rather light way, approaching time as just another 'space dimension'. (1983, p. 265)

In fact, Salter (1966) pointed out that a satisfactory system of analysis associated with productivity and output growth must take time into account. In his 'technical knowledge' analysis, new knowledge or advances in production techniques are allowed to flow from one time period to another. This continuous flow from one production technique to another is crucial to the evolution of technological progress. Hence, within Salter's framework, the evolution of technological progress is time dependent. As Salter stated:

> Techniques of production change through time for two reasons: improving technical

knowledge and changing factor prices. Both are continuous processes in time and together give rise to a stream of new techniques, each following the other in quick succession. The 'once-over' analysis of comparative statics is only appropriate to changes in technique which are sufficiently great to displace completely all pre-existing methods before they themselves are displaced. It hardly needs to be stressed that such cases are rare; in fact, many experienced observers rate the cumulative effect of small unnoticed modifications and improvements as equally great as the more significant changes normally regarded as innovations. Moreover, factor prices change slowly but continuously through time, and this alone is sufficient to produce a constant stream of new techniques of production. (1966, p. 5)

According to Harcourt (1976), the Cambridge capital controversy reached its climax in the reswitching and capital reversing debates during the mid-1960s. This climax, particularly the aggregation of capital, had involved considerable confusion and misunderstanding. As Harcourt (1976, p. 29) commented: 'It would be unfortunate, though, if it were to be deduced from this term that only aggregation and an index number problem are involved because this is not so.' He elaborated that Robinson argued that 'the problem is not the *measurement* of capital but its *meaning* – and that means specifying what sort of economy the writer has in mind – its institutional framework, "rules of the game", and social relationship' (p. 29).

In this book the links between capital and technological progress are of crucial importance. The relationship between capital and economic growth is not determined by the marginal productivity of capital but rather by the process of learning-by-doing following the propositions put forward by Young (1928), Myrdal (1957), Kaldor (1960), Salter (1966) and Arrow (1962). By acquiring and diffusing new technology or knowledge that is embodied in new capital investment, a society will be able to make advancement in their economic progress.

The Cambridge controversy highlighted the limitations of the neoclassical growth framework, particularly with the construction of capital stock, yet for a large proportion of mainstream economists it has become a neglected issue. Solow has now reached the view that it has been long and pointless debate. As he wrote, the 'whole episode now seems to have been a waste of time, a playing-out of ideological games in the language of analytical economics' (2000, p. xiii). However, Harcourt's view remains just as pertinent today:

The discussions themselves are about fundamentals, but the arguments tend to be highly technical and abstract, so much so that, in places, one side will accuse the other, often with some justice, of not knowing what is in fact being discussed. There are communication problems, both between the participants and for the spectators, partly because of the revolution in analytical techniques that has occurred, especially in the USA, over the last twenty-five years and partly because of ideological differences, which are often unconscious (and personality clashes, which are not). (1982, p. 225)

INCREASING GROWTH OF OUTPUT

The neoclassical growth model postulates that growth in output per capita may not be possible in the long run due to the constraint of diminishing returns. However, many empirical studies have revealed that output expansion has outpaced population growth since the 1820s (Maddison, 1991,1993; Grossman and Helpman, 1994). Marx (Baumol, 1986, p. 1073) remarked that: 'The bourgeoisie, during its rule of scarce one hundred years, has created more massive and more colossal productive forces than have all preceding generations together.' Maddison (1991, p. 8) wrote that: 'Since 1820 the total product of the advanced capitalist group has increased seventyfold, population nearly fivefold, and per capita product fourteenfold.' He reported that the growth rate of gross domestic product (GDP) in the US, in terms of person-hours (productivity growth), for the period 1870–1987, had been increasing at an average rate of 3.7 per cent per year. In a broader sample of the world, the growth trend of GDP per capita in the period 1870–1989 was increasing as shown in Table 2.1.

Table 2.1 GDP per head of population for 36 countries, 1870–1989 (at 1985 US prices)

Country	1870	1890	1913	1950	1973	1989
Leading Western economies						
Austria	1 442	1 892	2 683	2 869	8 697	12 519
Belgium	2 089	2 654	3 267	4 229	9 417	12 875
Denmark	1 543	1 944	3 014	5 227	10 527	13 822
Finland	933	1 130	1 727	3 481	9 073	14 015
France	1 582	1 955	2 746	4 176	10 351	13 952
Germany	1 251	1 660	2 506	3 295	10 124	13 752
Italy	1 216	1 352	2 079	2 840	8 631	12 989
Netherlands	2 065	2 568	3 179	4 708	10 271	12 669
Norway	1 190	1 477	2 079	4 541	9 347	15 202
Sweden	1 401	1 757	2 607	5 673	11 362	14 824
UK	2 693	3 383	4 152	5 651	10 079	13 519
Australia	3 143	3 949	4 553	5 970	10 369	13 538
Canada	1 330	1 846	3 515	6 112	11 835	17 236
USA	2 244	3 101	4 846	8 605	14 093	18 282
Average	*1 723*	*2 191*	*3 068*	*4 813*	*10 298*	*14 228*
European periphery						
Czechoslovakia	1 153	1 515	2 075	3 465	6 980	8 538
Greece	n.a.	n.a.	1 211	1 456	5 781	7 564

Table 2.1 (continued)

Country	1870	1890	1913	1950	1973	1989
Hungary	1 139	1 439	1 883	2 481	5 517	6 722
Ireland	n.a.	n.a.	2 003	2 600	5 248	8 285
Portugal	833	950	967	1 608	5 598	7 383
Spain	1 221	1 355	2 212	2 405	7 581	10 081
USSR	792	828	1 138	2 647	5 920	6 970
Average	*1 028*	*1 217*	*1 641*	*2 381*	*6 089*	*7 931*
Latin America						
Argentina	1 039	1 515	2 370	3 112	4 972	4 080
Brazil	615	641	697	1 434	3 356	4 402
Chile	n.a.	1 073	1 735	3 255	4 281	5 406
Colombia	n.a.	n.a.	1 078	1 876	2 996	3 979
Mexico	700	762	1 121	1 594	3 202	3 728
Peru	n.a.	n.a.	1 099	1 809	3 160	2 601
Average	*785*	*988*	*1 350*	*2 180*	*3 661*	*4 033*
Asia						
Bangladesh	n.a.	n.a.	519	463	391	551
China	497	526	557	454	1 039	2 538
India	490	521	559	502	719	1 093
Indonesia	585	640	710	650	1 056	1 790
Japan	640	842	1 153	1 620	9 524	15 336
Korea	n.a.	680	819	757	2 404	6 503
Pakistan	n.a.	n.a.	611	545	823	1 283
Taiwan	n.a.	564	608	706	2 803	7 252
Thailand	741	801	876	874	1 794	4 008
Average	*591*	*653*	*712*	*730*	*2 284*	*4 484*

Source: Maddison, 1993, pp. 4–5.

The long-run data for many countries show that the significant growth in output is inconsistent with the prediction of the neoclassical framework. Positive rates of per capita growth could persist over a century or more and these growth rates did not show any tendency to decline. Such inconsistencies prompted Romer to remark that:

> In a fully specified competitive equilibrium, per capita output can grow without bound, possibly at a rate that is monotonically increasing over time. The rate of investment and the rate of return on capital may increase rather than decrease with increases in the capital stock. The level of per capita output in different countries need not converge; growth may be persistently slower in less developed countries

and may even fail to take place at all. These results do not depend on any kind of exogenously specified technical change or differences between countries. Preferences and the technology are stationary and identical. Even the size of the population can be held constant. What is crucial for all of these results is a departure from the usual assumption of diminishing returns. (1986, p. 1002)

Table 2.2 shows that real GDP per capita experienced an increasing trend with an annual average growth rate of 2.4 per cent for OECD countries and 6.05 per cent annual average growth for the Asian NIEs. Even the worst-performing area, Sub-Saharan Africa, grew at 0.27 per cent annually. On average real per capita GDP increased on a worldwide basis for the period 1971–2000. As a result of the consistent increases in per capita growth in income since the 1820s, critics tend to question the validity of the postulation of diminishing returns.

Table 2.2   Average growth rate of real GDP per capita, major areas of the World, 1971-2000

	Annual Growth Rate (%)
China	6.75
Asian NIEs	6.05
East Asia and Pacific	5.75
India	2.82
Europe and Central Asia	2.57
OECD	2.40
Latin America	1.57
Middle East and North Africa	1.47
Sub-Saharan Africa	0.27
World average	1.72

Source: World Bank, 2002.

CONVERGENCE HYPOTHESIS

A major implication of the neoclassical growth model is the convergence hypothesis which states that countries with similar production technologies, savings and population growth rates should in the long run converge to similar steady state levels of per capita income. This convergence property means that poor countries starting with a relatively low standard of living and a lower capital–labour ratio will grow faster during the transition period. Both groups will ultimately arrive at the same level of per capita income. The convergence dynamics can be written as:

$$\dot{\gamma k} = \dot{k}/k = s\, f(k)/k - (n + g + \delta) \qquad (2.12)$$

where γ is the growth rate. The above equation is derived by dividing both sides of equation (2.11) by k. By taking the derivative of γk with respect to k, equation (2.12) becomes:

$$\partial \gamma k / \partial k = s\, f[f'(k) - f(k)/k]/k < 0 \qquad (2.13)$$

Equation (2.13) implies that smaller values of k are associated with larger values of γk. This means that economies with lower capital per worker would tend to grow faster in per capita terms.

A similar proposition was made by Gerschenkron (1962) who stated that a backward economy could take advantage of its relative backwardness to accelerate its growth performance. Gerschenkron argued that the pace of economic growth in European countries had been significantly affected by their initial economic growth levels. The greater the degree of relative backwardness of the latecomers, the faster the subsequent growth in their economies. This is based on the assumption that latecomers are able to adopt the advanced technology developed by advanced countries. A study conducted by Minami (1986) using Maddison's 1969 data found a clear correlation between relative backwardness and subsequent growth rates.

Sala-i-Martin (1996) defines two versions of convergence: β-convergence as absolute in that poor economies tend to grow faster than rich ones, and σ-convergence as a situation whereby a group of economies are converging in terms of σ, if the dispersion of their real per capita GDP levels decreases over time. The convergence hypothesis applies to a group of countries with similar economic structures in that they have similar values of parameters s, n, g and δ, and the same production function f, with the only difference among these economies being the initial quantity of capital per person, k. It follows that poor economies with lower values of k and y will have higher growth rates of k and y. Since all the economies have similar production structures, the dynamics of k among different economies will be determined in each case by the same $sf(k)$ and $(n + g + \delta)k$ curves. Hence, the growth rate of k will be larger for the economy with a lower initial value k.

Case for Convergence

Empirical evidence generated from the testing of the convergence hypothesis has created support for both sides of the argument (Maddison, 1983; Baumol, 1986; Barro, 1991; Sala-i-Martin, 1996; Smolny, 2000). There appears to be no cross-country evidence to support absolute or β-convergence. However, when factors such as technology, preferences and population growth rates are accounted for, there seems to be a conditional convergence taking place.[8] On the issue of conditional convergence, Maddison (1982) conducted a comprehensive empirical analysis and concluded that poorer countries are converging with richer countries. Maddison's (1982) findings were reinforced by Baumol (1986) who examined the convergence of 16 industrialized countries between 1870 to 1979 using Maddison's (1982) data. Baumol found the estimate of β to be almost equal to –1, indicating perfect convergence. With reference to the convergence of national productivity levels of the 16 economies surveyed, their productivity levels have tended to approach closer to one another. Baumol (1986) reported that in 1870, the ratio of output per work-hour in Australia, which was the leader during that period,[9] was about eight times as great as Japan (the laggard). By 1979, that ratio for the leader (US) to the laggard (Japan) had fallen to approximately 2. This led Baumol (1986) to conclude that poorer countries like Japan and Italy had substantially closed the per capita income gap with richer countries like the US and Canada between 1870 and 1970.

Subsequent research by Barro (1991) and Mankiw et al. (1992) on the US uncovered the presence of conditional convergence once differences in factor accumulation were controlled for. Poorer economies appear to approach their own steady states at a fairly uniform rate, say 2 per cent per year. Barro and Sala-i-Martin (1991, 1992) documented the existence of convergence in that economies tend to grow faster in per capita terms when they are further below the steady state position. This phenomenon shows up clearly for the US over various periods from 1840 to 1988. Poor states in the US tend to grow faster in per capita terms than rich states, even if variables other than initial per capita income were not held constant.

As for the OECD (Organisation for Economic Co-operation and Development) countries, Sala-i-Martin (1996) reported that poor and rich economies in that group[10] appeared to be converging towards each other at a uniform annual rate of 2 per cent. His findings of an annual convergence rate of 2 per cent in the OECD economies supported those of Dowrick and Nguyen (1989) and Jones (1997). According to the United Nations (1997), convergence over the 1950–92 period had been confined to a small group of industrialized economies, namely the OECD. Prior to 1950, the US led Western Europe by a significant margin, and thus opened up a large productivity and income gap within that region. Since the 1950s, most of the OECD countries have begun to close the gap, with an average growth rate of 2.4 per cent, thereby reducing dispersion of income by half. These findings have been treated as evidence of convergence, and that the neoclassical growth model is consistent with observed growth patterns.

A group of economies in East Asia also display the characteristics of catching up to the per capita level of the rich economies. Initially poor economies such as Singapore, Korea, Taiwan and Hong Kong have achieved per capita income levels of the OECD countries in a time span of less than four decades compared to 80 years or more for the UK, US, France and Germany to achieve such growth (Nelson and Pack, 1999). Table 2.3 provides an indication of the catching-up rate of the East Asia economies relative to the OECD countries.

Table 2.3   Growth in the world economy: catching up by developing economies on the OECD countries, 1960–90

GDP growth differential with OECD*	1960–90
More than 3 per cent	South Korea
	Singapore
	Hong Kong
	Taiwan
1–3 per cent	Botswana
	Malaysia
	Thailand
0–1 per cent	Indonesia
	Barbados
	Lesotho
	Morocco
	Tunisia
	Seychelles

Note: *Excess of average annual real GDP growth over the OECD average in percentage points.

Source: United Nations, 1997, p. 80.

The data show that in 1960–90, South Korea, Singapore, Hong Kong and Taiwan were catching up with the advanced countries at a rate of more than 3 per cent. During the same period, the catching-up rate in Malaysia relative to OECD nations averaged between 1 and 3 per cent.

Case against Convergence

When carried out on a larger sample or on a worldwide basis, many empirical studies reported divergence in growth rates (Romer, 1994). In fact, proponents of the convergence hypothesis found themselves in a difficult position in trying to explain the diverging trend found in a larger sample of countries. Baumol (1986) found a perfect convergence pattern for 16 developed economies but none among the less-developed economies. Jones (1997) stated that despite the fact that the OECD countries have tended to converge, per capita incomes have not converged in a large sample of countries (the world) during the post-war era. Sala-i-Martin (1996) reported strong convergence in the US among the poorer and richer states, in Japan among its prefectures, and within the OECD group, but he found no convergence for the whole world. In his study of 110 countries, in the period 1960–90, the dispersion, σ, was found to increase steadily from 0.89 in 1960 to 1.12 in 1990. These findings imply that economies had diverged over the 30-year period. Sala-i-Martin (1996, p. 1034) concluded that:

> the cross-country distribution of world GDP between 1960 and 1990 did not shrink, and poor countries have not grown faster than rich ones. Using the classical terminology, in our world there is no σ-convergence and there is no absolute β-convergence.

Similarly, Grossman and Helpman (1991) argued an absence of strong correlation between the initial levels of per capita income and growth of this income in the period since 1960. The United Nations (1997) also reported that over the 1960–90 period, developing countries as a whole had failed to move closer to the developed countries. In fact, it commented that: 'Simultaneously, there has been a strong divergence within the developing world itself whereby countries with low initial per capita incomes have fallen further behind the others' (p. 85).

The difference in growth trends between countries has a direct implication for the relative position of countries in the world economy. By classifying countries into quintiles, according to income shares, the United Nations (1997) showed that income divergence and increasing inequality in the world's population had been a persistent trend:

> The increase in the income share of the richest 20 per cent of the world population was significant; it rose by 14 percentage points from 1965 to 1990, to reach over 83 per cent of world GNP. Much of this increase occurred in the 1980s and was concentrated in the countries with the richest 10 per cent of the world population. The Gini Coefficient stood at 0.66 in 1965, rose slightly to 0.68 in 1980 and reached 0.74 in 1990. Perhaps more striking has been the enormous increase in the income gap between the richest and the poorest quintiles of the world population. In 1965 average GNP per capita in the poorest quintile was \$74 and in the highest \$2 281, a ratio of 31:1. By 1990 the figures were respectively \$283 and \$17 056, yielding a ratio of 60:1. There is little evidence to suggest that this tendency towards greater dispersion has been reversed. (p. 80)

The trend in income divergence is the result of rising share of income in the top quintile, and the widening of income gap in relation to other quintiles. Pritchett (1997) estimated that 'from 1870 to 1990 the ratio of per capita incomes between the richest and the poorest countries increased by roughly a factor of five' (p. 3). This points to a clustering of countries around the higher and lower growth poles.

Another limitation of the convergence hypothesis is that it fails to take into account the different growth experiences of different countries over long periods of time. Based on Maddison's figures in Table 2.1, the leading Western economies grew at a higher rate than the European Periphery, Latin America and Asia in 1870–1989. Every country within each of these groups also experienced different growth rates. In the leading Western group, Finland started with per capita GDP of US$933 in 1870 and ended with US$14 015 in 1989 compared to Belgium's US$2 089 in 1870 and US$12 875 in 1989, and Australia's US$3 143 and US$13 538 respectively. In Asia, Japan started with US$640 in 1870 and ended with US$15 336 in 1989, and China began with US$497 and ended on US$2 538. Bangladesh, on the other hand, experienced little or no growth at all. Hence, these data suggest that different countries vary in their economic performance over the long run. Maddison (1993, p. 9) stated that: 'in 1820 the intercountry income spread was probably about 4:1, in 1913 it was 10:1, in 1950 26:1, in 1973 36:1 and in 1981 39:1'. Maddison's findings were supported by Grossman and Helpman (1994).

The divergence in growth paths leading to rising inequality particularly in per capita output is presented in Table 2.4.

Table 2.4   Average values of dispersion of real GDP

	Entire sample	Poor	Middle	Rich
Sample size	113	42	32	39
Dispersion of RGDP 1962(1)	0.88	0.44	0.24	0.48
Dispersion of RGDP 1986(1)	1.07	0.59	0.62	0.57
Dispersion of RGDP 1962(2)	0.96	0.48	0.26	0.37
Dispersion of RGDP 1982(2)	1.06	0.62	0.62	0.42

Note: (1) denotes RGDP per capita, (2) denotes RGDP per worker.

Source: Dowrick, 1991, p. 4.

Based on the data in Table 2.4, the dispersion in income and productivity within and between the three income groups increased over time, leading to increasing inequality (Dowrick, 1991). In a study of 114 countries, Barro (1997) reported that the standard deviation of the log of real per capita GDP rose from 0.89 in 1960 to 1.14 in 1990, implying an increase in inequality. GDP growth rates can also differ, even in favourable periods (Lucas, 1988). During 1969–80, India grew at 1.4 per cent per year, Egypt at 3.4 per cent,

South Korea at 7 per cent, Japan at 7.1 per cent and the US at 2.3 per cent (Lucas, 1988). This diverse growth pattern prompted Lucas (1988) to question the ability of the neoclassical growth model to explain growth.

Furthermore, the studies carried out in the previous section tend to focus on countries with similar per capita income levels and countries that have converged. When explaining the lack of convergence pattern in developing countries, neoclassical economists defend their positions with the conditional convergence methodology. Developing countries possess the potential to grow faster than advanced countries, provided that they satisfy certain conditions. If these conditions are not satisfied, their growth rate may be below their potential, or even below that of richer countries.

Much of the recent empirical work on growth has struggled to interpret these findings in the context of neoclassical growth theory and to estimate the rate of convergence in different samples of countries and regions. De Long (1988) claimed that Maddison's data were subject to sample bias favouring convergence. He also demonstrated that Baumol's findings were faulty due to sampling error. De Long (1988) argued that since historical data were constructed retrospectively, the countries that had long data series were generally those that are the most industrialized today. Thus, countries that were not rich 100 years ago were typically in the sample only if they grew rapidly over the next 100 years. Countries that were rich 100 years ago, in contrast, were generally included even if subsequent growth was only moderate. Because of this, it is more likely that poorer countries were growing faster than richer ones in the sample of chosen countries even if there was no tendency for this to occur on average. De Long (1988) also pointed out the measurement errors in Baumol's study. Estimates of real income per capita in 1870 were imprecise. Measurement error again created bias towards finding convergence. He commented that when income in 1870 was overstated, growth over the period 1870–1979 would be understated by an equal amount, and vice versa. Thus, the measured growth rates would tend to be lower in countries with higher measured initial income even if there was no relationship between actual growth and actual initial income.

The validity of Baumol's (1986) findings was also questioned by Romer on the grounds of *ex post* sample selection bias. Romer (1994) argued that convergence takes place only in the post Second World War period. Between 1870 and 1950, income per capita diverged (Abramovitz, 1986). Those nations that did not converge were excluded from the sample, so convergence in Baumol's (1986) study was assured. As soon as Maddison's data set was expanded to include countries that appeared rich *ex ante* (that is, by 1870), convergence disappeared.

This view was shared by Durlauf and Johnson (1995) and Quah (1996a, 1996b). They argued that by using alternative econometric methods, the pattern of cross-country growth became inconsistent with convergence. Employing the Summers–Heston data set, which consists of 118 countries,

Quah (1996a) found few signs of negative correlation in the cross-section between initial conditions and time-averaged growth rates. Instead, overall data showed divergence. Quah remarked that:

> The picture that emerges is one of a world where countries tend – in the long run – towards either the very rich or very poor, with the middle income classes disappearing. The disparity between the rich and poor, further, appears to be widening. (1993, p. 39)

He argued that it is inappropriate to calculate a cross-section regression in order to explain time-averaged growth rates. This is because growth performance differs widely across countries, and the empirical findings of convergence are blurred by Galton's classical fallacy of regression towards the mean.[11] Quah's argument is supported by Hart (1995). Judging theories by simple correlations may be flawed if shocks are not properly accounted for. Quah stated that:

> Thus, the evidence on 'convergence' that different researchers have uncovered do not really bear on our empirical conclusions. Instead, the empirical results here simply highlight the error in interpreting previous findings as having demonstrated convergence ... That work concludes that much the same divergence and immobility results as obtained here remain, even after conditioning. (1993, p. 50)

The possibility of statistical errors is also reported by Levine and Zervos (1993) who pointed out that conceptual and statistical problems can hinder cross-country investigations. The previous finding that rich and poor economies are converging at a uniform annual rate of 2 per cent could be caused by factors that are unrelated to the dynamics of economic growth. Quah remarked that:

> The idea here is that such consistency might only reflect something mechanical and independent of the economic structure of growth. The working hypothesis, then, is that economic structure varies in many – explicable and inexplicable – ways across environments, and thus cannot be the source for the 2 per cent uniformity. Instead, that uniformity is due to something relatively uninteresting, namely, the statistical implications of a unit root in the time series data. (1995, p. 2)

He indicated that the usual empirical analyses – cross-section (conditional) convergence regressions, time series modelling and panel data analysis – can be misleading for understanding convergence.

Since Solow is the foremost authority on the neoclassical growth model, a quotation from him with reference to his view on the convergence hypothesis is most appropriate to conclude this discussion:

> It is enough to think of two countries. If they are described by altogether different

models, different technologies, different tastes, different rates of population growth, then of course convergence would simply not arise as an issue. You could ask how well a particular family of growth models fits each country, but that is all. For the convergence question even to arise these countries must have some relevant aspects of their economies in common. We know that population grows rapidly in some countries and slowly in others. We know for a fact that saving rates differ drastically from place to place, and it would seem implausible to suppose that the underlying taste parameters, rates of time preference or intertemporal elasticities of substitution, for example, should be the same in countries with different cultures and different histories ... A good illustration of this commonplace remark is the frequent finding that, while there may be some kind of convergence among the advanced industrial (OECD) economies, the poor countries of the world show no clear tendency to converge either with the OECD block [*sic*] or with each other (Pritchett, 1997). One is not surprised by the thought that poor countries may have institutional infrastructures that make them, for now, fundamentally different from rich countries. (Solow, 2000, p9. 103–4)[12]

Recently, there has been a shift towards the total factor productivity (TFP) approach to explain divergence in per capita income between developed and developing countries.

TOTAL FACTOR PRODUCTIVITY AND ECONOMIC GROWTH

The early 1990s saw a revival of the neoclassical growth framework to explain the economic miracle of East Asia (World Bank, 1993; Kawai, 1994; Kim and Lau, 1994; Krugman, 1994; Young 1994, 1995; Drysdale and Huang, 1995; Bosworth, 1996; Chen, 1997; Sarel, 1997; Dowling and Summers, 1998) with particular emphasis on TFP growth. In the standard production function, TFP which is a proxy for technological progress A, is estimated from the decomposition of economic growth into three factors. The first is due to growth in labour input, the second is due to growth in capital input, and the third is due to increase in the productivity of both capital and labour (TFP). The estimation of TFP based on the Cobb–Douglas production function is provided in Chapter 9 (equations 9.1 to 9.4). The aim of this section is to provide a brief general background to TFP in order to highlight some of the issues associated with the relationship between TFP and long-run economic growth. A systematic and comprehensive analysis of TFP is covered later in Chapter 9.

Accumulation and Assimilation of Factor Inputs

The findings and conclusions drawn from many studies[13] have led to the interpretations and reinterpretations of the relationship between TFP and long-run economic growth. For instance, Kim and Lau (1994), Young (1994,

1995) and Krugman (1994), on the one hand, stated that the levels of growth experienced by the East Asian economies are the result of high accumulation of both capital and labour with little or no role played by technological progress. In short, growth is input driven rather than productivity driven. If this is the case, growth for many of the East Asian countries will cease as soon as diminishing returns set in. On the other hand, several authors such as Kaldor (1960), Salter (1962) and Singh (1998) argued that diminishing returns to capital would not occur because technical progress is embodied in new capital goods as well as replacement capital. These expositions have led to the development of competing views, the accumulationists and the assimilationists, in the interpretation of the results generated from TFP estimates. Table 2.5 summarizes the basic principles of accumulation and assimilation theories.

Table 2.5   Accumulation and assimilation of factor inputs

Accumulation Theories	Assimilation Theories
Measurement: rate of factor accumulation	Measurement: rate of total factor productivity
Rapid economic development is caused by high investment rates, whereby the bulk of the share of increased output per worker is explained by increases in physical and human capital per worker.	Rapid economic development is linked to entrepreneurship, innovation and learning. New technologies from advanced nations also have to be adopted. Although investments in human and physical capital are pre-requisites, they are not sufficient.
Little attention is paid to firms as their behaviour is basically determined by the external environment.	Entrepreneurial firms and their ability to learn rapidly are critical factors behind the success of South Korea, Singapore, Taiwan and China.
Accumulation of human capital is treated as an increase in the quality or effectiveness of labour.	Sharply rising educational attainment means that well-educated managers, engineers and workers have a comparative advantage in terms of new opportunities and effective learning of new production techniques. Accumulation of human capital is an important factor for successful entrepreneurship.

Table 2.5 (continued)

Accumulation Theories	Assimilation Theories
Economies in which the stocks of physical and human capital are rising rapidly are expected to show a steep rise in manufacturing exports. There would also be a shift in comparative advantage towards sectors that employ these inputs intensively. Therefore, there is nothing commendable about a surge in manufacturing exports.	In order to compete effectively in world markets, firms require not only government support but must also acquire factors such as the necessary learning, entrepreneurship and innovation. Exports stimulate learning in two ways: (1) being forced to compete in world markets will make managers and engineers of firms pay close attention to best practice; and (2) the increase in exports is usually with US and Japanese firms which provide assistance in order to achieve their demanded high standards.

Source: Nelson and Pack, 1999.

ACCUMULATION THEORIES AND EAST ASIAN ECONOMIC GROWTH

The accumulationists claimed that the high-growth phenomenon of the East Asian economies is not sustainable because their expansion was derived from massive inputs of labour and capital and not from gains in efficiency. This is because labour and capital are subject to diminishing returns, as depicted by the transitional dynamics of Figure 2.1, and hence, an increase in capital and labour will only have level effects but not growth effects. Young's (1994) study on a sample of 118 countries during 1970–85 reported that the East Asian economies' TFP performance was not as spectacular as indicated by the World Bank (1993).

Table 2.6 shows that in the TFP league, Hong Kong ranked sixth, Taiwan twenty-first, South Korea twenty-fourth, Malaysia thirty-eighth and Singapore sixty-third. It is interesting to note that Young (1994) ranked Bangladesh higher than Taiwan, South Korea, Japan and Singapore. A later study conducted by Young (1995) supported his (1994b) findings of significantly lower TFP growth values in many East Asian economies relative to those in industrialised economies. TFP growth in Singapore, for example, was estimated to be 0.2 per cent for 1986–90. Young's findings are consistent with studies conducted by Yuan (1983, 1985) and Kim and Lau (1994). Yuan (1983) reported virtually no TFP growth for the average of 28 manufacturing industries in Singapore between 1970 and 1979; in fact, TFP growth was negative for 17 of them. In a subsequent application of the growth accounting approach, Yuan (1985) indicated that almost all of Singapore's output growth in 1966–80 could be explained in terms of increase in the quantities of factor inputs with negligible contribution from TFP growth.

Table 2.6   *Annual growth of total factor productivity of selected countries, 1970–85*

1. Egypt	3.5	23. Guinea	1.4	45. Turkey	0.8
2. Pakistan	3.0	24. South Korea	1.4	46. Netherlands	0.8
3. Botswana	2.9	25. Iran	1.4	47. Ethiopia	0.7
4. Congo	2.8	26. Burma	1.4	48. Austria	0.7
5. Malta	2.6	27. Mauritius	1.4	49. Australia	0.7
6. Hong Kong	2.5	28. China	1.3	50. Spain	0.6
7. Syria	2.5	29. Denmark	1.3	51. Kenya	0.6
8. Zimbabwe	2.4	30. Israel	1.2	52. France	0.5
9. Gabon	2.4	31. Greece	1.2	53. Liberia	0.4
10. Tunisia	2.4	32. Japan	1.2	54. Paraguay	0.4
11. Cameroon	2.4	33. Luxembourg	1.2	55. Honduras	0.4
12. Lesotho	2.2	34. Yugoslavia	1.1	56. Portugal	0.4
13. Uganda	2.1	35. Tanzania	1.1	57. USA	0.4
14. Cyprus	2.1	36. Colombia	1.1	58. Belgium	0.4
15. Thailand	1.9	37. Sweden	1.0	59. Canada	0.3
16. Bangladesh	1.9	38. Malaysia	1.0	60. Algeria	0.3
17. Iceland	1.8	39. Malawi	1.0	61. Cent. Af. Rep.	0.2
18. Italy	1.8	40. Brazil	1.0	62. India	0.1
19. Norway	1.7	41. Panama	0.9	63. Singapore	0.1
20. Finland	1.5	42. United Kingdom	0.9	64. Sri Lanka	0.1
21. Taiwan	1.5	43. W. Germany	0.9	65. Fiji	0.1
22. Ecuador	1.4	44. Mali	0.8	66. Switzerland	0.0

Note: Only the top 66 countries are presented out of the 118 countries.

Source: Young[14], 1994, p. 970.

Kim and Lau (1994) presented several reasons for the lack of measured growth in productive efficiency over time for the newly industrialised countries (NICs) in the post-war period. First, there is the possibility of scale effects. Second, research and development is actually relatively unimportant in the East Asian NICs due to the lack of investment in research and development as well as the scarcity of indigenous technological improvements. Third, the rapid capital deepening in the NICs is not knowledge-intensive nor technology-intensive. Fourth, the capital goods installed in the NICs are likely to be standardized and have limited possibilities for indigenous improvement. Fifth, technical progress is likely to be embodied in capital goods used in high-technology industries and NICs are limited in their ability to tap into these industries for technical progress. Sixth, the managerial methods, institutional environment and supporting infrastructure lagged behind so the NICs are unable to realize the full potential productivity of the imported goods. Finally, poor natural and human resource endowment may have nullified the potential gains in technical progress.

In a different context, Easterly and Fischer (1995) argued that the Soviet economy would inevitably run into diminishing returns due to the massive accumulation of capital not accompanied by technological progress. Such postulation, if correct, raises the question as to whether economies which invested heavily in capital, particularly in the past few decades, would experience sustainable growth. This prompted Krugman (1994) to draw a comparison between the Asian economies and that of the Soviet Union. In his paper which was based on Kim and Lau's (1994) and Young's (1992, 1995) empirical findings, Krugman concluded:

> The newly industrializing countries of Asia, like the Soviet Union of the 1950s, have achieved rapid growth in large part through an astonishing mobilization of resources. Once one accounts for the role of rapidly growing inputs in these countries' growth, one finds little left to explain. Asian growth, like that of the Soviet Union in its high-growth era, seems to be driven by extraordinary growth in inputs like labor and capital rather than by gains in efficiency. (1994, p. 40)

Krugman argued that it is unrealistic to expect these countries which are already investing 35–40 per cent of their GDP to be able to raise their rate of investment further. In addition, he argued that most of the East Asian economies have highly educated and high-quality labour forces, which limits the scope for further improvement in these spheres. Under such circumstances, without technical progress, eventual decreasing returns to investment will set in and the growth potential of these economies will be limited.

ASSIMILATION THEORIES

The main argument in assimilation theories is that the economy grows because it uses new technologies and becomes more efficient, creating more and more output per unit of inputs. The assimilationists challenged Krugman's analysis on a number of grounds. They argued that the decomposition of growth in output is difficult because technical progress is embodied in new capital. Accordingly, the effects of technical progress cannot be separated from the expansion of capital inputs. Technological progress can only take place through the introduction of new machines, that is, through an increase in capital inputs. In fact, this line of reasoning had been propounded in the 1960s by Kaldor. According to Kaldor:

> In a world in which technology is embodied in capital equipment and where both the improvement of knowledge and production of new capital goods are continuous, it is impossible to isolate the productivity growth which is due to capital accumulation as such from the productivity growth which is due to improvements in technical knowledge. There is no such thing as a 'set of blueprints' which reflect a 'given state of knowledge' – the knowledge required for making of, say, the Concorde is only evolved in the process of designing or developing the aeroplane; the costs of obtaining the necessary new knowledge is causally indistinguishable from the other elements of investment. (cited in Turner, 1993, p. 118)

Even replacement investment is associated, in this view, with technical progress. The rationale is that when a machine is being replaced by a new one, the latter is likely to be technologically more advanced and not simply a new copy of the old one (Singh, 1998). On this basis, decreasing returns are unlikely to occur because the higher the rate of investment, the greater would be the turnover of machines and the greater would be the technical progress. This in turn would lead to greater 'learning-by-doing' activities, thereby increasing technological progress. The high growth rates of the East Asian countries could thus be argued to be due to their high rates of capital accumulation which embodied technological progress.

There are many studies which emphasize the importance of capital accumulation in economic growth. Empirical evidence based on historical accounts of economic growth indicated the significant role played by capital accumulation particularly in the form of capital equipment. Nations and industries which increased their physical capital investment were found to grow more rapidly than those which did not (Gerschenkron, 1962; Landes, 1969; Pollard, 1981). Increases in capital investment would also increase the quality or effectiveness of labour (Nelson and Phelps, 1966; Schultz, 1975).

There is a growing literature on the importance of physical investment in the generation of higher rates of growth (Nelson and Winter, 1982; Rosenberg, 1994; Hobday, 1995). De Long and Summers (1991) reported that the real rate of return on equipment could be as high as 30 per cent. It was noted that capital accumulation, particularly in the form of equipment investment, resulted in higher social returns than other forms of investment (Jorgenson, 1988; De Long and Summers, 1991). The rationale is that equipment investment is the principal channel through which advances in technology are diffused both within a country and across countries. Several cross-country studies found a significant positive role played by capital investment in economic growth (Nelson and Winter, 1982; Dowrick and

Nguyen, 1989; Mankiw et al., 1992; Rosenberg, 1994; Barro, 1997). The analysis carried out by Khan and Kumar (1997) on 95 developing countries during 1970–90 found a positive relationship between gross national product (GNP) and public and private capital investment, with private investment having a larger impact than public investment. According to Nelson and Pack: 'The massive investment in physical and human capital made by the Asian newly industrialised countries is a sufficient explanation of the miracle' (1999, p. 4).

An increase in physical investment in the form of public infrastructure could significantly raise net output growth (Aschauer, 1989; Barro, 1990; Glomm and Ravikumar, 1994). Aschauer's (1989) study which employed time-series data of the US from 1949 to 1985 estimated an elasticity of output with respect to public capital of about 0.4. A similar magnitude was also found in other studies employing aggregate US data (Munnell, 1992). Thus in order to attain a higher growth of output, the equivalent stock of capital must grow faster than the input of labour. Referring back to Young's (1994) TFP analysis of 66 countries (Table 2.6), if TFP is the main determinant of economic growth as proposed by accumulationist theorists, then the top five TFP-performing countries – Egypt, Pakistan, Botswana, Congo and Malta – should experience not only high growth rates but also a significant level of structural transformation as in the East Asian countries. If TFP captures technological progress, then within the confines of the accumulationist paradigm this group of countries should be at the forefront of technical advancement. Yet this has not been the case. Egypt, Pakistan, Congo and Malta are still considered to be predominantly technologically backward compared to, for example, Singapore which ranked 63 on Young's TFP growth scale. Since the mid-1990s, Singapore has not only experienced one of the highest growth rates in the world but it is also one of the world's richest countries in terms of per capita income. None of the above-mentioned group of countries displayed any signs of converging towards the living standards of advanced nations at the speed experienced by Singapore. On this basis alone, a high TFP does not necessarily translate into high economic growth.

The estimation of TFP may also be subject to bias as a result of sensitivities associated with the variables which are incorporated in the estimation. Sarel (1994, 1997), Collins and Bosworth (1996) and Harberger (1996) reported that TFP is highly sensitive to the sample period, size of the capital share, and overall growth of the economy during the estimation period. Several studies (World Bank, 1993; Collins and Bosworth, 1996; Harberger, 1996; Sarel, 1996; Dowling and Summers, 1998; Gapinski, 1998), which employed different econometric methods including different methods of deriving capital and labour, reported that TFP growth in East Asia was much stronger than that reported by Young (1994, 1995).

A recent study conducted by Sarel (1997) found an impressive growth rate in the East Asian economies relative to that of the United States. Sarel's (1997) findings, in Table 2.7, suggest that TFP growth rates were strong in Indonesia, Malaysia, Singapore and Thailand. Singapore appeared to be the best performer, followed closely by Malaysia and Thailand. TFP growth accounted for a significant portion of growth rates of output per person.

Table 2.7   *Annual contribution to percentage growth in output per person in selected countries, 1978–96*

	Output per person	Capital per person	Effective labour	TFP
Average 1978–96				
Indonesia	4.74	8.97	0.93	1.16
Malaysia	4.54	6.86	0.58	2.00
Philippines	0.19	1.80	0.62	– 0.78
Singapore	5.09	6.45	1.06	2.23
Thailand	5.24	7.32	1.51	2.03
United States	1.07	1.63	0.43	0.29
Average 1991–96				
Indonesia	5.11	6.98	0.96	2.20
Malaysia	5.35	8.25	0.97	2.00
Philippines	1.63	1.15	0.87	0.67
Singapore	4.91	5.60	0.77	2.46
Thailand	6.51	11.13	1.37	2.25
United States	1.26	1.19	0.43	0.61

Source: Sarel, 1997, p. 29.

TFP growth rates estimated by Sarel (1997) were higher than those estimated by Young (1995). This difference may be due to the different time period and different size of capital share that were being utilised in these estimations. Sarel's findings were supported by Gapinski's (1998), who stated that TFP growth is a major determinant of economic growth for Hong Kong and Singapore. Furthermore, despite the low estimation of TFP reported by Kim and Lau (1994, 1995) and Young (1994, 1995), Dowling and Summers commented that:

> when the actual contribution to growth in percentage levels is compared the story is different. Because growth in Asia is so much higher, a small contribution of TFP is still as large or larger than it is in slower growing industrial countries, when measured in absolute percentage point additions to growth. (1998, p. 178)

With reference to the Malaysian experience, the estimates of TFP growth has produced mixed results. A study conducted by Tham (1995) seems to support Young's view based on a negative trend in TFP for the Malaysian economy. This is shown in Table 2.8.

Table 2.8   Sources of growth in Malaysia, 1971–87

Year (Average)	Rate of growth (%)				Contribution to growth (%)		
	Output	Capital	Labour	TFP	Capital	Labour	TFP
1971–75	6.7	10.24	3.77	−1.42	1.01	0.19	−0.21
1976–80	8.5	10.17	3.74	0.26	0.82	0.14	0.03
1981–87	4.6	9.26	3.16	−2.68	1.33	0.23	−0.58
1971–87	6.3	9.82	3.50	−1.44	1.04	0.18	−0.23

Source: Tham, 1995, p. 48.

Tham (1995) reported a low average rate of TFP for the manufacturing sector for 1971–87. He concluded that the growth and development of the Malaysian economy during this period was the result of input growth rather than productivity growth. There were also other authors who found a negative TFP growth for Malaysia (Drysdale and Huang, 1995; Alavi, 1996). Alavi (1996) reported that capital and labour inputs played predominant roles in output growth, with capital inputs as the most important contributor. She concluded that Malaysia experienced an insignificant TFP growth between 1979 and 1989. On the other hand, several authors had reported favourable TFP growth values for Malaysia. Table 2.9 lists some studies that reported a positive TFP growth for Malaysia. Thomas and Wang (1992) reported TFP growth of 2 per cent for 1960–90. The World Bank (1993) estimated 1 per cent TFP growth for 1970–90. These divergent estimates of TFP growth rates will be examined in Chapter 9.

Table 2.9   Studies which reported positive TFP growth for Malaysia: brief details

Author	Period of study	Method	TFP Growth (%)	
Syrquin (in Tham, 1995)	1960–89	Growth accounting	(1960–70)	3.0
			(1970–80)	0.5
			(1980–89)	0.5
Thomas and Wang (1992)	1960–87	Econometric estimation of Cobb–Douglas production function.		2.0
World Bank (1993)	1960–89	Econometric estimation of Cobb–Douglas production function.		1.0

Table 2.9 (continued)

Author	Period of study	Method	TFP Growth (%)	
Kawai (1994)	1970–90	Econometric estimation of Cobb–Douglas production function.	(1970–80)	2.5
			(1980–90)	0.7
Harberger (1996)	1970–91	Econometric estimation of Cobb–Douglas production function.	(1970–74)	7.2
			(1974–79)	1.2
			(1979–84)	−0.7
			(1984–89)	0.1
			(1989–91)	3.3
Malaysia (1996)	1971–95	Growth accounting	(1971–90)	1.2
			(1990–95)	2.5
Dowling and Summers (1998)	1961–95	Econometric estimation of Cobb–Douglas production function	a* (1961–95)	1.5
			b* (1961–95)	1.9
			c* (1961–95)	2.3
			e* 1961–95)	1.9
			f* (1961–95)	2.2
			g* (1961–95)	2.5

Notes:

a* based on 0.4 capital share using Nehru–Dhareshwar capital stock adjustment, World Bank data.

b* based on 0.35 capital share using Nehru–Dhareshwar capital stock adjustment, World Bank data.

c* based on 0.3 capital share using Nehru–Dhareshwar capital stock adjustment, World Bank data.

e* based on 0.4 capital share using King–Levine capital stock adjustment, Summers–Heston data.

f* based on 0.35 capital share using King–Levine capital stock adjustment, Summers–Heston data.

g* based on 0.3 capital share using King–Levine capital stock adjustment, Summers–Heston data.

CONCLUSION

The analysis of TFP growth is not without criticism. Shaikh (1974) argued that the Solow residual does not measure technical progress but only reflects distributional changes. TFP growth estimated from this residual may therefore be subject to measurement problems. While TFP estimates inform the sources of growth, the numbers represent only broad orders of magnitude and may be prone to significant errors (Scott, 1993; Singh, 1998). Nelson (1996, pp. 2–3) pointed out that:

to try to 'divide up the credit' for economic growth among different sources, assigning so much of the credit to technical advance, so much to growing capital intensity, so much to rising educational attainments – to list the sources generally treated as the most important ... this 'dividing up' exercise is nonsense.

In fact, one particular branch of endogenous growth model which is associated with the production function where $Y = AK$ (Rebelo, 1991)[15] proposes that the key to rapid long-run growth is found in cultures, institutions and tax policies with no explicit role for TFP. On the other hand, there is another branch of endogenous growth paradigm that seeks to explain rather than to downplay TFP growth. These theories emphasize human capital development. Because of its significance the next chapter will provide a brief review of this particular branch of endogenous growth models.

NOTES

[1]   The neoclassical growth model was originally developed by the independent works of Solow (1956) and Swan (1956). Due to the similarities in their approach, it is appropriate to refer to the neoclassical growth framework as a Solow–Swan growth model.

[2]   At a national conference on the growth and development of the Association of South East Asian Nations (ASEAN) in December 1995, the Prime Minister of Singapore, Dr Goh Chok Tong publicly repudiated Krugman's view (Wilson, 2000).

[3]   The different views are on subjects that range from the technical relationship between factor inputs to the role of political, social and cultural factors.

[4]   The higher the value A_t, the higher the effectiveness of labour input and therefore the greater the level of output Y. This type of technical specification is known as labour-augmenting. In the case of capital-augmenting, the production function is written as $Y_t = F(A_tK_t, L_t)$, and is Hicks-neutral when $Y_t = A_tF(K_t, L_t)$.

[5]   Inada (1963) imposed the technological restrictions that $f'(k) \to \infty$ as $k \to 0$ and $f'(k) \to 0$ as $k \to \infty$.

[6]   'Double-switching is associated essentially with the possibility that the same method of production may be the most profitable of a number of methods of production at more than one rate of profits (r) even though other methods are more profitable at rates in between. Capital-reversing is the value of capital moving in the same direction, when alternative rates of interest are considered, so that a technique with a lower degree of mechanization, as measured, for example, by its level of output per head and the value of capital per head, is associated with a lower rate of profits. That is to say, it is the most profitable technique at this rate of profits and, in particular, is more profitable than a more mechanized technique (in the two senses above) which was either equi-profitable or more profitable than this one at higher rates profits'. (Harcourt, 1972, p. 124)

[7]   It is important to note that Sraffa's (1960) *Production of Commodities by Means of*

Commodities: Prelude to a Critique of Economic Theory took a considerable time to complete, dating back at least to the mid-1920s (Harcourt, 1972).

[8] If in a group of countries, a rich country has a saving rate that is higher than a poor country, the *sf(k)* curve of the rich country will shift upward. This will increase the rich country's steady-state position, and the rich country will grow faster. In this situation, absolute β-convergence would not hold (Barro and Sala-i-Martin, 1995).

[9] According to Caves and Krause (1984), the leaders were Australia in the first decade of the 1870–1979 period, and the UK and the US during the post-Second World War era.

[10] The term 'grouping' includes different geographical regions, different regions within a country, different administrative units and even different time samples.

[11] Galton's (1886) research showed that the deviation of children's heights and other physical and mental characteristics from the mean of the population was positively correlated with their parents' deviation. He postulated that this amount of deviation would regress or converge towards zero. However, the population's distribution of heights was not found to narrow systematically over time.

[12] From Robert M. Solow, *Growth Theory: An Exposition*, 2000 Oxford University Press, New York. By permission of Oxford University Press, Inc.

[13] World Bank, 1993; Kawai, 1994; Kim and Lau, 1994; Krugman, 1994; Young 1994, 1995; Drysdale and Huang, 1995; Bosworth, 1996; Chen, 1997; Sarel, 1997; Dowling and Summers, 1998.

[14] Reprinted from European Economic Review, 38 (3/4), Young, A., Lesson from the East Asian NIC: a contrarian view, p. 970, © Elsevier 1994, with permission from Elsevier.

[15] *Y* is output, *A* is a constant and *K* is physical capital that is augmented with human capital which may prevent diminishing returns from setting in.

3. Endogenous growth: the evolution of technological progress

INTRODUCTION

The recent trend in the application of growth accounting methodology to explain the East Asia miracle clearly points to the importance of technological progress as captured by TFP growth. However, the validity and applicability of the TFP approach for explaining East Asia growth performance had been criticized on numerous occasions. Singh (in Thompson, 1998, p. 79) argued that:

> TFP growth does not imply that a country has had no or slow technical progress in the ordinary meaning of these terms. That would be a silly conclusion for a country like South Korea in the light of its extraordinary success in continually upgrading its export structure. Thirty years ago it was exporting mainly textiles. Today much the larger part of its exports come from cars, computer chips and other technologically advanced products … In a non-neo-classical analysis where technical progress is embodied in new capital goods as well as replacement capital, there is no reason to expect that high rates of investment will necessarily lead to decreasing returns.

The main concern about neoclassical growth analysis, as pointed out by Singh (1998), arose from the assumption of diminishing returns to factors input. Long-run growth will cease once the economy arrives at its steady state. However, empirical evidence is not consistent with the assumption of diminishing returns as growth in per capita income was positive and non-declining in many countries for prolonged periods of time as indicated earlier in the discussion of the convergence controversy. In fact, Kaldor (1960) observed that growth of output per worker rose continually and productivity growth rates showed no tendency to decline. Grossman and Helpman (1991, p. 4) stated that:

> If production of output is characterized by diminishing returns to the accumulated factors, the incentive to investment may disappear in the long run in the absence of productivity gains. The fact that investment has continued for more than two hundred years since the industrial revolution suggests that technical change has played a major role in the growth process.

This points to the notion that growth in output cannot be entirely accounted for by growth in inputs, and within the neoclassical growth framework, the residual is postulated to be attributed to exogenous technological progress. Endogenous growth theories, on the other hand, attempt to explore and understand this unexplained residual by endogenizing it.

There have been a number of attempts to endogenize technological progress. Early attempts, however, faced a major problem in dealing with increasing returns within a dynamic general equilibrium framework. If technological progress is to be endogenized, then the decision to make it grow must be rewarded, just as capital and labour must be rewarded.

The standard production function can be written as $Y = F(A,K,L)$. If F exhibits constant returns in K and L when A is held constant, it must exhibit increasing returns on three factors: K, L and A. This difficulty was acknowledged by Solow (1957), who assumed technological progress to be exogenous not because it was realistic, but because it was the only manageable assumption. Kaldor (1960) suggested abandoning altogether the notion of an aggregate production function and the distinction between increases in productivity due to capital and those due to technological progress. Instead, he proposed a technical progress function where the rate of output is directly related to the rate of investment.

Solow (2000) pointed out two popular approaches to rectify this deficiency. The first method drops the assumption of diminishing returns as revealed by the production function, $Y = AK$, with A as a constant (Romer, 1986; Lucas, 1988; Easterly et al., 1991). Physical capital is augmented by human capital so that diminishing returns would not occur. The second approach provides a theory to explain the evolution of technological progress, A. The central feature of this approach is that technological progress (leading to or generating productivity growth) is primarily driven by theoretical constructs which take the form of innovations, new consumer goods (Aghion and Howitt, 1992), research and development (Romer, 1990) and international trade (Grossman and Helpman, 1991).

The aim of this chapter is to provide a brief overview of the development of endogenous growth models, paying particular attention to the accumulation of human capital in driving A. In doing so, a theoretical foundation for the study is provided. In order to introduce the relevant concepts of endogenous growth models, it is sufficient to work with a 'reduced form' or 'bare structure' of endogenous production technology. It is not the intention of this exercise to go over the models step by step as it would not only lengthen this book considerably, but also add to unnecessary complications without making any new and significant contributions to the existing literature. It would only be repeating what has already been proposed by Grossman and Helpman (1991), Barro and Sala-i-Martin (1995), Aghion and Howitt (1998), Solow (2000) and others.

Many endogenous growth models (particularly those associated with human capital accumulation, learning by doing, and research and development– R&D) share similar structures with the standard neoclassical production framework. What differentiates the standard neoclassical production framework from endogenous growth models is that the latter provides a theory accounting for the evolution of A to explain output growth (Casaratto, 1999; Solow, 2000). It complements the neoclassical framework to explain technical change. This chapter will focus primarily on the evolution of A and not the microeconomics of endogenous production technology.

OVERVIEW OF ENDOGENOUS GROWTH MODELS

Often, the literature has led us to believe that endogenous growth began with Romer's 1986 paper. This is not entirely true. According to You (1994), it was Kaldor (1960) who pioneered the work on endogenous technical change by introducing the technical progress function. Harcourt (2001, p. 45) clarifies:

> Kaldor has come back even though he has not been acknowledged on the whole in the new growth theory – Lucas, Romer, Helpman and Grossman. Sometimes they remember to say that these ideas actually came from Kaldor, Myrdal and Allyn Young, but since the way they now train youngsters in America is that economics began ten years ago, these writers are unknown to them. What is worthwhile in the new growth theory is the taking up of the ideas of Kaldor, Myrdal and Young.

Solow (2000), with reference to Romer's growth model on endogenizing technological progress, said that 'Kaldor's "technical progress function" was an earlier and less successful, attempt to accomplish the same thing' (p. 46). Solow (2000) also pointed out that the AK models[1] of Romer and Rebelo (primarily responsible for the expansion of the endogenous paradigm) share many similarities to Domar's growth analysis which was introduced in the 1940s. In Solow's (2000, pp. 123–24)[2] words:

> That device amounts to little more than going back to Domar (1946, 1957). A typical example will show that a substantial part of the modern literature consists of a complicated way of disguising the fact that it is returning to the Domar model, and, as with Domar, the rate of growth becomes endogenous.

Palley (1996, p. 125) stated that: 'such models implicitly embody a Kaldorian technical progress function in which the symbols K and I are replaced by the stock and flow of R&D. This reveals how Kaldor (1957) is the progenitor of endogenous growth.'

Myrdal (1957) endogenized technological progress by linking it to capital investment. The evolution of technological progress is driven by 'the principle of circular and cumulative causation'. Accordingly, the mechanism behind the 'cumulative causation' is increasing returns found in the manufacturing sector. Myrdal (1957) argued that industrialization is the key to economic development. Those countries that concentrated on activities with increasing returns (mainly manufacturing) are those that have become rich. This, according to Myrdal (1957), explains the polarization of the world between the rich and the poor countries. Earlier, Young (1928) pointed out that increasing returns is the driver of technological progress. In Young's framework, increasing returns is not just about economies of scale in production, but more importantly, it is a cumulative process associated with learning-by-doing activities during the production process. In Young's (1928, p. 537) words: 'for it involves a particular thesis with respect to the way in which increasing returns are reflected in changes in the organization of industrial activities'. This in turn will lead to the specialization of human capital. He cited Adam Smith's principle of the division of labour, whereby during the production process, labour began to acquire new skills. One important implication of this type of technological progress is that it will lead to new forms of production techniques which in turn will spill over into the production of new products or the expansion in the variety of products.

According to Barro and Sala-i-Martin (1995), the first economist to use a production function of this type was Von Neumann (1937). In fact, as early as 1890, Marshall argued that technological progress in the form of knowledge accumulation is central to the production of material goods, knowledge, organization and investment thereby leading to increasing returns. These increasing returns are driven by spillovers from other firms. Schumpeter (1934) postulated that knowledge accumulation was facilitated by entrepreneurship. In his creative destruction analysis, technological progress is primarily driven by entrepreneurs, who are constantly seeking improvements, changes and progress to enhance their profit margins during the production of goods and services. He stated that competition is not simply about prices but also about better production techniques (innovation and technological progress). He viewed growth as a dynamic process, occurring intermittently over time. The introduction of a new innovation or new production technique by one entrepreneur would affect the production structures of other entrepreneurs through spillover of knowledge.[3] This would facilitate other entrepreneurs in their decisions about their own production frontiers. As time progresses, the pace of spillover or diffusion would slacken and so would growth. In order to sustain long-run growth, incentives must be given to stimulate the accumulation of knowledge (in the form of better linkages between investment and other areas of the economy) needed to drive technological progress.

Hirschman (1958) built on Schumpeter's concept of linkages and diffusion by postulating that growth could be generated through the promotion of leading industrial sectors which would, in turn, provide linkages with other industries in the economy. This is based on the notion that linkages would make it easier (or perhaps less risky) for other firms to undertake further investment as a result of externalities from the initial investment.[4] According to Hirschman, the leading sectors in an economy could generate the most externalities so the diffusion of knowledge to other sectors of the economy could take place at a rapid rate. This view was supported by Schmockler (1966) who argued that innovations are driven by the same factors which determine other investments, namely the perceived economic value of innovations. He stated that innovations are determined endogenously and are related to the rate of investment in physical capital.

Recently, Aghion and Howitt (1998) extended Schumpeter's approach of endogenous generation of new technology. They incorporated Schumpeter's exposition of creative destruction into their model by suggesting that successful R&D may render technology invented by previous R&D unprofitable. Rents acquired from successful innovations are viewed to be temporary, thereby affecting the entrepreneurs' R&D spending decisions. Hence, it is in the interest of entrepreneurs to pursue further innovation in order to capture the temporary monopolistic rents (until it has been replaced by the next innovation). In doing so, technological progress, A, will continue to rise.

In Aghion and Howitt's (1998) framework, output depends on the input of an intermediate good, x:

$$y = AF(x) \tag{3.1}$$

Function F is positive with diminishing marginal product. Technological progress is derived from the invention of a new variety of intermediate good which replaced the old one, and in the process raises the technological parameter, A, by a constant factor of $\gamma > 1$:

$$A_{\Phi + 1}/A_{\Phi} = \gamma \tag{3.2}$$

where Φ denotes the ith innovation.

Labour is assumed to be fixed but has competing usages. It can either be utilized for the production of intermediate goods, x, or it can be employed in R&D, n. Hence:

$$L = x + n \tag{3.3}$$

The amount of n being employed in R&D would generate an amount of innovations at a random Poisson arrival rate of λn, where $\lambda > 0$ (a parameter capturing the productivity of R&D).

The amount of labour being devoted to R&D is derived from:

$$w_{\Phi} = \lambda p_{\Phi + 1} \tag{3.4}$$

where w_{Φ} is the wage paid to the Φth innovation, and $p_{\Phi + 1}$ is the discount rate or expected payoff of the $(\Phi + 1)th$ innovation.

The value of $p_{\Phi+1}$, is determined by:

$$r\,p_{\Phi+1} = \pi_{\Phi+1} - \lambda n_{\Phi+1}\,p_{\Phi+1} \tag{3.5}$$

The expected income or rate of profit (being generated by the $(\Phi + 1)th$ innovation), $rp_{\Phi+1}$, is equal to the profit flow, $\pi_{\Phi+1}$, minus the expected loss, $p_{\Phi+1}$, that will be incurred by an entrepreneur when the $(\Phi + 1)th$ innovation is being replaced by a new invention. The Schumpeterian effect can then be captured by:

$$P_{\Phi+1} = \pi_{\Phi+1}/(r + \lambda n_{\Phi+1}) \tag{3.6}$$

The technically detailed mechanism for tracing the flows of both profit, $\pi_{\Phi+1}$, and labour, x, can be found in Aghion and Howitt (1998). Briefly, the arbitrage in relation to flows of profit, π_Φ, and flows of demand for labour in the production of intermediate goods, x_Φ, is where 'both the allocation of labor between research and manufacturing and the productivity-adjusted wage rate remain constant over time, so that wages, profit, and final output are all scaled up by the same $\gamma > 1$ each time a new innovation occurs' (Aghion and Howitt, 1998, p. 57).

In a steady state, the flow of final output produced during the interval period between the Φth and the $\Phi + 1th$ innovation is:

$$y_\Phi = A_\Phi \tilde{x} = A_\Phi\,(L - \tilde{n}) \tag{3.7}$$

where ~ denotes the steady-state equilibrium.

This implies that:

$$y_{\Phi+1} = \gamma y_\Phi \tag{3.8}$$

Since the flow of output does not occur in time but in a continuous sequence of innovations, and in order to trace the rate of growth of output, it is necessary to trace the evolution of final output in real time, φ. Using equation (3.8), and taking logs, the final output $ln\,y\,(\varphi)$ increases by an amount equal to $ln\,\gamma$ each time a new innovation occurs. Since the real time interval between two successive innovations is random, the time path of the log of final output $ln\,y\,(\varphi)$ will also be a random step function as shown in Figure 3.1.

Accordingly, the size of each step is equal to $ln\,\gamma > 0$ and the time interval between each step is exponentially distributed with parameter $\lambda\tilde{n}$. Taking a unit-time interval between φ and $\varphi + 1$:

$$ln\,y\,(\varphi + 1) = ln\,y\,(\varphi) + (ln\,\gamma)\,v\,(\varphi) \tag{3.9}$$

where $v(\varphi)$ is the number of innovations between φ and $\varphi + 1$.

The Poisson distribution of $v(\varphi)$ is with parameter $\lambda\tilde{n}$, so:

$$V[ln\,y\,(\varphi + 1) - ln\,y\,(\varphi)] = \lambda\tilde{n}\,ln\,\gamma \tag{3.10}$$

In the steady state, average growth rate is given by:

$$g = \lambda \tilde{n} \ln \gamma \qquad (3.11)$$

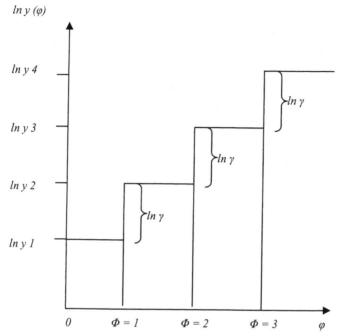

Figure 3.1   A random step function of output growth

Based on equation (3.11), the expected rate of growth is proportional to $\tilde{n}$. This endogenous rate of growth will depend on anything that will help to increase $\tilde{n}$. Increases in labour, L, will increase $\tilde{n}$ and thereby g. Increases in the size of innovation γ and/or in the productivity of R&D, λ, will also foster growth, directly by increasing the factor $\lambda \ln \gamma$, and indirectly through increasing $\tilde{n}$.

Kaldor (1960), on the other hand, put forward a proposition that technical progress is diffused into the economic system through the creation of new equipment, which is dependent upon current investment. He suggested that rate of growth output per worker, $\dot{y}/y$, is a function of the rate of growth of capital per worker, $\dot{k}/k$:

$$\dot{y}/y = F(\dot{k}/k) \qquad (3.12)$$

This relationship is captured in Kaldor's 'technical progress function' in Figure 3.2.

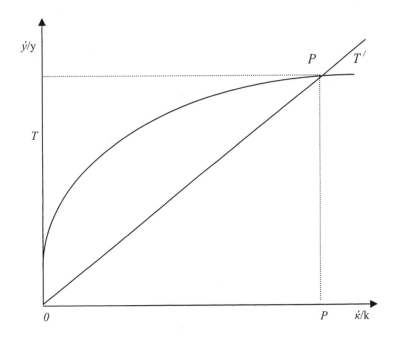

Source: Kaldor, 1960.

Figure 3.2   Kaldor's technical progress function

The shape and position of the TT' curve reflects both the magnitude and character of technological progress. The TT' curve slopes upward because increases in the rate of growth of capital per worker are postulated to be associated with increases in the rate of growth of output per worker. Accordingly, a series of new innovations could shift the TT' curve upward leading to a fall in capital–output ratio, and technological progress will take the form of capital-saving. A downward shift in the TT' curve is interpreted as predominantly a labour-saving production process which is associated with the drying up in the flow of new innovations (and as such productivity will be lagging behind). P is the steady state, where the rate of growth of capital and the rate of output are equal. In short, towards the left of P in the TT' curve, innovations will be predominantly capital-saving in nature, and towards the right of P, innovations will be labour-saving. The TT' curve does not start from the origin because 'some increase in productivity would take place even if capital per man remained constant over time' (Kaldor, 1960, p. 596).

In the reworked version of Kaldor's (1960) technical progress function, Kaldor and Mirrlees (1962) showed that technological progress is driven by the rate of improvement in the design of a newly produced capital good. Here, the driver of technical progress is more specific in that it is driven by the desire to replaced outmoded capital equipment. The rationale for doing so is linked to the obsolescence of capital equipment. Not only is the profitability of older plant and equipment assumed to diminish over time, but more importantly, equipment and plant of subsequent dates are likely to be superior. An important implication of this reworked version is that the acceleration of the retirement of old equipment will accelerate technical progress. Kaldor and Mirrlees (1962) went on to suggest that it is not possible to increase the productivity of labour by reducing the number of workers in relation to the existing capital equipment. Rather, productivity of labour is governed by the amount of capital equipment available for workers to operate, that is: 'by the amount of investment per operative' (Kaldor and Mirrlees, 1962, p. 175).

In his later writings, Kaldor (1966) extended the technical progress function, whereby the evolution of A occurs in the form of Verdoorn's (1949) Law in that productivity growth is an increasing function of output growth leading to increasing returns. Kaldor's propositions drew upon Verdoorn's (1949) framework to explain the behavioural relationship between productivity growth and the expansion of the manufacturing sector. This, according to McCombie (1998, p. 353), 'does shed light on the growth process'. Verdoorn's exposition was expanded, and two additional propositions were incorporated into Kaldor's (1966) analysis to explain the differences in growth rates among developed countries. Accordingly, the rate of output growth is substantially determined by the impact of economies of scale, leading to increasing returns through the division and specialization of labour. Since the manufacturing sector offers more scope for increasing returns, it constitutes the main determinant of productivity growth. Kaldor (1966) proposed that the faster the rate of growth in the manufacturing sector, the faster would be the growth of total output. The faster the growth of labour productivity in manufacturing, the faster would be the growth of manufacturing output. This causal relationship is summarized in Box 3.1.

Kaldor's three propositions (which will be discussed in detail in Chapter 7) suggest that a substantial part of productivity growth (technical advancement) is endogenous to the growth process. It is driven by the rate of expansion of output through the effect of economies of scale brought about by spillover effects.

In summary, Kaldor's endogenous growth analysis is considered to be a cumulative and path-dependent process. Kaldor's view on endogenous technical progress focused on three distinctive stages. It started with the technical progress function to demonstrate that capital investment drives technical progress. This was then reworked; the driver of technical progress became more specific and took the form of replacement capital. Later, Kaldor's growth analysis climaxed on a grand scale with the manufacturing sector driving increasing returns for the whole economy. One can only regret that Kaldor did not integrate these three distinctive components into one coherent framework.

BOX 3.1   KALDOR'S THREE PROPOSITIONS OF ECONOMIC
           GROWTH

The faster the rate of growth of the manufacturing sector, the faster will be the rate of growth of Gross Domestic Product, not simply in a definitional sense in that manufacturing output is a large component of total output, but for fundamental economic reasons connected with induced productivity growth inside and outside the manufacturing sector. It is summed up in the maxim that the manufacturing sector of the economy is the "engine of growth".

The faster the rate of growth of manufacturing output, the faster will the rate of growth of labour productivity in manufacturing owing to static and dynamic economies of scale, or increasing returns in the widest sense.

The faster the rate of growth of manufacturing output, the faster the rate of transference of labour from other sectors of the economy where there are either diminishing returns, or where no relationship exists between employment growth and output growth. A reduction in the amount of labour in these sectors will raise productivity growth outside manufacturing. As a result of increasing returns in manufacturing on the one hand and induced productivity growth in non manufacturing on the other hand, we expect the faster the rate of growth of manufacturing output, the faster the rate of growth of productivity in the economy as a whole.

Source: Thirlwall, 1983, p. 345.

A similar view that predates the Kaldor–Mirrless technical progress function is found in Salter's (1966, p. 21) analysis of 'the flow of technical knowledge'. Salter first documented this proposition in his 1954 PhD dissertation at the University of Cambridge. The flow of technical knowledge is a production technique (at each date) that employed the most recent technical advances, and these technical advances are derived from the additions or replacements of the pre-existing capital stock. According to Salter (1966), the flow of new knowledge generated during the production process from one time period to another is an important source of technological progress. As workers learnt how to utilize a piece of equipment more efficiently, advances are made to improve the existing methods of production. This will lead to a continuous flow of new knowledge and in the process continuously changing the production function of each commodity. Salter (1966) captured this flow by using a series of dated production functions, one for each time period:

$$Y = f_n(a, b, c...), \ Y = f_{n+1}(a, b, c...), \ ...Y = f_{n+t}(a, b, c....),$$

where Y is output; $a, b, c, ...$ are inputs of factors of production and $n, n+1, ...n+t$ are consecutive time periods.

An important consequence of the new advances in the production techniques is that the new techniques will be superior to their predecessors. As pointed out by Salter (1962, p. 138): 'These standards of technique differ from those of pre-existing capacity which, to a greater or lesser degree, has been outmoded by changes and improvements in technical knowledge and changes in factor prices since its construction date.' Salter (1966) then combined the flow of technical knowledge with changing relative factor prices so that firms could arrive at their best-practice method. According to Salter (1966, p. 23): 'The best-practice technique at each date is the appropriate technique having regard to both economic and technical conditions; it is the technique which yields minimum costs in terms of the production and relative prices of each date.' Salter (1966) went on to argue that an expanding labour force, if not accompanied by an appropriate increase in new capital investment, would eventually lead to a dilution in the amount of capital per worker, and through this, increase the risk of a lower rate of productivity increase. An important policy implication of the Salter model is that an increase in the rates of investment or replacement capital will lead to a more rapid increase in the utilization rates of new methods of production brought into general use. Salter (1966, p. 72) stated that:

> Thus all investment, net investment and replacement investment, is important in economic growth. An increasing supply of real gross investment per worker allows progress on two frontiers: the mechanisation frontier as best-practice techniques become progressively more mechanised, and the obsolescence frontier as the gap between co-existing techniques is steadily narrowed.

The importance of the spillover effects of increased knowledge was further extended by Arrow (1962). It was Arrow (1962) who found a way around the requirement of rewarding a factor share to A, in the form of spillover generated by knowledge. He indicated that through spillover generated by knowledge in the form of learning-by-doing, K and L could continue to receive their marginal products because in a competitive equilibrium, no additional compensation would be paid to A and as such A becomes endogenous.

In his learning-by-doing assessment,[5] Arrow indicated that during the production process, firms learn from both their previous investment experience and the investments of others. Any investment in physical capital would, in turn, increase the stock of knowledge. Under Arrow's framework, knowledge is taken to be a function of total capital stock. Investment is not regarded as a carrier of technical progress as in the vintage models, but instead represents its source. Arrow's analysis can be captured by the following Cobb Douglas production function:

$$Y_t = K^\alpha_t (A_t L_t)^{1-\alpha} \tag{3.13}$$

The evolution of A in Arrow's learning by doing analysis can be traced by employing Frankel's (1962) technology:

$$\dot{A} = A(K/L)^\beta \tag{3.14}$$

Frankel (1962) assumed that $\alpha + \beta = 1$. Combining equations (3.14) and (3.13):

$$Y = AK \tag{3.15}$$

According to equation (3.15), as capital increases, so will output in a proportional manner, because knowledge automatically increases in proportion, even if there is a continuous full employment of labour and substitutability of labour and capital in the aggregate production function.

Another interpretation of the evolution of A in Arrow's learning by doing approach is also given by Shell (1966):

$$\dot{A}_t = \theta\sigma_t Y_t - \beta A_t , \quad 0 < \theta < 1, 0 < \sigma < 1, \beta > 0 \tag{3.16}$$

where θ is the research success coefficient, σ represents the fraction of output being utilized for inventive purposes and β denotes the rate of decay of technical knowledge.

Because equation (3.16) has two state variables, deriving a solution is not an easy task, and as such, no solution on the dynamics of the model was given by Shell (1966). However, Sato (1966) pointed out that this difficulty lies in the specification of A, which ties A to Y. Instead, Sato suggested that A could evolve as follows:

$$\dot{A}_t = \theta\sigma - \beta A \quad \text{or} \quad \dot{A}/A = \theta\sigma/A - \beta \tag{3.17}$$

Equation (3.17) shows that as long as $\theta\sigma - \beta > 0$, there is no constraint to the growth of knowledge.

Many recent endogenous growth models (Romer, 1986, 1990; Lucas, 1988; Grossman and Helpman, 1991) have been constructed based on Arrow's learning-by-doing framework. In Romer's (1986) framework, A was primarily driven by R&D as knowledge,[6] and all types of knowledge shared an essential feature in that they were non-rivals. An important implication of this non-rival property is that the production and allocation of knowledge cannot be completely governed by competitive market forces. Marginal cost of supplying an item of knowledge to an additional user, once the knowledge has been discovered, is zero. There is thus no need to reward A. Romer's (1986) production technology shared similar features to that proposed by Frankel (1962), but assumed that $\alpha + \beta > 1$ instead of $\alpha + \beta = 1$ as found in Frankel's (1962) analysis.

As with Romer (1986), Lucas (1988) also stressed the importance of human capital. Lucas postulates that human capital is linked to formal education and on-job training in the form of learning-by-doing. By participating in the learning process, human capital could increase and this could increase new knowledge and lead to greater productivity. In short, the higher the level of human capital, the greater the spillover effects on the productivity of others. Accordingly, it is the level of human capital that drives the level of productivity which, in turn, drives growth rates. Lucas's analysis of human capital is as follows:

$$Y = K^{\alpha} \; (uHL)^{1-\alpha} \qquad (3.18)$$

where H is current human capital stock, u denotes fraction of labour time being allocated to the production of consumer goods, and K denotes physical capital stock, which evolves over time according to the neoclassical production function.[7] Since human capital, H, is the driver of technological progress, the evolution of H is given as:

$$\dot{H} = H^{\varepsilon} \; \delta \; (1 - u), \quad \varepsilon = 1 \qquad (3.19)$$

where $1-u$ is the share of labour being utilized in the production of consumer goods,[8] and ε denotes knowledge intensity.

If $u = 1$, no effort is made to increase human capital accumulation as all of the society's labour force is devoted to the production of intermediate goods. Hence, there is no accumulation of human capital. If $u = 0$, then H will grow at the maximum rate δ. In between, there are no diminishing returns to the stock H. This, according to Lucas (1988), is because a given percentage increase in H would require the same effort no matter what level of H has already been attained. Hence, technological progress is dependent upon the term $1-u$, which is the amount of resources being devoted to the accumulation of human capital. Based on such a rationale, the growth rate of an economy can then be summarized as:

$$g = \psi \; (1 - u^{*}) \qquad (3.20)$$

where u^{*} is the optimal allocation of individuals' time between production and education.

In constrast, Romer's (1990) endogenous technological progress is expressed as:

$$H = H_{Y} + H_{A} \qquad (3.21)$$

Human capital H is assumed to be constant but is allocated according to preference between the production of final output H_Y, and the production of new varieties of capital H_A.

The evolution of A is constructed as shown below:

$$\dot{A} = \psi H_A A$$

In that:

$$\dot{A}/A = \psi H_A A > 0 \qquad (3.22)$$

where ψ is a productivity parameter.

Equation (3.22) specifies that endogenous growth is derived from the rate of growth in output which is proportional to the amount of human capital allocated to research in discovering new varieties of capital goods. According to Romer (1990), the key to growth is that A is linear in A. It is also interesting to note that a similar idea existed earlier as proposed by Sato (1966) to ensure unbounded progress as indicated in equation (3.17). What differentiated Sato's proposition from Romer's was that in the latter, σ was replaced by human capital H_A.

The production of the final output can be expressed as follows:

$$Y = H_Y{}^\alpha L^\beta \sum_{i=1}^{A} xi^{1-\alpha-\beta}, \qquad \alpha + \beta > 1 \qquad (3.23)$$

where Y is final aggregate output, L is stock of ordinary labour, and xi is an index of the different types of capital goods ($i = x_1, x_2, x_3,...$)[9] employed in the production of final output.

Because the integer i (different varieties of goods) is treated as a continuous variable, equation (3.21) can be replaced by an integral as shown below:

$$Y = H^\alpha L^\beta \int_0^A xi^{1-\alpha-\beta}\, di \qquad (3.24)$$

Since each good is assumed to have the same production cost and marginal productivity, xi is substituted with X to get:

$$Y = H^\alpha L^\beta \int_0^A X^{1-\alpha-\beta}\, di$$

$$= X^{1-\alpha-\beta} \int_0^A di$$

$$= AX^{1-\alpha-\beta} \qquad (3.25)$$

Equation (3.23) can now be written as:

$$Y = H_Y{}^{\alpha} L^{\beta} AX^{1-\alpha-\beta} \qquad (3.26)$$

The rest of Romer's (1990) analysis is devoted to the construction of a competitive market structure which H_A constant and positive. It will not be pursued in this brief overview. As remarked by Solow (2000, pp. 151–153)[10]:

> Most of the words in the Romer paper are devoted to talking about a complicated structure in which there are firms that manufacture these capital goods. There are other firms that do research on new varieties of capital goods and have a monopoly on the capital goods that they invent and then rent or sell to the manufacturing firms … You could just as well cut through all that if you were prepared to say that the economy has a stock of human capital H that is given and a fraction of γ of H is devoted to H_A. Then the rate of growth of output would just be: $(\alpha + \beta) \gamma H$, … .

Grossman and Helpman (1991) argued that A can be driven by the diffusion of new knowledge which is linked to international trade. Accordingly, if the local residents meet and interact with their foreign counterparts, they may find occasions to learn technical information that contributes to their country's stock of general knowledge. The Grossman and Helpman (1991) model can be expressed as:

$$K_{nt} = F(n_t \, O_t) \qquad (3.27)$$

where K_{nt} denotes the stock of knowledge capital in an economy.

Growth of K depends not only on spillover from local research but also from the international community. O is the cumulative volume of trade as captured by exports plus imports. The function F is assumed to be increasing in both arguments and is homogenous of degree one.

The Grossman–Helpman model shows that growth in international trade will increase the rate of knowledge spillovers. Grossman and Helpman (1991) indicated that in addition to the spillovers generated by international trade, there are also other avenues for knowledge transmission as listed below:

1. The flow of mainly non-rival knowledge through networking, the movement of researchers, information exchange and so on.
2. Intra-industry trade between oligopolistic competitors. In this framework, competition is based on product differentiation with respect to both increases in product variety and quality of existing

products. The knowledge is transmitted in the products traded. There is additional pressure for further innovation in the form of international competition.

3.   Inter-industry trade in the traditional sector is based on the notion of comparative advantage. Knowledge is transmitted through goods that are traded and, because there is perfect competition, there is less pressure to innovate and differentiate the product.

In short, the Grossman–Helpman model postulates that by increasing the investment in innovation (particularly by the R&D sector), through trade expansion, the variety of products available or improvement in the quality of existing products, the growth rate will increase. This is because innovation has the capacity to increase the overall stock of knowledge capital. Since knowledge possesses public good characteristics, there will be positive externalities to other firms and to the economy as a whole.

Grossman and Helpman's (1991) analysis of the impact of international trade on technological progress, A, can be interpreted by utilizing Romer's (1990) production technology of the following sort:

$$Y = L_Y^a \sum_{i=1}^{A} x_i^{1-\alpha}, \quad 0 < \alpha < 1 \qquad (3.28)$$

It is assumed that the two trading economies have similar production structures as put forward by Romer (1990). The evolution of new innovations, A, is expressed as:

$$\dot{A} = \psi L_A A \qquad (3.29)$$

where ψ is a productivity parameter.

If the production of intermediate goods occurs in isolation, the evolution of A would take the form of equation (3.29). If on the other hand, trade is allowed into the production process, equation (3.29) becomes:

$$\dot{A} = \psi L_A 2A \qquad (3.30)$$

The doubling of A is a result of the flow of ideas between trading partners. This is because trade is not only confined to physical goods but also includes ideas, as suggested by Grossman and Helpman (1991). Through trade, exchange of ideas is made possible and this will increase the rate of adoption and diffusion of new ideas into the production process. This will in turn have additional spillover benefits to other sectors of the economy, thereby further increasing A. Romer (1990) pointed out that raw materials that are employed to produce all types of goods have not changed. What changes is how they are manufactured and processed as a result of trial and error, experimentation and refinement, and so forth. In Romer's (1990, p. 72) words: 'One hundred years ago, all we could do to get visual stimulation from iron oxide was to use it as a pigment. Now we put it on plastic tape and use it to make video cassette recordings.' The point is that the new idea is the key to the production process, and trade is an important source for discovering new ideas.

International trade has two important effects on the economy's steady-state growth level. First, it has a direct positive impact on the rate of growth of the domestic knowledge stock, A, regardless of the value L_A, leading to higher productivity level. Second, productivity increases in research will increase the utilization of L_A, which in turn will further increase A.

CONCLUSION

The endogenous growth models have important implications for national policies development. For instance, initiatives implemented to increase the size of innovation or research, γ, will foster growth in the Schumpeterian framework. In Kaldor's technical progress analysis, policy initiated to expand the manufacturing sector could increase growth of output as captured by spillover effects. Based on Arrow's perspective, expansion of formal education could increase the stock and quality of the workforce, a pre-requisite for technological progress. In Hirschman's approach, policies initiated to promote the leading industrial sectors would in turn provide linkages to other industries in the economy. In the models constructed by Lucas and Romer, policy could be developed to channel more resources to the accumulation of human capital, and this can take the form of expanding the provision of formal education.

Government policies too can influence long-run growth patterns through international trade. Grossman and Helpman (1990) indicated that through international trade, a country could explore the wealth of knowledge that is available in the international communities. In summation, any incentives that are available and able to affect productivity, A, even if it is only temporary in nature, can dramatically alter the course of economic history. In addition to opening up technological progress and innovation to systematic analysis,[11] there is also the possibility of opening up the institutional structure, based on a historical perspective, which is often regarded by economic historians as crucial in terms of the resource allocation process underlying endogenous growth outcomes (Crafts, 1997). This would provide new insights into the growth process. Crafts (1997) highlighted the likely areas to benefit from the endogenous framework. These are as follows:

1. Unlike traditional neoclassical growth economics, the new models can readily allow scope for divergence and for a much richer menu of influences on growth outcomes. The dangers of a Panglossian view of the past and a selective and

restrictive search for evidence in evaluating growth performance should be much reduced for the next generation of cliometricians. This branch of growth theory offers improved hypotheses to economic historians unhappy with earlier formal models of induced technological change based on arguments familiar to historical research, these models deserve to be taken seriously in economic history.

2. Institutions (and policymaking) can be placed right at the heart of the growth process in a rigorous way. This should help to focus attention on the detailed characteristics of these arrangements and to explain why they really matter. Institutional arrangements will be an intrinsic part of historical accounts of economic growth partly because they exhibit substantial continuity, and windows of opportunity for their reform may well be both narrow and infrequent. There is an opportunity to assimilate key arguments of traditional historians which were previously either excluded by assumption or treated at best discursively. (Crafts, 1997, p. 68)

This chapter has provided the theoretical basis for examining the growth process of Malaysia. Growth analysis starts with the proposition put forward by Crafts (1997) that institutions matter to economic growth. This will be attempted in the next chapter.

NOTES

1   $Y = AK$, where Y is output, A is a constant and K is physical capital that is augmented with human capital which may prevent diminishing returns from setting in.

2   From Robert M. Solow, *Growth Theory: An Exposition*, 2000 Oxford University Press, New York. By permission of Oxford University Press, Inc.

3   Knowledge required to produce new innovation is assumed to be non-rival.

4   The act of investment creates knowledge that can be used by both the original investor and other firms to make better-informed decisions about future investments.

5   Gross investment is the measure of the amount of 'doing' that results in 'learning' (technological progress).

6   Knowledge takes many forms. At one extreme is basic scientific knowledge with broad applicability, such as the Pythagorean theorem and theory of quantum mechanics. At the other end is knowledge about specific goods, such as starting a particular lawn mower on a cold morning. In between is a wide range of ideas, from the design of transistors to a recipe for a better-tasting soft drink (Romer, 1996).

7   Lucas (1988) model is consistent with the Solow–Swan growth model as outlined in Chapter 2, except for the $(1 - u)$ term.

8   This implies that a society can determine the efficiency of the forthcoming generation of workers by making a choice between present consumption of consumer goods and future investment in educational activities.

[9] $Y = HY^{\alpha}L^{\beta} (x_1^{1-\alpha-\beta} + x_2^{1-\alpha-\beta} + x_3^{1-\alpha-\beta} + x_4^{1-\alpha-\beta} + ...)$, suggesting that the final output (Y) is made up of infinite types and designs of capital (x_i), including those that have not yet been invented at the present time.

[10] From Robert M. Solow, *Growth Theory: An Exposition*, 2000 Oxford University Press, New York. By permission of Oxford University Press, Inc.

[11] Including the role of the state in the accumulation of human capital and industrial policies targeted to increase the spillover effects from leading industrial sectors to other sectors.

4. Initial conditions and economic development: the Malaysian case

INTRODUCTION

Although technological progress is the driver of economic growth as discussed in the previous chapters, initial conditions can also affect the growth process of an economy. Malaysia is no exception. Since gaining political independence in 1957, initial conditions in the form of political instability and international trade have played a large role in restructuring the nation's economy. The aim of this chapter is to set a background for economic analysis found in the following chapters, and to examine the impact of initial conditions on the economic development of Malaysia. In keeping this book to a manageable size, 1960 is taken as the starting year for Malaysia's modern economic growth. It was during this period that the modernization of the Malaysian economy took off at a rapid pace.

INITIAL CONDITIONS AND ECONOMIC DEVELOPMENT

Initial conditions can affect economic development in several ways. Based on the path dependency theorem, what happens to the system today can profoundly influence how the system will behave well into the future (Setterfield, 1998). As Nelson (1996) pointed out, history matters. Accordingly, the existence of a destabilizing feedback mechanism, for instance, in the form of political instability or deterioration in the terms of trade, could imply that temporary disturbances would have large and cumulative effects. Short-term sequential patterns therefore become critical to the state of the economy, and 'cannot be predicted except as a result of the sequence of events in previous periods which led up to it' (Kaldor, 1972, p. 1244). Even if the sources of instability can be defined in terms of economic variables, the instability of the economic process is likely to provoke institutional and political changes, possibly abrupt and violent changes, in political and social institutions such as those associated with the 1969 racial crisis experienced by Malaysian society, and late 1990s political unrest in Indonesia. A major distinction between the endogenous growth models and the neoclassical framework is that the former models take into consideration other non-economic factors that have the potential to affect the growth process. For instance, Crafts (1997) raised the possibility of incorporating institutional structures into the endogenous growth frameworks. Crafts went on to suggest that:

> one of the most exciting avenues of research for economic historians and economists to pursue together using an endogenous innovation framework is the political economy of growth. This should aim for an understanding both of what the key effects of policy on growth have been and also of how the incentive structures facing politicians and private agents generate growth-retarding or growth-enhancing interventions. This will more likely be successfully achieved through a portfolio of detailed case studies of individual countries than through regressing growth rates against standard political variables. (1997, p. 69)

Efficient and effective resource allocation and distribution require a stable environment. This is because economic decisions (that is, allocation and distribution of resources) do not exist in a vacuum but as outcomes of the interactions between economic agents, which consist of individuals, firms (domestic and foreign), markets and governments. It is therefore essential that a stable economic environment exists so that resources could be allocated and distributed with minimum frictions. Only then can transactions between the different sets of economic agents be undertaken at maximum efficiency. If a developing country is engulfed in political rivalry or unrest (generating social tensions), it is highly unlikely that the economic environment will be stable. This can hinder long-run growth. Galbraith pointed out that political stability is an important factor in economic development:

> A stable political system accords people the personal security that is the first requisite of economic success ... The importance of political stability in the sequence of development cannot be too strongly emphasized. There is today no country with a stable, participatory, and honest government that does not have – or has not had – a reasonably satisfactory state of economic progress. There are few without such a government of which this can be said. (1983, pp. 13–14)

Easterly and Levine (1997) and Collier and Gunning (1998) reported that Africa's poor growth performance is related to political instability. Ndulu and O'Connell commented on the circumstances faced by sub-Saharan Africans, 'where political instability continues or the interests of the military and other privileged classes cannot be accommodated with a pluralist regime, economic gains may well be negligible or reversed' (1999, p. 64).

Initial conditions in the form of political instability can affect the savings variable in the Solow–Swan growth model. When a political regime is unstable, consumers reduce their savings for fear that their savings become worthless. Political instability also often displaces people or deprives them of jobs, making saving money more unrealistic. Investors similarly will decrease investment in fixed capital stocks such as factories or land, preferring to keep their properties and portfolios in liquid and portable forms such as in foreign currencies or gold which stand a better chance of retaining value. In extreme cases, the ruling elites may send their savings to more secure financial institutions, robbing their nations of the much needed investment funds. The implication of declining savings is especially detrimental to the early stages of economic development. Not only will it suffocate physical capital investment, but above all it will deny the society of the valuable learning-by-doing activities and the new technological progress embodied in new equipment.

The relationship between political instability, private investment and economic growth has been documented by Knack and Keefer (1995), Mauro (1995), Clague et al. (1996), Barro (1997) and Keefer and Knack (1998). Their results found strong correlations between political instability, lower investment and lower growth. Recently, Yi Feng (2001) conducted a study on 42 developing countries covering the period 1978–88, and found that political instability has a negative impact on private investment. Yi Feng concluded that:

> the countries that have difficulties initiating or executing successful development programmes are typically those with political systems that make it difficult to develop freedom, with governments that do not have consistent policy strength or with political regimes that are simply unstable. I am tempted to argue that their negative effects on private investment far exceed the unwholesome impact of monetary or fiscal policies on private investment. (2001, p. 288)

The dominant perception is that only a democratically elected government can enhance the performance of the economy, and that an authoritarian form of government serves as a constraint to economic growth.[1] This is based on the perception that authoritarian regimes are more likely to exercise their powers to deplete the nation's wealth and to carry out non-productive investments (Barro, 1997).[2] According to Shah (1991), dictatorship is a form of risky investment. However, the relationship between democracy and economic growth is not as clear-cut as indicated by the mainstream views. For instance, Schwarz (1992) reported that most OECD countries began their modern economic development in institutions with limited political rights, with full-fledged democracy occurring only much later. Barro (1997, p. 58) revealed that 'the effect of more political freedom on growth is theoretically ambiguous'. He went on to argue that:

> nothing in principle prevents non-democratic governments from maintaining economic freedoms and private property. A dictator does not have to engage in central planning. Examples of autocracies that have expanded economic freedoms include the Pinochet government in Chile, the Fujimori administration in Peru, the Shah's regime in Iran, and several previous and current governments in East Asia. (p. 50)

The results from his regression of more than 100 countries found that the estimated coefficients on democracy and its R-square were statistically significant ($p = 0.001$) with a positive coefficient on the linear term and negative coefficient on the square, implying 'that growth is increasing in democracy at low levels of democracy, but the relation turns negative once a moderate amount of political freedom has been attained' (p. 58). According to Barro, the estimated turning point occurs at an indicator value of around 0.5,[3] which corresponds to the levels of democracy in 1994 for Malaysia and Mexico.

Although Barro (1997) and several others have provided empirical evidence on the existence of a causal relationship between political freedom and economic growth, it is not the intention of this chapter to analyse the state in terms of a rigid polarity of 'autocracy versus democracy'. Nor is it intended or even possible in this chapter to establish a causal relationship between political freedom and economic growth. Instead, this chapter points to the role of the state in providing a stable base or conditions for economic agents to perform their economic function as efficiently as possible. It should be noted that there is no *a priori* optimal mix of state intervention. This can only be achieved on a pragmatic, case-by-case, country-specific examination which is based on inherited conditions (reinforcing further the need to examine economic growth from a case-study perspective).

POLITICAL INSTABILITY AND ECONOMIC DEVELOPMENT IN MALAYSIA

A survey conducted by Doraisami (1996) on members of the Malaysian Economic Society identified political stability as the leading factor behind Malaysia's economic success. When asked to rank their perceptions of the factors responsible for Malaysia's economic success, the results in Table 4.1 suggest that a majority of the Malaysian economists considered political stability to be the most important factor in the achievement of long-term economic growth. Political stability ranks higher than the widely held belief that the economic success of Malaysia is largely linked to foreign investment and a literate and disciplined workforce.

Table 4.2 presents the Malaysian economists' view on Malaysia's manufacturing export success. Again political stability is ranked first among other factors. It is interesting to find that the Malaysian economists ranked political stability to be far more important for Malaysia's export success than low wages. This raises an important question as to whether the export success of many of the East Asia countries can be largely explained by low wages, as often argued in the mainstream literature.

Table 4.1   Factors associated with Malaysia's economic success

Rank	Category	Score
1	Political stability	547
2	Foreign investment	419
3	Good macro management	371
4	Development planning	331
5	Good resource endowment	324
6	Literate and disciplined workforce	294
7	Good infrastructure	280
8	Government guidance	274
9	Labour market flexibility	218
10	Minimal government intervention	202

Source: Doraisami, 1996, p. 32.

Table 4.2   Factors associated with Malaysia's manufacturing export success

Rank	Category	Score
1	Political stability	488
2	Foreign investment	454
3	Export promoting incentives	414
4	Literate and disciplined workforce	317
5	Good macro management	297
6	Resource endowment	270
7	Development planning	254
8	Labour marketing flexibility	234
9	Government guidance	231
10	Low wages	209

Source: Doraisami, 1996, p. 32.

In order to understand why political stability is a significant factor for Malaysia's economic success, it is necessary to provide a brief background of the Malaysian political and social structures.

POLITICAL AND SOCIAL STRUCTURES OF MALAYSIA: A BRIEF HISTORICAL BACKGROUND

The Federation of Malaya gained its independence from Britain in 1957. In 1963, the British colonial Borneo territories of Sabah and Sarawak, and Singapore joined the Federation of Malaya, and Malaysia was formed. In 1965, Singapore was expelled from Malaysia due to the bitter political rivalry between the Malay-based political party, the United Malay National Organisation (UMNO), under the leadership of Tunku Abdul Rahman, and the Chinese-based political party, the People's Action Party, under the leadership of Lee Kuan Yu (Means, 1991).

Composition of Malaysian Society

On the eve of its independence in 1957, Malaysia was made up of three major ethnic communities – indigenous Malays or Bumiputeras (who accounted for 50 per cent of the population at that time), and two sizeable immigrant communities: Chinese (37 per cent) and Indians (11 per cent) (Federation of Malaya, 1961).[4]

The Malays were heavily concentrated in rural areas where they were primarily engaged in subsistence agriculture (Anand, 1983; Onn, 1989; Snodgrass, 1980). In the urban areas, most of them were employed as labourers by the construction industry. The few educated Malays during that period formed the elite strata of civil servants (Means, 1991). As such, the Malays represented an extreme case in both the Malaysian political and economic spectrums. At one end of the spectrum, the Malays were well represented among the most politically powerful positions (state bureaucracy), while at the other end, they dominated the ranks of the least well-off urban proletariat and rural peasantry. According to Puthucheary (1960), there was no Malay ownership in tin mining and manufacturing prior to independence in 1957. A possible reason is that taking up new and untried economic roles was not an attractive option as their economy was quite adequate for a modest living (Lim, 1973). The Malays were mostly associated with the traditional agricultural sector, such as rice cultivation, fishing, small cottage industries and coconut growing. On the eve of independence, more than 740 000 Malays were employed in the agricultural, fishing and forestry sectors compared to 310 000 Chinese and 174 000 Indians. The Malays also made up the largest labour force in rice cultivation at 381 000 during this period relative to 9 000 Chinese and 500 Indians (Jesudason, 1989).

Table 4.3 shows the 1957 and 1967 occupational distribution of each ethnic group. The data show that the agricultural sector was dominated by the Malays, while the manufacturing and commerce sectors were dominated by the Chinese. Malay ownership in the commercial sector was also limited during this period.

Table 4.3   Employment by occupational group and ethnic group, 1957 and 1967 (%)

	1957			1967		
Occupational group	Malay	Chinese	Indian	Malay	Chinese	Indian
Professional, technical, etc.	41	39	11	47	36	11
Administrative, managerial, etc.	17	62	12	21	64	9
Clerical	27	46	19	30	51	15
Sales & related	16	66	17	26	65	9
Agricultural	62	24	13	65	22	12
Miners	8	86	5	16	76	8
Transport & communication	41	40	39	45	38	15
Craftsmen, labourers, etc.	24	56	20	36	49	14
Service	40	33	13	38	47	14
Total	47	36	15	50	40	13

Source: Snodgrass, 1980.

Malays owned only 10 per cent of registered businesses, paid only 4 per cent of income taxes and held only 1.5 per cent of shares in publicly listed companies (Bowie, 1988). Ownership of share capital of registered limited companies in Table 4.4 shows that in 1969, Malays owned around 1.5 per cent of total share capital compared to 22.8 per cent owned by the Chinese, 0.9 per cent by the Indians and 62.1 per cent by foreign interests.

Snodgrass (1975a) also indicated that in the late 1950s, the Malays were at a disadvantage in the consumption of services allocated by the state: 'This differential was evident in transportation, communication, utility, education, health, housing and other social services' (p. 281). Public investment was also biased against the Malays during this period (Snodgrass, 1975a).

The Malays lacked institutions that could mobilize capital and pool economic resources effectively. The Europeans had their international financial networks while the Chinese had clan-based organizations. The latter were so ubiquitous that even when Chinese took up agricultural cultivation in smallholdings, they carried it out in *kongsi* (partnership) form, unlike the more individualistic methods of the Malays which were more prone to failure

(Lim, 1973). The incidence of poverty was also the highest among the Malays compared to non-Malays, as shown in Table 4.5.

Table 4.4   Ownership of share capital of limited companies in Malaysia, 1969

Malaysian companies	All industries	
	(RM '000)	%
Companies registered in Malaysia		
Residents		
Malays	49 294	1.0
Malay interests	21 339	0.5
Chinese	1 064 795	22.8
Indians	40 983	0.9
Federal & state governments	21 430	0.5
Nominee companies	98 885	2.1
Other individuals & locally controlled companies	470 969	10.1
Foreign controlled companies in Malaysia	282 311	*6.0
Non-Residents	1 235 927	*26.4
Malaysian branches of companies registered abroad		
Net investment by Head Office	1 391 607	*29.7

Note: *These items show foreign ownership totalling 62.1%.

Source: Malaysia, 1971, p. 40.

During 1970, the Malays experienced the highest incidence of poverty at 64.8 per cent compared to 26 per cent for the Chinese and 39.2 per cent for the Indians. Although the incidence of poverty of Malays declined to 46.4 per cent in 1976, it was still significantly higher than those of the Chinese (17.4 per cent) and Indians (27.3 per cent). Malays earned significantly less than the Chinese and Indians. In 1969, 48.8 per cent of Malays earned less than RM150 per month compared to 18.1 per cent of Chinese and 29.9 per cent of Indians. Only 1.3 per cent of Malay households earned above the monthly RM1 000 bracket, as shown in Table 4.6.

These findings were also consistent with the studies conducted by Anand (1983) and Snodgrass (1975b). Snodgrass (1975b) reported that the Malays received the lowest mean monthly household income during the period 1957–58 and 1970 compared to the non-Malays. For instance, in the 1957–58 period, the Malays received RM139 per month compared to the monthly income of RM300 for the Chinese and RM237 for the Indians. During 1970, the amounts were RM177, RM 399 and RM310 respectively. A survey conducted by Anand (1983) for the World Bank estimated that the 1970 mean monthly household income varied from RM172 for Malays to RM394 for Chinese and RM304 for Indians. The racial disparity ratio of Chinese to Malays was 2.29, and 1.77 for Indians to Malays. Rural and urban disparities were also prominent. The estimated average monthly household income for 1970 was RM428 in the urban areas and RM200 in the rural areas, implying a disparity ratio of 2.14. The Malays also experienced imbalances in the educational composition of the population.

Table 4.5   Incidence of poverty by ethnic group in Malaysia, 1970 and 1976

	1970		1976	
	Total poor households ('000)	Incidence of poverty (%)	Total poor households ('000)	Incidence of poverty (%)
All ethnic groups	791.8	49.3	688.3	35.1
Malays	584.2	64.8	519.4	46.4
Chinese	136.3	26.0	109.4	17.4
Indian	62.9	39.2	53.8	27.3
Others	8.4	44.8	5.7	33.8

Source: Jomo, 1994.

Table 4.6   Percentage of Malaysian households by race and income, 1969

Income (RM)	Malays (%)	Chinese (%)	Indians (%)	Others (%)	Total (%)
<150	48.8	18.1	29.9	6.8	35.6
151–300	31.2	38.0	33.6	8.5	33.4
301–500	13.1	23.5	20.6	32.2	17.8
501–1000	5.6	15.6	12.4	27.1	10.1
>1000	1.3	4.8	3.5	25.4	3.1

Source: Rao, 1980, p. 210.

Table 4.7 indicates that a third of the employed Malay population had no formal education during 1967 compared to 18 per cent and 25 per cent for the Chinese and Indians respectively.

Table 4.7   Educational attainment of employed persons by race, 1967

Educational Attainment	Malays (%)	Chinese (%)	Indians (%)
No formal education	33.3	18.4	25.3
Primary education	57.3	58.7	54.8
Higher than primary	9.4	22.9	19.9

Source: Rao, 1980.

The Chinese, originally drawn to the Malay peninsula by the lure of profits from trade and tin mining, represented a substantial permanent community by the time of Malaysia's independence. Among the three major ethnic communities, the Chinese were the most economically advantaged, dominating both small and medium-sized industries (usually associated with the processing of raw materials from the agricultural sector), while the large companies were mainly foreign-owned during this period (Malaysia, 1971). Snodgrass pointed out that:

> Economically the Chinese were in by far the strongest position, not only because they had amassed relatively large amounts of wealth, education, and experience but also because of their demonstrated capacity to adopt to changing circumstances and seize newly-offered opportunities. (1980, p. 42)

The Malayan Indian community originated from the Malaysian rubber boom at the turn of the nineteenth century. According to Thorburn (1977), the Indian Immigration Committee was established in 1907 to implement a comprehensive scheme for the importation of labour from South India on a large scale. By 1922, 78 per cent of total estate labour force was Indian (Jesudason, 1989). The result was a substantial permanent population of Indians, comprising, as was the case with the other ethnic groups, a mixture of rich and poor, of proletarian and bourgeoisie, and of rural and urban dwellers.

Divisions of Political Power

In Malaysia, the contest for political power is one between the dominant racial groups. The Malays or Bumiputeras claim legitimacy and political supremacy on the basis of being the original inhabitants of the nation. The non-Malays (the Chinese and Indians), who like other migrant groups, were gaining in status as nationals after Malaysia's independence, began to challenge the Malay claim (Fisk and Osman Rani, 1982; Means, 1991; Snodgrass, 1980). This kind of ethnic-based political structure has deep historical roots. When the British acquired colonial control over Malaya and the Borneo territories, the old political structure of the sultanates was retained and modernization proceeded with as little interference as possible. Political management remained, at least on the surface, a Malay prerogative. In exchange, the Malay rulers, and the Malays in general, normally did not interfere with or even participate in the modern economy. Large-scale British businesses in tin and in rubber planting were accompanied by Chinese entrepreneurship in tin mining, commerce and petty manufacturing (Kasper, 1974). This separation of spheres was to a large extent inherited by independent Malaysia. Prior to 1969, there appeared to be an accord struck between the Malays and non-Malays in which political power remained the domain of the Malays while the non-Malays, specifically the Chinese, were allowed full participation in economic and commercial activities. The decision to leave industrial investment to the private sector was largely a political compromise reached between the parties making up the ruling alliance (Bowie, 1991). The acceptance of the UMNO's political domination by the Chinese and Indians largely rested upon the state's non-interference (beyond its regulatory role) in private commerce and industry. In other words, the UMNO accepted the dominance of the Chinese and Indians in businesses and commerce in exchange for their acceptance of its political domination and its efforts to increase Malay participation in the rural sector, transportation, mining, construction and timber industries (Bowie, 1991; Spinanger 1986).

Chinese businesses were able to make impressive gains in the 1960s by taking advantage of the loss of the foreigner's political position in the colonial era and the government's greater national orientation in its development programmes. Some Chinese businesses succeeded in becoming large conglomerates involved in nearly every kind of business. Even small businessmen found many opportunities for growth because of the Malayan Chinese Association's (MCA) role in preventing excessive bureaucratic interference in private business. The greatest expansion was probably in property development and banking (Kasper, 1974).

This trade-off is sometimes referred to as the special position of the Malays, which includes quotas in favour of Malays in public service recruitment in exchange for the granting of citizenship to the non-Malays (Means, 1991). The bases of this arrangement had important implications for the development and implementation of economic policies.

Operating on such a trade-off, Malaysia's economic policy (prior to 1969) had involved minimum government interference, indeed less than that in the more liberally managed economies of the West (Kasper, 1974). Although there were some shifts in basic government policy towards more public enterprise over the decades, it could be argued that the Malaysian economy was run along the lines of the laissez-faire capitalist model. This trade-off approach, which was augmented with the laissez-faire framework, created an informal convention encouraging an unequal distribution of economic wealth. In its earlier days, such institutions appeared to be appropriate for achieving balance and racial harmony. But as each ethnic group's aspirations and expectations grew, they began to question the structure that was forced upon them by their colonial masters. The Malays, in particular, did not see any benefit in the existing economic arrangements and began to harbour resentment of marginality and being economically disadvantaged in their own society.[5]

Although the Malays were the predominant ethnic group in the population and electorate, they constituted a majority of the poor or economically disadvantaged. They were also discontented with the pace of modernization as well as with the notion that their main activity was limited to politics. As more Malays moved to towns and into industrial professions, they began to question their predetermined social and economic standing. On the other hand, the Chinese wanted a more prominent political role. According to Snodgrass (1980), the withdrawal of the Chinese support from the MCA, which was part of the Alliance (see below), alarmed the Malays as their withdrawal was interpreted as a direct challenge to the Malays' inherited political supremacy: 'since Malay economic backwardness had not been overcome while awareness of the disparities and determination to do something about them had increased such a challenge was frightening to the Malays' (pp. 55–6). Given these socio-economic conditions,[6] racial harmony was not achieved (Jomo, 1994). These resentments erupted in May 1969.

The May 13 Political Crisis

Taking into account the complex mixture of ethnic communities, the Malaysian political system had evolved around the significance of and need for accommodative solutions to address important public issues (Jomo, 1990). In order for the political elites to gain a broad base of support, the three major political parties formed a coalition called the Alliance. This Alliance coalition comprised the United Malays National Organisation (UMNO), the Malayan Chinese Association (MCA) and the Malayan Indian Congress (MIC), respectively representing the Malays, Chinese and Indians. It was within the governing councils of the Alliance that the most difficult and contentious issues of politics were resolved by representatives from each of these three political parties. By forging the basis for multi-ethnic cooperation, the Alliance was able to form a consensus and obtain public support to win elections (Jomo, 1990).

However, the 1969 general election results exerted a great strain on the Alliance system. In the election, a majority of the electorate rejected the then ruling Alliance government, resulting in the Alliance losing its two-thirds majority in parliament. The MCA party, in particular, experienced the largest loss of seats contested. For instance, in the 1964 election, it won 27 seats out of the 33 it contested, but in the 1969 election, it won only 13 seats. The results of the 1959, 1964 and 1969 elections are presented in Table 4.8.

Table 4.8   Parliamentary Election Results, Malaysia, 1959–69

Parties	1959 Won	1959 Contested	1964 Won	1964 Contested	1969 Won	1969 Contested
Alliance	74	104	89	104	66	103
UMNO	52	70	59	68	51	67
MCA	19	31	27	33	13	33
MIC	3	3	3	3	2	3
Opposition						
PAS	13	58	9	52	12	59
DAP	-	-	1	11	13	23
Gerakan	-	-	-	-	8	14
Others	17	-	5	-	4	-
Total	104		104		103	

Notes: UMNO = United Malays National Organisation; MCA = Malayan Chinese Association; MIC = Malayan Indian Congress; PAS = Partai Islam Se Malaysia; DAP = Democratic Action Party.

Source: Jesudason, 1989.

It was reported that about half the Malays voted against the Alliance together with about two-thirds of the non-Malays (Means, 1991). Despite the massive defeat, the Alliance managed to retain control of federal government because of the rural and Malay bias associated with the gerrymandering of the electoral system, and the ethnically divided nature of the opposition. However, the Alliance lost the state elections in Kelantan and Penang, and barely held on to the states of Selangor, Perak and Trengganu. The UMNO blamed the MCA for the Alliance's losses. Because of the weak mandate, the MCA (under the leadership of Tan Siew Sin) withdrew from representation of the new federal cabinet. According to Means (1991, p. 7): 'this move raised the spectre of no inter-ethnic bargaining mechanisms being in place in the new government'.

What happened next was the exchange of racial epithets and threats between the supporters of the opposition parties (the Gerakan and the Democratic Action Party) and the Malay bystanders during a staged parade in Kuala Lumpur. In response, the embattled Chief Minister of Selangor, Harun bin Haji Idris, called upon the Malays for a mass pro-government demonstration (and show of force) on the evening of May 13.[7] Many Malays, armed with parangs (machetes) and other weapons, looted and burned Chinese-owned shops. The Chinese mounted stubborn resistance and some launched retaliatory counter-attacks. Although the police mounted a strong force to stabilize the situation, they were overwhelmed by the larger number of rioters. As the rioting intensified, the Army was called in. Acting on the basis of ethnic and political sympathies, the Army directed most of their measures against the Chinese. Despite curfews and heavy military presence, severe rioting, arson and looting continued. When the authorities finally restored order, approximately 6 000 residents in Kuala Lumpur (about 90 per cent of whom were Chinese), had lost their homes and properties. The official estimate of fatalities from the riots was 178, but other non-official sources claimed a much higher figure (Means, 1991). In addition to the destruction of life and property, the May 13 incident provoked a crisis within the highest level of government, in particular over the appropriate mechanisms for inter-ethnic accommodation.

The Rukunegara was proclaimed on 31 August 1970 for the recovery process. It is in essence a national ideology to assert the fundamental agreements among the different ethnic groups. It is understood that these agreements are not to be challenged in the ongoing process of politics. Challenges to the principles of the Rukunegara would result with severe penalties. In effect, the Rukunegara is a formal declaration of a National Compact, or what later came to be called The Racial Bargain. While the Rukunegara might promote racial harmony through the bargaining process in the political system, it failed to address the underlying factors that led to the May 13 incident. Over the period of 1957–70, development planning, while successful in generating rapid economic growth, was ineffective in bringing about adequate employment opportunities and a reduction in income inequality, as discussed earlier. Given the socio-economic conditions prevailing in the country, this meant that the basic aim of racial harmony was not achieved (Jomo, 1994).

In response to maintaining political stability, the state adopted the view that the laissez-faire approach may not be appropriate under these circumstances. Although the laissez-faire system was relatively successful in generating national income and diversifying the economy, it had its limitations, particularly in the political and social spheres. It contributed to the process of ethnic polarization in the Malaysian society. Each ethnic group began to take its own resource monopoly for granted and saw itself, in what it lacked, as being deprived in comparison to other groups (Jomo, 1994). The urgency to end racial compartmentalization of interest in the economy meant that the old framework would have to be replaced. This was explicitly laid out in the Second Malaysia Plan and thereafter where it was acknowledged that a policy of complete economic laissez-faire had retarded the economic advancement of the Malays (Mahathir, 1970). This led to intense discussion which resulted in a new strategy for development, which will be discussed in greater detail in the next chapter.

In the meantime, we will turn our attention to the impact of external shocks on the Malaysian economy. This is important because on various occasions, external shocks in the form of the deterioration of the terms of trade had threatened to derail Malaysia's economic growth momentum. More importantly, these external shocks had served as a catalyst in accelerating the pace of the structural transformation of the economy. The early and mid-1980s economic recessions clearly demonstrated that the agricultural sector could no longer support the Malaysian economy.

INITIAL INEFFICIENCIES: EXTERNAL SHOCKS AND ECONOMIC DEVELOPMENT IN MALAYSIA

External trade had had a substantial adverse effect on the Malaysian economy, as demonstrated by the 1980s economic recessions. This is not surprising because Malaysia is one of the world's most trade-dependent economies, as shown in Table 4.9. During 1955, exports contributed more than 49.8 per cent of Malaysia's GDP compared to 4.4 per cent for the US, 17.7 per cent for Australia, 22.4 per cent for Sweden, 21.6 per cent for the UK, 11.5 per cent for Japan, 1.8 per cent for Korea and 12.7 for the Philippines. In 1996, Malaysia's export contribution to GDP rose to 92 per cent in comparison to 11.8 per cent for the US, 19.8 per cent for Australia and 29.3 per cent for the UK. A prominent feature of Table 4.9 is that Malaysia became even more trade-dependent after 1980 and Table 4.10 provides an indication of the extent to which foreign trade dominated the composition of Malaysia's output.

The data in Table 4.10 suggest that fluctuations in output growth could not be adequately explained by consumption and investment components because exports and imports contributed a high proportion towards aggregate output growth. In 1959, exports contributed 51 per cent to GDP, and this figure rose rapidly over the next 40 years peaking at 125 per cent in 2000. Contribution of exports to GDP growth had also increased consistently and rapidly since 1986.

Table 4.9   *Export share of gross domestic product of selected countries, 1955–96 (%)*

Year	US	Australia	Sweden	UK	Japan	Korea	Philippines	Malaysia
1955	4.4	17.7	22.4	21.6	11.5	1.8	12.7	49.8
1960	4.9	13.9	22.9	20.0	9.7	2.7	10.6	50.6
1965	5.0	15.0	22.0	20.0	10.9	13.4	17.2	44.7
1970	5.6	25.3	24.1	22.5	11.3	14.0	19.1	46.1
1975	8.5	15.3	28.2	32.3	13.7	26.7	18.5	45.5
1980	10.2	17.5	29.8	27.4	16.1	33.1	20.2	57.3
1985	0.7	16.8	35.3	29.5	16.8	34.5	20.7	55.0
1991	10.2	17.8	27.9	23.3	10.2	28.2	29.6	82.1
1995	11.3	19.6	40.9	28.4	9.4	33.1	36.4	95.4
1996	11.8	19.8	40.0	29.3	9.9	32.4	42.0	92.0

Sources: International Monetary Fund, 1986, 1998.

Table 4.10   *Percentage contribution of major components to Malaysian GDP, 1959–2003*

Year	Private Consumption	Public Consumption	Private Investment	Public Investment	Exports	Imports
1959	64	15	9	2	51	38
1960	62	14	11	2	54	44
1965	62	17	11	8	48	46
1970	61	19	10	6	48	45
1975	61	18	16	10	49	51
1980	52	17	20	12	63	63
1985	56	16	17	15	61	63
1990	55	15	22	12	80	78
1995	50	13	32	13	86	86
2000	43	11	13	13	125	105
2003	47	15	9	15	117	97

Sources: Bank Negara Malaysia, 1994; Ministry of Finance, Malaysia, 1996, 2000, 2004.

It appears that as Malaysia shifted from the commodity-driven era of the pre-1970s towards an export-oriented manufacturing base, the economy became even more dependent on external trade. It seems that the rate of output growth of the Malaysian economy from 1980 to 2000 had been largely dependent on external trade, suggesting an export- oriented industrialization.

Prior to 1970, Malaysia not only depended heavily on agricultural products for its export earnings but it also relied on a limited number of primary exports. Most of the export income was derived from rubber and tin earnings, as shown in Table 4.11. In 1947–70, total exports averaged 48 per cent of GDP. Out of this, exports of rubber and tin averaged 37 per cent of GDP.

Table 4.11   Malaysia's Gross Exports of Rubber and Tin and Total Gross Exports as a Percentage of GDP, 1947–70

Year	Total gross exports	Gross exports of rubber	Gross exports of tin	Total gross exports of rubber & tin
1947	31.5	22.1	4.3	26.4
1950	63.0	43.8	10.7	54.5
1955	55.5	37.1	10.2	47.3
1960	58.9	36.9	10.2	47.1
1965	47.2	20.8	13.3	34.1
1970	49.5	19.6	12.0	31.6

Source: Lee, 1978, p. 26.

It is reasonable to conclude that from 1947 to 1970, Malaysia represented a typical case of a developing economy, which was largely dependent on a limited number of primary export products that were subjected not only to large price fluctuations but also faced prospects of a long-term decline. This is shown in Figure 4.1 for rubber.

Annual changes were considerable, ranging from over 64 per cent in 1950 to slightly less than 0.5 per cent in 1965. The year-to-year fluctuations in export unit values had been substantial, particularly during the 1950s. Although these fluctuations were reduced in the 1960s, they remained significant. A similar trend was also found for the tin industry as shown in Figure 4.2.

Both Figures 4.1 and 4.2 show that rubber and tin could no longer support the growth of the economy. Their export prices and export revenues were subjected to large fluctuations, and continued to decline over the years. The demand and prices for natural rubber dropped from 1960 onwards due to a new family of synthetics called stereo regular. As a result, the growth rates of rubber output declined rapidly from 7 per cent in 1966–70 to 3.1 per cent in 1971–75, and continued to decline to 0.06 per cent in 1981–85 (Drabble, 2000).

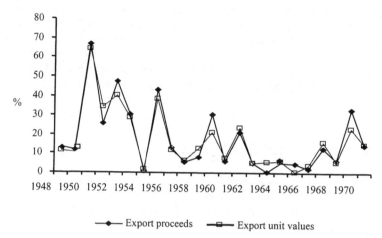

Source: Lee, 1978.

Figure 4.1 Malaysia's year-to-year fluctuations of export proceeds and export unit values of rubber, 1948–70 (based on gross exports)

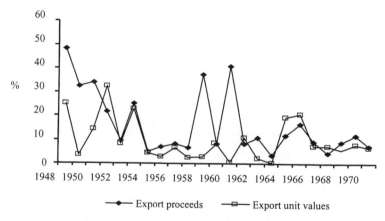

Source: Lee, 1978.

Figure 4.2 Malaysia's year-to-year fluctuations of export proceeds and export unit values of tin, 1948–70 (based on gross exports)

The future of the natural rubber industry appeared bleak, and future reliance on it as a major source of economic growth was questioned. A major problem faced by the Malaysian tin industry was the rapid depletion of known tin deposits brought about by a lack of mining land. After several decades of mining, Malaysia's tin resources had passed their peak production and were clearly being depleted (Department of Statistics, 1982, 1983). In 1967–72, Malaysia produced between 73 000 and 77 000 tonnes of tin annually. This dropped to 60 000 tonnes in 1980–81, and further fell to 52 342 tonnes in 1982. In response to the reduction in earnings from rubber and tin exports, Malaysia began to reduce its dependence on these two commodities by diversifying its sources of export income.

TRENDS IN EXPORT EARNINGS

Although Malaysia's exports were more diversified in the early 1980s than in the 1960s, a bulk of its export earnings in the early 1980s still consisted of five major commodities which accounted for approximately 75 per cent of total exports, as indicated in Table 4.12.

Table 4.12   Malaysia's key commodity exports, 1970–85 (RM million)

	1970	1971–5	1980	1981	1982	1983	1984	1985
Rubber	1 724	2 016	4 618	3 713	2 655	3 664	3 672	2 864
Palm oil	263	1 268	2 515	2 725	2 656	2 977	4 531	3 944
Tin	1 013	1 217	2 505	2 138	1 484	1 718	1 163	1 595
Crude petroleum	156	123	6 709	6 922	7 694	7 871	8 737	8 970
Sawn timber	201	363	1 178	971	1 035	1 221	994	1 020
Saw logs	643	632	2 616	2 473	3 378	2 792	2 790	2 667
Manufactures	392	1 912	6 269	6 328	7 398	9 502	12 148	12 229

Sources: Malaysia, 1976, 1986.

The diversification of Malaysia's exports may, to some extent, provide some stability to external shocks in that the decline in the prices of some commodities may be offset by others. For instance, rubber experienced a drop in unit price (cents per kilogram) from 303 in 1980 to 250 in 1981, while unit price (RM per tonne) for crude petroleum increased from 597 in 1980 to 683 in 1981. Despite this, the Malaysian economy in the early 1980s was still very much subject to the shock of world commodity prices. A prominent feature in

Table 4.12 is that both rubber and tin exports continued to experience a decline in export value. In 1970, rubber outperformed all other exports, with an export value of RM1 724 million, followed closely by tin with an export value of RM1 013 million. The export values for palm oil, crude petroleum, saw logs and the manufacturing sector were RM263 million, RM156 million, RM643 million and RM392 million respectively. By 1985, the export value of rubber dropped to RM2 864 million from RM4 618 million in 1980. Tin experienced a similar trend, peaking in 1980 with an export value of RM2 505 million, and decreasing to RM1 595 million in 1985.

Despite the diversification in export earnings to reduce its dependence on rubber and tin, Malaysia's export earnings, up to 1985, were heavily reliant on the primary sector. As shown in Table 4.12, exports generated by the manufacturing sector were significantly less than those from primary exports. During the recessions of the early and mid-1980s, all key primary exports, with the exception of crude petroleum, experienced a significant decline in prices, leading to a fall in export earnings. This is illustrated in Table 4.13.

Table 4.13   Export value, volume, price and terms of trade in Malaysia, 1979–82

	1979	1980	1981	1982
Total export value				
(RM million)	24 222	28 172	27 100	26 640
% change	42	16	− 4	− 2
Export quantum index				
Index (1970 = 100)	209	203	204	221
% change	21	10	− 11	1
Export price index				
(1970 = 100)	231	254	238	217
% change	16	10	− 6	− 10
Import price index				
(1970 = 100)	223	268	306	306
% change	7	20	15	1
Terms of trade				
(1970 = 100)	103	95	78	71
% change	8	− 9	− 8	− 9

Source: Khor, 1983, p. 34.

The data in Table 4.13 also show that the export quantum index dropped by 11 per cent in 1981 from a high of 21 per cent in 1979. In 1982, it recovered only marginally by an estimated 1 per cent. Between 1980 and 1982, import prices grew at double the rate of export prices. For instance, in 1980, the import price index experienced a 20 per cent rate of change, compared to 10 per cent rate of change for the export price index. The decline in export prices was reflected in the fall of overall export price index from a maximum of 254 in 1980 to 217 in 1982. The situation worsened in 1981, with the export price index falling from 10 per cent in 1980 to –10 per cent, and the import price index continuing to rise by 15 per cent in 1981 and 1 per cent in 1982. By 1982 standards, the export prices were 6 per cent lower than in 1979, while import prices were 37 per cent higher. As a result, the terms of trade fell from 103 in 1979 to 71 in 1982 (January to July average), which is a significant drop of 31 per cent in just three years (Khor, 1983).

The decrease in the terms of trade caused by the fall in export earnings had a significant negative impact on the overall economy. The 31 per cent drop in the terms of trade means that Malaysia was only able to pay for 69 units of its imports for every 100 units of exports. Purchasing power equivalent to 31 per cent of the current export value was therefore lost. In 1982, Malaysia's export earnings totalled RM26 640 million. The subsequent loss in purchasing power was equivalent to RM8 258 million. The drop in the terms of trade was so serious as to cause the real income of the country to fall in 1982 despite the rise in GDP during that year (Khor, 1983). According to the Ministry of Finance (1982), real GDP grew by 2.8 per cent in 1982. However, based on January to July figures for that year, the terms of trade fell by an estimated 9 per cent. Since commodity exports comprised 46 per cent of GDP, the 9 per cent drop in terms of trade had the effect of reducing the purchasing power of GDP by 4.1 per cent.

There were also social pressures resulting from the traditional export system which came in the form of a rising level of unemployment. During the late 1950s and early 1960s, the natural rate of increase in population had risen to more than 3 per cent per year, making such a rise one of the highest recorded in the world (Lim, 1973). According to Lim (1973), the high rate of population increase had created a severe strain on the resources of the economy. These pressures had necessitated a restructuring of the economy. Initially, the rubber and tin industries were able to absorb the increases in the labour force. However, with the decline in the prices of rubber and tin, and the depletion of known deposits of tin, the two industries found it increasingly difficult to maintain their traditional roles as the main sources of employment. The level of unemployment, particularly among young Malays, began to rise and the ensuing social pressures led to yet another call for change in the colonial patterns of production. In 1982, for instance, the significant decline in rubber prices drastically cut into the income of 500 000 smallholder families, and another 100 000 estate families, whose wages were partly determined by the price level (Khor, 1983). The small producers were hit the hardest. On the one hand, they were faced with lower prices for their products and higher production costs for their products. On the other hand, they had to pay higher retail prices for the goods they consumed in exchange for rubber. In fact, the 1982 real income of smallholders was similar to the dismal levels of November 1974 when thousands of smallholders staged a demonstration in Baling (a town in Malaysia) to draw attention to their plight (Khor, 1983). In the rubber estate sector, the higher production costs (as a result of higher retail prices due to differences between the goods needed for production and the exchange prices for rubber) had resulted in the loss of 15 549 jobs, which was 6 per cent of the total workforce (Khor, 1983). Employment opportunities in the tin industry were also affected by a reduction in tin prices. The level of employment dropped from 40 080 in July 1980 to 29 804 in October 1982 (a loss of 10 276 jobs since July 1980) due to the closure of several mines.

The decline in export prices also had a significant impact on the employment front of other sectors in the economy in terms of slower job creation and higher retrenchment. Between December 1981 and August 1982, employment in selected industries which accounted for 75 per cent of total manufacturing sales fell from 324 029 to 323 261. In the public sector, the job freeze in some services slowed down job creation. Compared to an average annual job creation of 51 000 in the period 1977–81, government jobs increased by only 22 000 in 1982 and were expected to rise by only 15 000 in 1983 (Khor, 1983). As a result, unemployment rate grew from 5.7 per cent in 1980 to 6.2 per cent in 1982.

The government subsequently initiated a series of industrial policies in order to accelerate the shift of the nation's production structure from an agricultural base to one that is centred on export-oriented industrialization. Despite the commitment given to the expansion of a manufacturing base, the government was faced with a dilemma, particularly during the initial stages of economic development, as to whether to embark fully on an agricultural or industrial restructuring. By promoting agricultural development, the Malaysian economy would be vulnerable to global market fluctuations in commodity prices. On the other hand, the promotion of industrial development would mean that the Malay community would be further left behind on the path to economic prosperity relative to other ethnic groups, in particular the Chinese. As Dr Mahathir pointed out:

What is clear is that unless the Chinese in particular are willing to hold themselves back and appreciate the need to bring the Malays up in the economic field, not even the determination of the Malays and schemes of the Government can help to solve the Malay economic dilemma. (1970, p. 32)

There was a concern that the Malays had yet to acquire the necessary skills to undertake the challenge of the industrial sector (Mahathir, 1970). The demographic distribution of the ethnic groups and a weighting system in the allocation of parliamentary seats also played an influential role in shaping the development of the agricultural sector. Since the bulk of political support for the dominating political party, the UMNO, comes from the rural areas, in which a majority of Malays reside, it would be to the advantage of the

UMNO to concentrate its strategies on the modernization of rural development programmes. The rural development initiatives were also highly political in that successive Ministers of Agriculture would often use these initiatives to gain 'support among the rural Malays, if not indeed for leadership of UMNO itself' (Snodgrass, 1980, p. 167). The livelihood of these rural inhabitants was largely subsistence. They constituted mainly the poor of the country and the backward sector of the economy (Lim, 1973). The UMNO's strategy, since independence in 1957, had been to raise the living standards in the rural areas and rural income to a more decent level, even more so after the May 1969 racial riots. This was indicated in the Second Malaysia Plan: 'The measures to raise incomes in rural areas, where Malays and other indigenous people predominate, will not only help to eradicate poverty, but also serve the objective of correcting racial economic imbalance' (Malaysia, 1971, p. 3).

The government recognized the gravity of the ethnic politics, and responded with development initiatives for the rural sector during the period 1971–90, which encompassed the Second, Third, Fourth and Fifth Five-Year Plans.[8] Restructuring and eliminating poverty entailed considerable modernization of the Malays' attitudes. In addressing this concern, the government initiated a series of agricultural reforms to increase the productivity of the rural sector and the living standards of the rural population. Many quasi-government agencies were established to implement integrated agricultural schemes (the Muda Agricultural Development Authority), to develop farmers' associations (the Farmers' Organisation Authority), to encourage rural credit (the Agricultural Bank), to administer land settlement (the Federal Land Development Authority), to handle agricultural marketing (the Federal Agricultural Marketing Authority) and to coordinate commodity matters (the National Rice Board).[9]

It was only in the mid-1980s that the government began to take the manufacturing sector seriously as the traditional sector was no longer able to support the growing economy. The declining commodity prices put enormous pressures on the objectives of the New Economic Policy (to be discussed in the next chapter). There were also few downstream and value-added activities generated by this sector. Rather than wait for world commodity prices to increase again, initiatives were put in place to make manufacturing the key leading sector and the economy's engine of growth.

CONCLUSION

The dynamics of the Solow–Swan growth model imply that in the long run, countries will converge to similar steady-state levels of per capita income. Poor countries starting with a relatively low per capita income and lower capital–labour ratio will grow faster during the transition period. The implication of this convergence property to developing nations is that they can take advantage of their relative backwardness to accelerate their growth potentials. However, there are many empirical studies to indicate that this has not been the case. The per capita income gap between the rich and poor countries is not closing. If the stocks of capital K and labour L are relatively low in poor economies, the return to these factors should be relatively high. This alone should see K and L flowing from rich to poor economies because these two factor inputs display decreasing marginal productivities. Why is it then not the case? Technology is now more readily transferable across nations than ever before as a result of progress in transport, telecommunications and computers. Since the early 1980s, economic activities and technological progress have been evolving towards (and increasingly dependent upon) a global structure.

The problem lies with the fact that political instability makes investment risky. In addition to taking into account the rates of return to investment in their decision-making process, firms place a premium on risks. Adam Smith once wrote:

> In those unfortunate countries, indeed, where men are continually afraid of the violence of their superiors, they frequently conceal a great part of their stock, in order to have it always at hand to carry with them to some place of safety, in case of being threatened with any of those disasters to which they consider themselves as at all times exposed. (1776, p. 268)

With reference to the endogenous growth models, political instability can have a negative impact on human capital accumulation by hindering and disrupting education and physical capital investment.

In light of the 'instabilities' generated by political and social tensions, and deterioration in the terms of trade, the Malaysian government embarked on a series of development strategies to minimize their impact on the economic system. The elimination of poverty, which was achieved through rapid growth rather than by redistribution of wealth from one section of the community to the other, was primarily aimed at minimizing social tension, which was the source of political instability. Manufacturing was earmarked as the engine of growth as a result of the deterioration in commodity prices, and the inability of the agricultural sector to support the growing economy. The expansion of the manufacturing sector was geared to the generation of employment opportunities, thereby reducing the incidence of poverty and interracial economic disparities, which was believed to be the fundamental cause of the 1969 racial crisis. The expansion of the manufacturing sector also minimized the impact of the massive fluctuation in the agricultural sector in terms of export revenue and employment generation. The next chapter will examine the role of the state in minimizing these shocks from political instability and external trade, through an expansion of the manufacturing sector.

NOTES

[1] Earlier, Lipset (1959) wrote about the relationship between political institutions (democracy) and economic outcomes (prosperity), and this hypothesis has since been well established as an empirical regularity (Barro, 1997).

[2] Examples are the governments in Africa, Latin America, planned economies of Eastern Europe, and the former Marcos administration in the Philippines.

[3] Barro (1997) used the Gastil (1991) indicator of political rights. The original ranking from 1 to 7 was converted to a scale from 0 to 1, where 0 corresponds to the fewest political rights (Gastil's rank 7) and 1 to the most political rights (Gastil's rank 1).

[4] In 1995, the Malays, who descended from migrants who had traversed the land-bridge from Central Asia, made up 61.5 per cent of the population; the Chinese, Indians and others constituted 27.4 per cent, 7.7 per cent and 3.4 per cent respectively.

[5] In the early 1960s, the state was unable to absorb the increasing numbers of emerging university-trained middle class, particularly the Malays. With limited options at its disposal, the ascendant Malay middle class turned its attention to business. The first Bumiputera Economic Congress in 1965 led to the establishment of Malaysia's national bank, Bank Bumiputera, and the reorganization of the Rural Industrial Development Authority in the form of Majlis Amanah Rakyat or the Council of Trust for the Bumiputeras (Jomo, 1994). According to Jomo:

> The second Bumiputera Economic Congress in 1968 continued to reflect the dissatisfaction of sections of the growing Malay elite with the ethnically accommodative policies of Tunku Abdul Rahman's Alliance government. Not surprisingly then, criticisms against the Tunku – variously associated with so-called 'young turks' and 'ultras' – grew. Some of those involved – including Mahathir and his erstwhile deputy, Musa Hitam – were punished by the Tunku after May 1969, before Tunku Abdul Rahman himself was slowly eased out of the leadership of the Government, UMNO and the Alliance. (1994, p. 5)

[6] Between the mid-1950s to late 1960s, rapid economic growth was ineffective in bringing about adequate employment opportunities and a reduction in income inequality.

[7] Means (1991, p. 7) observed that: 'Malay politicians recounted the "insults" and interpreted the earlier "victory parade" as evidence that Malay supremacy in government was being challenged by "infidels". They argued that counter-demonstrations were needed "to teach the Chinese a lesson"… in the atmosphere of crisis and with the irrational mechanisms of crowd psychology, primal emotions surged in uncontrollable waves combining racial antipathies, anger, fear, hatred, and self-justifying rationalizations for barbarous behaviour.'

[8] During this period (1956–70), the main priorities were: (1) the redevelopment of the rubber industry; (2) general agricultural development; (3) mining development; and (4) the determination of a sound policy of land utilization.

[9] Snodgrass (1980) provided a detailed and comprehensive account of the policies and programmes in the development of the Malaysian agricultural sector.

5.   The role of the state in the development of the manufacturing sector

INTRODUCTION

The previous chapter discussed the importance of political stability in the economic development of Malaysia. However, this does not in the strictest sense imply that gaining political stability is enough to put a country on the path to sustainable growth. Political stability, in itself, is not a means to an end. What political stability does is to allow the unhindered flow and exchange of resources among economic agents, domestic as well international. Once political stability has been established, the pace of the modernization process will be to a large degree determined by the structure and characteristics of the government. Several authors (Nelson and Pack, 1999; Rowan, 1998; World Bank, 1993) have argued that the high growth rates experienced by the newly industrialized countries (NICs) are largely due to government initiatives put in place to channel resources to growth-enhancing activities, such as expanding human capital accumulation and physical infrastructure.

There is a view which suggests that efficient market allocation and distribution of economic resources cannot be attained with state intervention. However, this need not be the case. Greenwald and Stiglitz (1986) argued that a state–market relationship can have a positive and complementary role in improving market efficiency. Stern (1991a, p. 250) highlighted five areas justifying state intervention:

1. market failure, which may arise from many possible sources including externalities, missing markets, increasing returns, public goods, and imperfect information;
2. a concern to prevent or reduce poverty and/or to improve income distribution;
3. the assertion of rights to certain facilities or goods such as education, health and housing;
4. paternalism (relating, for example, to education, pensions and drugs); and
5. the rights of future generations (including some concerns relevant to the environment).

Empirical evidence on the relative magnitude of the role of government and market failure are inconclusive, despite claims that government failure outweighs market failure (Srinivasan, 1985; World Bank, 1983). Fishlow (1990, p. 66) stated that: 'in sum, no one has yet shown that the failure of government intervention necessarily outweighs market failure'. This view is shared by Lipton (in Crabtree and Thirlwall, 1993, p. 163):

> Yet markets need states – and states that do more, better, than most states in the Third World now. States are not just needed to organize roads and schools, laws and police. They also ensure a competitive framework by providing, or regulating, commodities normally undersupplied privately, and/or supplied by monopolies and/or in non-contestable markets. Nor will market outcomes be generally acceptable in a free society unless there is a sense of fairness. To create that, states may need to attack socially intolerable levels of poverty and inequality: intolerable especially if they are not related to market performance or marginal product, but are inherited. Nor can markets be sustained unless states protect physical environments.

Chang (1998, p. 64), reported that:

> Firstly, it has become increasingly clear over the years that the spectacular successes of the East Asian countries of Japan and the so-called first-tier Newly Industrialized Countries (NICs) and then of the second-tier NICs of Southeast Asia could not be easily explained by pure market economies. This has raised the question: What, if not the market? The obvious answer to this question was the strong, pro-business development state, and especially the elite bureaucracy as its core institution ... Secondly, in contrast to the East and the Southeast Asian experiences, market-oriented reforms in many developing and transition economies over the last two decades have often dismally failed.

Thirlwall (1999, pp. 80) wrote:

> The Cambridge development economist Ajit Singh tells the story of when he first went to Cambridge as a student of Kaldor that Kaldor taught him three things: first, developing countries must industrialise; second, they can only industrialise by protection, and third, anyone who says otherwise is being dishonest!

Singh (1994, p. 1821), referring to East Asia, commented that:

> There is now general agreement that governments in these countries intervened heavily in all spheres of the economy in order to achieve rapid economic growth and fast industrialization.

Furthermore, the state could play a positive role in the development of the exports sector in a country. It is generally assumed that government intervention is lower in countries that are integrated with the global markets. However, a study of 23 OECD countries conducted by Rodrik (1998) found a relationship between openness and size of government. Highly open economies such as Austria, the Netherlands and Norway were reported to have some of the world's highest shares of government spending in GDP. Rodrik's (1998) findings have important implications, particularly with reference to a country in which its comparative advantage is in tradeable goods. If Rodrik's (1998) analysis is correct, government intervention in the economy must be larger, not smaller as suggested by the proponents of free trade. The explanation given by Rodrik (1998) for this recommendation is that government expenditure can be used to provide social insurance against external risk. There are also the added spillover benefits suggested by Grossman and Helpman (1991) in that technological progress, A, can be driven by the diffusion of new knowledge which is linked to international trade.

The aims of this chapter are to examine the role of the state in the development of the Malaysian manufacturing sector, and to analyse empirically the structure of output growth. It begins with an overview of the government's key initiatives for restructuring both the economy and society. This is followed by the empirical estimation of Malaysia's structure of output growth based on the model of Chenery and Taylor (1968). This is important because 'productivity growth is influenced by changing output' (Cornwall and Cornwall, 1994, p. 240). Any potential efficiency gains, as postulated by the Solow–Swan and endogenous growth models, and whether it is caused by technological advancement or by policy implementation, will only be realized at a pace determined by the shift in the sectoral composition of the Malaysian economy. As Harcourt (2001) commented, when referring to Kaldor's views on economic growth:

> He [Kaldor] argued that both the Keynesian and the neoclassical growth models were in essence single sector and so could not handle the basic *complementarity* of an integrated world. The latter requires a multi-sector model to do it justice, to tackle the mutual interdependence of different sectors where the development of each depends on and is stimulated by the development of the others. (p. 247)

STATE AND ECONOMIC PLANNING IN MALAYSIA

Planning constituted the institutional centrepiece of the Malaysian economic development effort. Although Malaysia maintains a market economy, planning has served as a significant and increasingly comprehensive instrument of economic management and development, particularly in minimizing both internal and external shocks.[1] These shocks served as a catalyst in the restructuring process of the Malaysian economy.

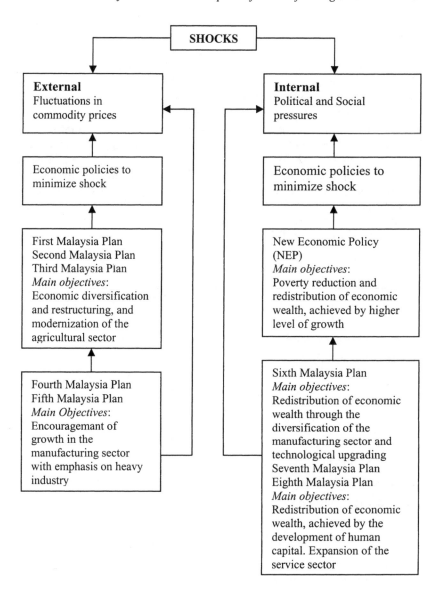

Sources: Malaysia, 1971; 1976; 1981; 1986; 1991; 1996; 2001.

Figure 5.1   Strategies used by the Malaysian government to minimize shocks in its economic system

Figure 5.1 shows two prominent features. First, the Malaysian economic transformation was shaped by two major shocks – political and terms of trade. Second, the state has played an important role in minimizing the impact of these shocks. The 1985–1986 recession is often cited as an example of Malaysia's vulnerability to external shocks. Malaysia's rapid recovery from that recession was due to not only its favourable external conditions but largely its shift in government action. Fluctuation and reduction in export earnings had been cushioned by policies initiated to either minimize these shocks or encourage growth in other sectors of the economy which were less prone to such shocks. For example, when Malaysia experienced massive fluctuations in its agricultural sectors, the government introduced new initiatives to diversify its agrarian economy. The result was that rubber and tin were no longer the main export earners.

Supporting the various Malaysia Plans was the allocation of public expenditure, as shown in Table 5.1.

Table 5.1   Total development allocations under the Malaysia Plans, 1956–2005

	RM (million)	%
Agricultural & rural development	48 767	9.7
Mineral resources development	233	0.05
Commerce & industry	142 415	28.5
Transport	79 296	15.8
Communications	17 089	3.4
Utilities	40 668	8.2
Research & development	3 976	0.8
Education & training	53 728	10.8
Health & family planning	17 395	3.6
Social & community services	25 095	5.1
General administration	23 848	4.7
Security	46 717	9.4
Total	499 226	100

Sources: Malaysia, 1971; 1976; 1981; 1986; 1991; 1996; 2001.

During the NEP (New Economic Policy) plan period of 1971–90, the Treasury bureaucracy and other bureaucratic organizations under the administrative guidance of the Prime Minister's office became progressively involved in the planning process, as shown in Figure 5.2.

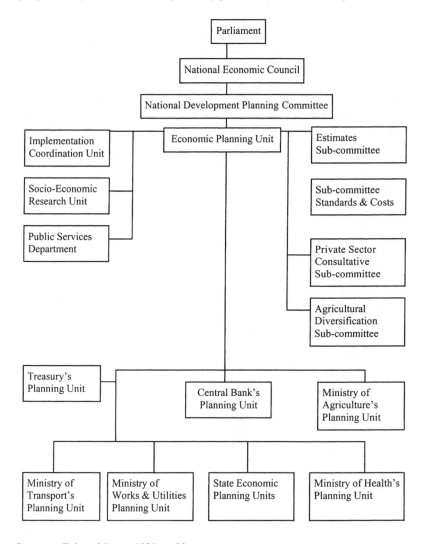

Source: Toh and Jomo, 1983, p. 32.

Figure 5.2   Organizational set-up of the Malaysian planning machinery

Although there have been amendments and changes to this structure since 1990, on the whole, the principal framework remained intact until early 2000.

Since gaining independence in 1957, Malaysian development planning has undergone five successive historical phases of role expansion. They are as follows:

1. Phase I: an initial forward-budgeting phase represented by the colonial-style First Five-Year Plan (1956–60).
2. Phase II: a second public investment phase denoted by the Second Five-Year Plan (1961–65) and First Malaysia Plan (1966–70).
3. Phase III: more broadly interventionist phase inaugurated by the NEP and carried forward in the Second Malaysia Plan (1971–75), Third Malaysia Plan (1976–80) and heavy industrialization under the Fourth Malaysia Plan (1980–85) and Fifth Malaysia Plan (1986–90).
4. Phase IV: Sixth Malaysia Plan (1991–95) – diversification of the manufacturing base, promotion of linkages through the development of small and medium-sized-industries, and acceleration in the restructuring and modernization of the lagging industries.
5. Phase V: Seventh Malaysia Plan (1996–2000) and Eighth Malaysia Plan (2001–05) which emphasizes the importance of human capital development and the service sector for new sources of growth.

It was during the Phase III period and thereafter that the state intervened heavily in restructuring the nation's economic system. The NEP became the foundation of and the yardstick for all economic and social policies (the NEP was operationalized in the Second, Third, Fourth, Fifth and Sixth Malaysia Plans). Because the NEP formed the basis of Malaysia's development strategies, it is appropriate to review briefly the success of the NEP, prior to examining the development of the country's manufacturing sector. The NEP had two main objectives:

> The Plan incorporates a two-pronged New Economic Policy for development. The first prong is to reduce and eventually eradicate poverty, by raising income levels and increasing employment opportunities for all Malaysians, irrespective of race. The second prong aims at accelerating the process of restructuring Malaysian society to correct economic imbalance, so as to reduce and eventually eliminate the identification of race with economic function. (Second Malaysia Plan, Malaysia, 1971, p. 5)

These changes were planned to occur over a 20-year Perspective Plan period (1971–90), and the initiatives and strategies were carried out in the Second Malaysia Plan, Third Malaysia Plan, Fourth Malaysia Plan and Fifth Malaysia Plan. In operational terms, the restructuring had two explicit goals imposed by the planning authorities:

1. Employment by sector should reflect the racial composition of the

population, which was 54 per cent Malays, 35 per cent Chinese, 10 per cent Indians and 1 per cent others.

2. By 1990, the Malays and indigenous groups in Malaysia should own and manage at least 30 per cent of the share capital of the corporate sector, compared to their 2.4 per cent share in 1970. As for the other Malaysian ethnic groups, the target was an increase from 34.3 per cent to 40 per cent, while foreign share was a decrease from 63.3 per cent to 30 per cent.

The achievement of the second prong of the NEP inevitably meant expanding Malay participation in the formal sectors and the creation of a Malay commercial culture:

This process involves the modernization of rural lives, a rapid and balanced growth of urban activities and the creation of a Malay commercial and industrial community in all categories and at all levels of operation, so that Malays and other indigenous people will become full partners in all aspects of the economic life of the nation. (Second Malaysia Plan, Malaysia, 1971, p. 5)

Since the development of a sizeable Malay commercial and industrial community would take time, the government embarked on establishing and operating Malay enterprises, both wholly government-owned and private–public joint ventures. The plan for achieving the objectives of the NEP stipulated massive public sector participation in the economic and commercial spheres, as well as government intervention in legal and administrative aspects. Thus, a host of statutory corporations such as the National Corporation (PERNAS) and the State Economic Development Corporation (SEDC), and business ventures under the government umbrella, were established. A major objective of the government's participation in the corporate sector of the economy was to increase the ownership and control of the corporate wealth for the Malay community. In addition, the government initiated legislation (the Industrial Coordination Act, 1975) to redress the racial economic imbalance through the provision of more opportunities for Malay participation in the private sector. As a result, Malay-controlled companies began purchasing plantations (foreign capital was gradually displaced by Malay trusts in several large plantations), mines and other commercial activities, including the media (Gomez and Jomo, 1997; Means, 1991; Rasiah and Shari, 2001). During 1971–75, the government allocated RM362.1 million (2 per cent of total government expenditure) for the development of a Malay commercial base. This amount was further increased to RM1 924.1 million (5.1 per cent of total government expenditure) for the 1976–80 period, and to RM3 455 million (4.2 per cent of total government expenditure) in 1981–85.

Public expenditure for the development of the rural sector totalled RM2 127.4 million (11.8 per cent of total government expenditure) in 1971–75 (Malaysia, 1971), RM4 427.7 million (11.6 per cent of total government expenditure) in 1976–80 (Malaysia, 1976), and RM6 245.5 million (7.6 per cent of total government expenditure) in 1981–85 (Malaysia, 1981). Table 5.2 gives an indication of the allocated expenditure for poverty eradication and restructuring of society under various Malaysia Plans.

Table 5.2   Allocation for poverty eradication and restructuring of society under various Malaysia plans, 1971-1990, RM million

	Poverty eradication	Restructuring	Overlapping	Total
Second Malaysia Plan	2 350.0	508.3	3.4	2 861.7
Third Malaysia Plan	6 373.4	2 376.0	149.0	8 898.4
Fourth Malaysia Plan	9 319.2	4 397.6	300.5	14 017.3
Fifth Malaysia Plan	15 445.7	5 076.2	n.a.	20 521.8

Sources: Malaysia, 1971, 1976, 1981, 1986.

THE NEW ECONOMIC POLICY RECORD

When the NEP expired in 1990, it was widely viewed as a success in that it achieved its two major objectives: reduction of poverty and a more equitable distribution of wealth among the ethnic groups.

Poverty reduction

Table 5.3 shows that the poverty rate dropped from 49 per cent in 1970 to 15 per cent in 1990, a reduction of more than 50 per cent.

Table 5.3   Incidence of poverty (%), Malaysia, 1970–2002

	1970	1975	1980	1985	1990	1995	1997	1999	2002
Rural	58.7	54.1	43.1	24.7	19.3	14.9	10.9	12.4	11.4
Urban	21.3	19.0	15.8	8.2	17.3	3.6	2.1	3.4	2.0
Total	49.3	43.9	33.8	18.4	15.0	8.7	6.1	7.5	5.1

Sources: Malaysia, 1971, 1981, 1986, 2001; Ministry of Finance, Malaysia, 2003.

The figure continued to decline to 8.7 per cent in 1995 and 5.1 per cent in 2002. However, in 1999, the poverty rate increased to 7.5 per cent as a result of the 1997 financial crisis.

Inter-Ethnic Redistribution

Over the years, the second prong, which was committed to restructuring the Malaysian society in order to eliminate the identification of race with economic function, became the main item on the NEP agenda, particularly the target of 30 per cent Malay participation in the economy (in terms of ownership of the modern corporate sector). Despite the fact that the NEP's target of 30 per cent was not met, Malay participation in the corporate sector, measured in terms of share ownership in publicly listed companies, rose significantly from 2.4 per cent in 1970 to 7.8 per cent in 1975, 12.5 per cent in 1980 and 20.3 per cent in 1990, before falling to 19.1 per cent in 1999 as a result of the 1997 financial crisis. This is shown in Table 5.4.

Table 5.4   Percentage ownership of share capital in limited companies, Malaysia, 1970–99

	1970	1975	1980	1985	1990	1995	1999
Malays	2.4	7.8	12.5	17.8	20.3	20.6	19.1
Other Malaysians	34.3	37.3	44.6	56.7	46.2	43.4	40.3
Foreigners	63.3	54.9	42.9	25.5	33.5	36.0	40.6
Total	100	100	100	100	100	100	100

Sources: Malaysia, 1971, 1981, 1986, 2001.

In addition, the private share in the total Malay stake increased significantly, from 39 per cent in 1975, to 41 per cent in 1983, 68 per cent in 1990 and 87.6 per cent in 1992, reflecting the new emphasis on private Malay wealth accumulation under the Mahathir administration (Jomo, 1994).

EMPLOYMENT BY OCCUPATION AND RACE

The target set out by the NEP that employment should reflect the racial composition of the population (54 per cent Malays, 35 per cent Chinese, 10 per cent Indians, and 1 per cent others) was approximately achieved by 1990, as indicated in Table 5.5.

Despite the success of the NEP (under the various Malaysia Plans) in achieving political stability through poverty eradication and inter-ethnic redistribution, there have been many criticisms of the large amount of public expenditure allocated to achieve the NEP's main objectives. Jomo (1990, 1994), for instance, argued that the reduction in poverty had been primarily attributed to economic growth brought about by an increase in productivity rather than by distributional policies. The government itself acknowledged that only 40 per cent of the RM30 billion that was spent on poverty eradication from 1971 to 1988 reached the targeted poverty groups, with the balance going to administration and infrastructure costs (Jomo, 1991).

Table 5.5   Employment by occupation and race, Malaysia, 1970–2000

1970	Malay	Chinese	Indian	Others
Professional & technical workers	47.2	37.7	12.7	2.4
Administrative & managerial workers	22.4	65.7	7.5	4.4
Clerical workers	33.4	51.0	14.3	1.3
Sales workers	23.9	64.7	11.0	0.4
Agricultural workers	68.7	20.8	9.6	0.9
Production workers	31.3	59.9	8.6	0.2
Service & other workers	42.9	42.5	13.4	1.2
Total	*51.4*	*37.0*	*10.7*	*0.9*
1990				
Professional & technical workers	60.3	30.8	7.7	1.2
Administrative & managerial workers	33.3	58.7	5.3	2.7
Clerical workers	54.9	36.9	7.8	0.4
Sales workers	36.0	56.5	6.5	1.0
Agricultural workers	76.4	15.8	7.0	0.8
Production workers	48.5	40.4	10.7	0.4
Service & other workers	61.5	27.0	10.6	0.9
Total	*57.8*	*32.9*	*8.5*	*0.8*
2000				
Professional & technical workers	63.9	25.8	7.6	2.7
Administrative & managerial workers	37.0	52.3	5.5	5.2
Clerical workers	56.8	32.9	8.6	1.7
Sales workers	37.3	49.8	6.8	6.1
Agricultural workers	61.2	10.3	6.9	21.6
Production workers	44.7	33.8	10.0	11.5
Service & other workers	57.7	21.8	8.5	12.0
Total	*51.5*	*29.7*	*8.3*	*10.5*

Sources: Malaysia, 1971, 1981, 1986, 2001.

There is also the issue that the key policy instrument used by the Malaysian government to reduce inter-racial economic differences is the discriminatory allocation of public expenditure in favour of the Malays. In order to improve the economic conditions of Malays, the government significantly increased its expenditure on projects designed exclusively for Malays participation (Lim, 1973, 1983). As a result, resources were often allocated inefficiently (Jomo, 1990). In fact, the then Prime Minister Mahathir (Khoo, 1994, p. 150) pointed out that:

> Malay businessmen had been nurtured on easy credit, business licenses, government contracts, and other forms of preferential treatment ... they did not fulfill NEP's vision of a class of competitive Malay entrepreneurs. Malay professionals were raised in 'MARA Colleges' and trained abroad on state scholarship to form a 'permanent middle class' but clung to the state for employment. NEP's restructuring appeared to have removed the racial imbalances only in form because in reality NEP fostered a 'dole', 'subsidy' or 'get-rich-quick' mentality among the Malays. State protection had perpetuated Malay dependence on the state.

If efficiency is used as the main criterion to judge the allocation of public expenditure on restructuring Malaysian society, then without doubt the ethnic-based distribution policies have failed. This is because many of the programmes and projects initiated by the government since 1970 were riddled with corruption and crony interests (Gomez and Jomo, 1997; Jomo, 1994). On the other hand, if political stability forms the basis of efficient economic production, and if initial conditions and shocks matter (Crafts, 1997; Kaldor, 1972; Keynes, 1936; Nelson, 1996; Setterfield, 1998), then undoubtedly the amount of expenditure which was allocated to establish stability (at an annual average of about RM2.2 billion for the period 1970–2000, and constituting approximately 2 per cent of total government expenditure) was a small price to pay in return for rapid economic growth.[2] As Rasiah and Shari (2001, p. 75) pointed out:

> While ethnic-based distribution policies, especially those involving the promotion of crony interests, sapped the economy of rents, many critical instruments assisted poverty alleviation and distribution, which helped enhance political stability.

In addition, Khong (1991) and Rasiah and Shari (2001) reported that the discriminatory allocation of public expenditure in favour of the Malays actually strengthened intra-ethnic solidarity amongst the Chinese. According to Rasiah and Shari (2001, p. 72): 'It is believed that the Chinese, fearing increased ethnic encroachment into the market by the state, started ethnic networks to protect their interests in the private sector, thus uniting even the once clannishly divided Chinese.' This uniting gesture further minimized ethnic political tensions. When examining the economic history of Malaysia,

Drabble (2000, p. 275) pointed out that: 'the pattern of income distribution has implications for a country's standard of living, level of savings (and thereby investment and the rate of economic growth), as well as overall political and social stability'. Perhaps Aghion and Williamson (1998, p. 33) were correct in asserting that:

> Overall, inequality actually proves *bad* for growth in several circumstances. Redistribution is then growth enhancing because it creates opportunities, improves borrowers' incentives and/or because it reduces macroeconomic volatility. In such instances, there is no longer a tradeoff between equity and efficiency goals, and policies designed to tackle one then have a positive impact on the other.

When the Seventh Malaysia Plan expired in 2000, Malaysia had successfully transformed from an agricultural production structure towards a modern manufacturing structure. Table 5.6 show the rising trend in the manufacturing sector. Although the growth was modest during the 1960s, the manufacturing sector surpassed the agricultural sector in 1990 in terms of its contribution to GDP growth.

Table 5.6   Gross domestic product by sector, Malaysia, 1960–2003 (%)

	1960	1970	1980	1990	1995	2000	2003
Agriculture	40.5	30.8	22.8	18.7	10.3	8.7	8.2
Mining	6.1	6.3	10.0	9.7	8.2	6.6	7.2
Manufacturing	8.6	13.4	20.0	27.0	27.1	33.4	30.6
Service	44.8	51.3	47.2	42.3	51.3	52.6	56.8

Sources: Malaysia, 1971, 1981, 1986, 1991, 2001; Bank Negara Malaysia, 2004.

By 1990, the economy had reduced its reliance on primary products, such as rubber and tin, and in the process became one of the world largest manufacturers of semiconductors, and a sizeable producer of electronic and electrical products. This seems to suggest that manufacturing is the engine of Malaysia's economic growth, and it is in this sector that the evolution of technological progress is at its most intense. Accordingly, the subsequent sections will examine this growth trend.

MALAYSIAN INDUSTRIAL DEVELOPMENT

Manufacturing had played a minor role in the economic development of Malaysia during the British occupation. Although policy initiatives were implemented to establish a manufacturing base as soon as Malaysia gained its political independence in 1957, manufacturing during this period contributed only a few percentage points to GDP and employed 110 000 workers, including craftsmen and workers in handicrafts industries, and factory workers (Snodgrass, 1980). The manufacturing sector did not take off until the early 1980s. Prior to 1980, the economy was dominated by the export of rubber and tin, largely due to the inherited colonial economic structure. Accordingly, the evolution of the manufacturing sector was greatly influenced and shaped by the export of rubber and tin. The manufacturing sector during the 1950s and 1960s was largely confined to the processing of raw materials (Snodgrass, 1980). Manufacturing products were generally associated with low-value products such as bricks, beer, soft drinks, ice and lumber. Exports often 'consisted mainly of simple manipulations of local primary products to raise their value-to-weight ratios and make them more portable: the smoking of rubber, milling of coconut oil and so on' (Snodgrass, 1980, p. 207). Domestic firms that wished to establish production other than processing raw materials were effectively discouraged by colonial policies (Jomo, 1994). Reflecting that pattern of production, and the recommendation of the International Bank of Reconstruction and Development (1955), import substitution industrialization was favoured to diversify Malaysian exports in order to minimize the impact of fluctuations in rubber and tin prices during the 1960s. However, employment generation and the anticipated linkages to other sectors of the economy did not eventuate, leading to a shift in favour of export-oriented industrialization.

Since 1971, Malaysia's manufacturing structure had evolved under the initiatives of the NEP and the impact of the terms of trade. In addition to the Five-Year Plans, a supplementary series of industrial plans were implemented to broaden the output base of the economy. Development allocation for the manufacturing sector rose significantly during the Second Malaysia Plan period with the primary aim of rectifying the discrepancy in income between the Malays and non-Malays, and to reduce the high levels of unemployment in urban centres. During this period, government initiatives were implemented to accelerate growth in the manufacturing sector and were favourably received by both domestic and foreign firms. Manufacturing output rapidly rose from 8.2 per cent of GDP in 1955 to 16.4 per cent in 1975, and 20 per cent in 1980. Nonetheless, the agricultural sector still dominated the production capacity of the economy, contributing 40.2 per cent, 27.7 per cent and 22.8 per cent of GDP in 1955, 1975 and 1980 respectively.

In early 1980s, the Malaysian economy spiralled into a recession as a direct consequence of a massive fall in commodity prices. This prompted the government to evaluate other development options. As a result of the commitment of the then Prime Minister, Dr Mahathir Mohamad, heavy industrialization was pursued as the engine of economic growth (Jomo, 1993). However, the unsustainable mounting public expenditure being channelled into heavy industry projects, and the lack of linkages between heavy industries and other sectors of the economy, resulted in a shift towards an emphasis on the development of human capital (Malaysia, 1991, 1996). The subsequent release of the Sixth and Seventh Malaysia Plans meant that Malaysia's economic growth would be derived from gains in productivity rather than through accumulation of capital and labour. Figure 5.3 provides a summary of the Malaysian industrial policies from 1958 to 2005.

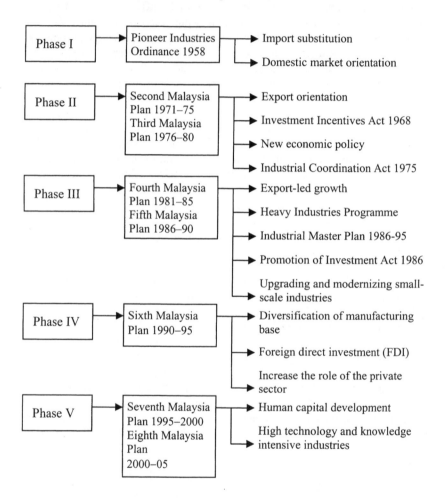

Sources: Ali, 1992; Malaysia, 1991, 2001.

Figure 5.3   Industrial development and major policy initiatives, 1958-2005

GROWTH OF THE MANUFACTURING SECTOR

Immediately after independence, the Pioneer Industries Ordinance 1958 was introduced under the recommendation of the World Bank (IBRD, 1955), marking the beginning of an import substitution manufacturing structure which lasted until the late 1960s. The first policy measure taken for the stimulation of industrial development was tariff protection. Complementing tariff protection were tax incentives in the form of two years tax exemption (which were later extended to three years for a fixed capital expenditure of more then RM100 000 and to five years of expenditure exceeding RM250 000) for any new manufacturing establishment approved as a 'pioneer'. The exemption was later extended to cover the non-manufacturing sector.

During the Phase I period (1958–71), firms responded positively to government initiatives. Industrial growth consequently averaged 17.4 per cent per year in 1959–68, and manufacturing share of GDP rose from 8.5 per cent in 1959 to 12.7 per cent in 1968. Employment in the manufacturing sector also significantly increased from 6.4 per cent in 1957 to 8.1 per cent in 1965, involving a rise from 135 700 to 214 800 workers (Malaysia, 1971). The number of companies which received pioneer status and entered commercial production also rose from 18 in 1959 to 246 in 1971. During 1981–85, the number of projects that were approved totalled 431 with a total capital investment of RM3785 million (Malaysia, 1986). The growth in the pioneer sector is shown in Table 5.7.

Although the number of companies established under the pioneer status was small during the period 1959–71, these pioneer companies produced a substantial share of the total manufacturing output and employment. As shown in Table 5.7, output of the pioneer companies rose from 0.8 per cent of total manufacturing output in 1959 to 33.5 per cent in 1971, and employed 28.8 per cent of the total manufacturing sector in the same period.

Table 5.7   Growth of the pioneer sector in Malaysia, 1959-1971

Year	No.	% (a)	Output (RM'000)	% (a)	Value added (RM'000)	% (a)	Fixed capital (RM'000)	% (a)	Employ-ment no.	% (a)
1959	18	0.4	10 671	0.8	4 305	1.5	n.a.	n.a.	1 296	2.1
1968	146	1.6	895 126	29.3	278 274	32.2	449 027	50.4	23 115	17.7
1971	246	n.a.	1 393 361	33.5	450 933	35.6	699 947	54.3	43 624	28.8

Note: (a) % of manufacture.

Sources: Department of Statistics, Malaysia, *Census of Manufacturing Industries*, 1963, 1968, 1973.

In terms of fixed capital and valued added, the pioneer companies represented 54.3 per cent and 35.6 per cent of the total manufacturing sector respectively.

Despite the significant growth in the manufacturing sector during Phase I, the absorptive capacity of the manufacturing sector in terms of employment opportunities was comparatively low. The number of workers employed in the manufacturing sector was still significantly lower than those in other sectors of the economy. From 1960 to 1970, employment in the manufacturing sector averaged 11.4 per cent of the total workforce compared to 47.5 for the agricultural sector (Malaysia, 1981). This may be due to the fact that large foreign capital-intensive firms were outpacing small labour-intensive domestic enterprises, constraining employment creation.

In addition to employment constraints, there were other factors which highlighted the limitations of the import-substitution manufacturing structure that was used to propel Malaysia to a higher level of economic growth. According to Jomo and Edwards (1993), the import-substitution initiatives had created an environment in which manufacturing firms failed to see the need to compete in the international market to increase their profits. Rather, they were more inclined to produce for domestic consumption as they were guaranteed substantial profits under the protection umbrella. Jomo and Edwards (1993) calculated that the average effective rate of protection (EPR) increased from 25 per cent on value added in 1962 to 70 per cent in 1972. Based on an EPR of 70 per cent, a profit of 1000 per cent could be generated for a firm. Other problems associated with the import-substituting industry phase included the following:

1. There were limited incentives and pressures for firms to export. Firms that benefited from government initiatives, such as subsidies and tariff protection, contributed only 4 per cent of total exports.
2. Foreign firms dominated the import-substituting industries. More than three-fifths of all manufacturing outputs (including mining) were produced by foreign firms. The protection initiatives not only gave rise to high profits at the expense of domestic consumers but these profits were remitted out of Malaysia (Jomo and Edwards, 1993).

Jomo and Edwards (1993, p. 24) aptly described the situation:

> The net result of this first phase of industrialization was that the mass of the population in Malaysia was being charged (as consumer) above world prices and receiving little or no benefits from the industrialization. On average in 1970 the domestic prices of goods manufactured in Malaysia were about 25 per cent above world prices. The surcharge to consumers in the form of protection amounted to as much as M$500 million or about M$50 per Malaysian ... These 'infant' industries were not being forced or induced to grow up. There was little pressure to transfer technology or skills. There was admittedly some growth in manufacturing employment between 1957 and 1970, but it was small.

Import substitution in Malaysia had generally involved domestic assembly, packaging and final processing of finished goods – previously imported from abroad – using domestic labour but machines and materials that were largely imported from abroad. The employment-generating capacity of such industrialization was limited due to the utilization of capital-intensive foreign technology and the existence of weak linkages to the rest of the national economy.

Towards the early 1970s, the limitations of the Malaysian import-substitution strategy became clear. It had failed to address the pressing unemployment problem. The number of people unemployed was 180 000 or 6.5 per cent of the labour force in 1965, and 280 000 or 8 per cent in 1970 (Malaysia, 1971). Throughout the 1960s, in terms of location, the urban areas experienced unemployment rates of around 10 per cent, with more than 75 per cent of that associated with the 15–25 age group (Malaysia, 1971).

During the Phase II period (1971–80), the government targeted two types of export-oriented industries: resource-based and non-resource-based. Resource-based industries consisted of the older industries (rubber and tin) and the new industries (palm oil, petroleum, timber) that processed raw commodities for export. However, from 1970 onwards, growth of the resource base sector in terms of total output and export contributions declined rapidly relative to other manufacturing sectors. This was largely due to a fall in export contributions by rubber and tin, which were once Malaysia's main export earners. In 1960, rubber and tin contributed more than 60 per cent towards total export earnings but that percentage dropped to less than 10 per cent by 1980 (Bank Negara Malaysia, 1988). The only commodity that defied this declining trend was crude petroleum. In 1960, petroleum accounted for around 4 per cent of total exports. By 1980, petroleum's share of total exports had increased to more than 11 per cent. As a result of the deterioration in revenues from the resource-based exports, there was a shift towards non-resource-based manufacturing. This marked the end of the import-substitution industrialization and the beginning of export-oriented industrialization. Due to technological constraints, the fastest way to redress technological deficiency is through foreign direct investment (FDI).

The government put in place several measures, such as taxation incentives, free trade zones and labour laws, to attract foreign capital to develop an export-oriented manufacturing sector. A comprehensive list of the taxation incentives can be found in the investors' guide in the various issues of the *Economic Report* published by the Ministry of Finance, Malaysia. Briefly, a firm that is granted Pioneer status will be exempted from tax for five years, and firms that are producing goods that are encouraged by the Malaysian government will be granted an investment tax allowance of 60 per cent for capital expenditure incurred within five years. In addition, certain expenses (overseas promotion, export market research, and so on) are entitled to double tax deduction. With reference to labour laws, workers from electronic factories were forbidden to form unions. Similarly, textile and garment workers were prohibited from establishing a single national union (Jomo and Todd, 1994).

During the Phase III and IV periods (1981–85 and 1990–2000 respectively), FDI flows rose significantly, particularly from 1991 onwards. Table 5.8 shows the total FDI inflows to Malaysia for 1980–2002.

Table 5.8   Total FDI inflows to Malaysia, 1980–2002

Period	US$ millions
1980–2002 (annual average)	1 083
1986–90 (annual average)	1 126
1991–95 (annual average)	4 907
1996–2002 (annual average)	3 970
Annual average	
1996	5 300
1997	4 534
1998	1 484
1999	3 230
2000	5 223
2001	4 975
2002	3 046

Sources: Asian Development Bank, 1998; Bank Negara Malaysia, *Annual Report*, various years; Ministry of Finance, Malaysia, 1998, 2003.

Total FDI inflows to Malaysia peaked in 1996 at US$5 300 million but declined to US$1 484 million, primarily due to the mid-1997 financial crisis. FDI inflows rose again from 1999 onwards, peaking at US$5 223 million, and from then on began to decline to US$3 046 million. From 1980 to 2002, on average, Japan was the highest investor constituting more than 30 per cent of total FDI, followed by Singapore at 20 per cent and the US at 14 per cent. The dominance of foreign investments in 1985–98 was confined to petroleum and gas, and the electrical and electronic sectors. Both of these sectors experienced rapid growth. In the petroleum and gas sector, FDI inflows started at a modest US$330 000 and expanded to more than US$1 082.9 million in 1997. Inflows for the electrical and electronic sector amounted to US$45.8 million (12.4 per cent of FDI) in 1985 and US$740.9 million (25.1 per cent of FDI) in 1997. Other industries which experienced an increase in FDI were metal products, chemicals and textiles as shown in Table 5.9.

Table 5.9   *Amount of foreign investments (US$ million) in approved projects by industry, 1985–2002*

Industry	1985	%	1995	%	2000	%	2002	%
Food manufacturing	25	7	47	1	142	3	113	4
Textiles	13	4	187	5	192	4	9	0
Paper and printing	42	11	39	1	56	1	47	2
Chemicals	12	3	719	20	154	3	131	4
Petroleum and gas	0	0	155	4	844	16	1 261	42
Rubber products	12	3	30	1	176	3	58	2
Non-metallic mineral products	46	12	494	14	402	8	26	1
Basic metal products	61	17	187	5	113	2	42	1
Fabricated metals	18	5	112	3	43	1	56	2
Electrical and electronic products	46	12	935	26	2 687	51	1 005	34
Transport equipment	77	21	182	5	72	1	37	1
Miscellaneous	19	5	515	14	342	7	214	7
Total	371	100	3 600	100	5 222	100	2 998	100

Sources: Ministry of Finance, Malaysia, 1993, 1994, 1998, 2004.

However, in the late 1990s there was a switch from the traditional manufacturing sector to the service sector. For instance, during the period 1993–97, the manufacturing sector made up 66 per cent of FDI with 21 per cent going to the service sector and the remaining 13 per cent going to oil and gas. In the 1998–2002 period, the share in FDI was 38 per cent manufacturing, 38 per cent services, and 24 per cent oil and gas. It was also during the Phase III and IV periods that the electrical and electronic industry experienced the most rapid growth, which accounted for 49 per cent of manufacturing exports in 1985, and expanded to 67 per cent of total exports in 1998, amounting to RM89 372 million (Ministry of Finance, Malaysia, 1998). According to Drabble (2000), it is in this sector that FDI expansion has been most beneficial, particularly for employment opportunities for women from the rural areas (which will be discussed in greater detail in the next chapter). Figure 5.4 shows the proportion of electrical and electronic exports to total manufacturing exports.

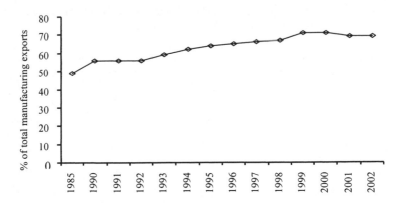

Sources: Das, 1998; Ministry of Finance, Malaysia, 2003.

Figure 5.4   Proportion of electrical and electronic exports to total manufacturing exports, 1995–2002

The contribution of Malaysia's electrical and electronic exports to total manufacturing exports is significant when compared to other countries, as shown in Table 5.10.

Table 5.10   Contribution of electronics exports to growth of total merchandise exports in selected Asian economies (%)

	1986–90	1991–95
Malaysia	58	66
Korea	39	43
Singapore	62	79
Taiwan	18	23
Indonesia	1	28
Philippines	21	38
Thailand	26	35
China	8	28
India	4	4

Source: Das, 1998.

With the exception of Singapore, Malaysia's dependence on this sector for export revenue was significantly higher compared to various countries listed in the table. Between 1996 and 1997, the electronic and electrical exports contributed to more than 75 per cent of total exports but this figure declined to 67 per cent in 1998 (January–July) as a result of slower demand, in particular for integrated circuits, radios, air-conditioners, household refrigerators, and insulated wires and cables. This is shown in Table 5.11

Table 5.11   *Production of selected electrical and electronic products (January–July) in Malaysia*

Products	1997	1998	Annual Change (%)
Electronic transistors (million units)	7 558	7 635	1.0
Integrated circuits (million units)	6 944	6 803	− 2.0
Television sets ('000 units)	4 186	4 683	11.9
Radios ('000 units)	19 093	18 393	− 3.7
Room air-conditioners ('000 units)	1 594	930	− 41.7
Household refrigerators ('000 units)	135	121	− 10.4
Insulated wires and cables (tonnes)	69 800	50 676	− 27.4

Source: Ministry of Finance, Malaysia, 1998, p. 76.

However, by 1999, the electronic sector exports began to pick up again from RM119 025 million to RM209 062 million in 2002, an increase of more than 50 per cent in absolute value. As the electronic sector constituted more than 50 per cent of Malaysia's exports, a downturn in exports would have a significant impact on export revenues. Based on the strong growth during 1995–2002 (Figure 5.5), it is possible that the electronic sector will continue to grow, at least into the near future.

Figure 5.5 shows that the demand for electronic products was increasing over the 1995–2002 period. The demand for semiconductors was strong, rising from RM33 197 million to RM71 070 million in 2000, and declined momentarily to RM60 778 million in 2001 before rising again to RM72 467 million in 2002 (Ministry of Finance, 2003). This was also the case for the exports of the electronic equipment and electrical products.

Although the incentives set out in the various Malaysia Plans had brought about significant changes to both the production structure and exports of the Malaysian economy, the industrialization programme was not without criticism, particularly with the heavy industrialization strategy implemented during the Phase III period (1981–85). Several authors (Gomez and Jomo, 1997; Jomo, 1990, 1994) argued that the push for heavy industrialization by the Mahathir administration was an expensive mistake. They argued that the economy had been burdened with unnecessary protectionist measures which sheltered the infant industries from competition.

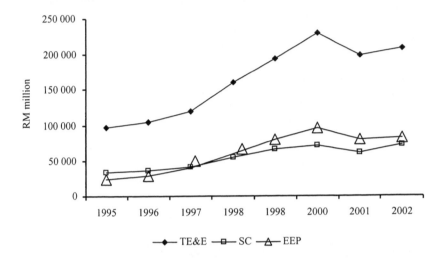

Notes: TE&E: Total electronics & electrical exports
          SC: Semiconductor
          EEP: Electronic equipment & parts

Sources: Ministry of Finance, Malaysia, 2001, 2003.

Figure 5.5   Exports of electronics and electrical products, Malaysia, 1995–2002

The scale of investments in terms of capital meant that there was less capital for other uses, leading to additional foreign borrowings and mounting foreign debts incurred by the public sector to finance the massive industrialization projects which peaked at RM28 310 million in 1986. Heavy industrialization had also failed to develop strong and extensive linkages with other sectors of the economy (Cheong and Lim, 1981; Jomo, 1990; Malaysia, 1986). The outputs of most of the heavy industries chosen by the Mahathir administration for development, such as steel, cement, petrochemicals, shipbuilding and repairs, faced strong international competition due to excessive global production capacity with little likelihood of viability. This led Jomo (1990, p. 128) to comment that: 'for a more integrated and balanced industrialization programme, the question is not whether or not to develop heavy industries, but rather which ones to support, for what ends, and under what conditions'.

The need to reassess the heavy industrialization policy was reflected in a shift in policy from a redistributive approach (in order to met the NEP objectives) based on heavy industrialization to an approach which emphasized the role of human resources in the development of the economy. A comprehensive analysis of human capital development in Malaysia will be covered in Chapter 8. In the meantime, it is essential to trace empirically the changing structure of outputs.

CHANGING STRUCTURE OF OUTPUTS IN MALAYSIA: AN EMPIRICAL ANALYSIS

This section sets out to analyse empirically the shifts in the production structure and the growth rate of per capita income in Malaysia from 1957 to 2003. This will provide an indication of the productivity growth in the various sectors of the economy, and is linked to the analyses undertaken in Chapters 6, 7 and 9. This is important because growth-enhancing activities, as discussed in Chapters 2 and 3, in the various growth models hinged on the flows of factor inputs from one sector to another. If factors inputs, such as capital and labour or both, do flow to the highest returns (as postulated by the Solow–Swan growth model), then it would be expected that these factors would flow from the agricultural sector to the manufacturing sector because the latter has a greater potential for increasing returns (Kaldor, 1966). Thus, by tracing this shift, it is possible to account for their impact on output growth.

According to Chenery and Taylor (1968),[3] as per capita income rises, the share of industry in gross domestic product also rises. Chenery and Taylor (1968) categorized development patterns into three distinct types: (1) large countries (2) small industry-oriented countries and (3) small primary export-oriented countries. Given the dominance of the agricultural sector in contributing to the economic growth of Malaysia, the third pattern fits Malaysia's development experience.[4] Since 1957, per capita income had been consistently increasing but it was during the mid-1980s that per capita income began to rise rapidly. This is displayed in Figure 5.6. It was also during the mid-1980s that the share of the primary sector to GDP significantly decreased as indicated in Figure 5.7.

Figure 5.7 shows that during the early stages of economic development, the agricultural sector dominated the production of output. During the 46-year period, the primary sector's contributions declined significantly from more than 50 per cent in the early 1960s to less than 20 per cent towards the end of the 1990s. The secondary sector, however, experienced a rapid rise in growth of output particularly from 1980 onwards, as shown in Figure 5.8.

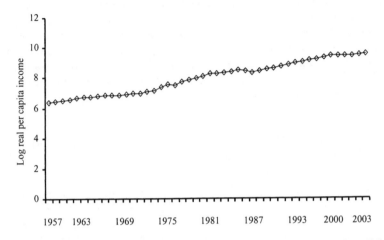

Sources: Malaysia, 1965, 1971, 1976, 1981, 1986, 1991, 1996; Rao, 1980; Ministry of Finance, Malaysia, 1998, 2000, 2004.

Figure 5.6   Per capita income in 1960 prices, Malaysia, 1957–2003

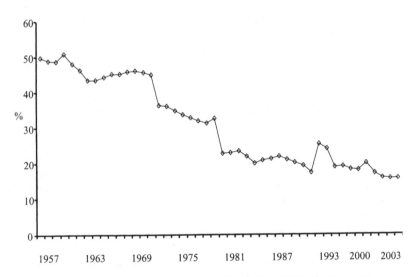

Sources: Malaysia, 1965, 1971, 1976, 1981, 1986, 1991, 1996; Ministry of Finance, Malaysia,1998, 2000, 2004; Rao, 1980.

Figure 5.7   Percentage contribution of primary sector to GDP at constant prices, 1957–2003

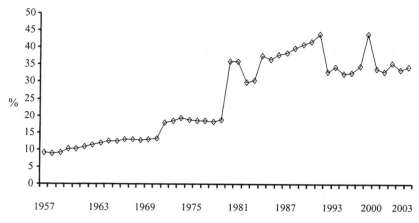

Sources: Malaysia, 1965, 1971, 1976, 1981, 1986, 1991, 1996; Rao, 1980; Ministry of Finance, Malaysia, 1998, 2000, 2004.

Figure 5.8 *Percentage contribution of secondary sector to GDP at constant prices, 1957–2003*

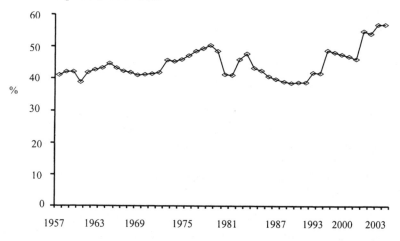

Sources: Malaysia, 1965, 1971, 1976, 1981, 1986, 1991, 1996; Rao, 1980; Ministry of Finance, Malaysia, 1998, 2000, 2004.

Figure 5.9 *Percentage contribution of tertiary sector to GDP at constant prices, 1957–2003*

While both the primary and secondary sectors experienced significant changes in their contributions to GDP, the tertiary sector remained more or less the same, hovering between the 42 and 48 percentage mark, but increased more rapidly from 2000 onwards. This is shown in Figure 5.9.

Based on Figures 5.6 to 5.9, it is reasonable to state that the structural patterns in Malaysia resembled those described by Chenery and Taylor (1968). The rapid increase in per capita income during the mid-1980s coincided with a rapid decline in the share of the primary sector to aggregate output, and a sharp increase in industry share of production output. This trend is further supported by the large difference in value added between the agricultural and manufacturing sectors.

Value added from the agricultural sector decreased from an annual average growth of 4.9 per cent for 1971–80 to an average of 1.6 per cent for 1996–98. In contrast to other sectors, the manufacturing sector contributed the largest increase in value added. This is shown in Table 5.12.

Table 5.12   Growth rate of value added in primary, secondary and tertiary sectors, Malaysia, 1971-1998 (average per annum in %)

Sectors	1971–80	1981–90	1991–98
Primary	4.9	3.9	1.6
Secondary	9.6	7.3	10.7
Tertiary	8.3	3.9	8.5

Sources: Asian Development Bank, 1993, 1998.

Since 1960, the composition of exports had also undergone changes reflecting the changes in production structure. In the early stages of economic development, Malaysia depended upon the agricultural sector for the bulk of its foreign earnings. This dependence gradually declined over time and by 1990, the manufacturing sector overtook the agricultural sector. This trend is reflected in Figure 5.10.

The rapid increase in manufacturing exports particularly from the late 1980s onwards may indicate a productivity-driven sector[5] (to be discussed in Chapters 7 and 9). Although the rising share of manufacturing in GDP and the declining share of agriculture is a pattern common to all developing and developed economies, the rate of change differs among countries due to the different inherited characteristics of an economy (Chenery and Taylor, 1968). This suggests that history or initial condition matters for output growth (Crafts, 1997; Kaldor, 1972; Nelson, 1996; Setterfield, 1998; Solow, 1994). The sector share elasticities of small primary-oriented countries estimated by Chenery and Taylor (1968) are presented in Table 5.13.

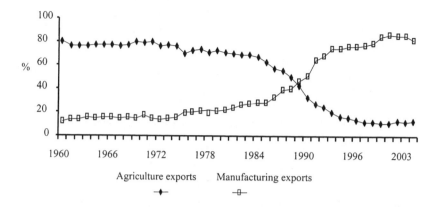

Sources: Malaysia, 1965, 1971, 1976, 1981, 1986, 1991, 1996; Rao, 1980; Ministry of Finance, Malaysia, 1998, 2000, 2004.

Figure 5.10   *Percentage share of agriculture and manufacturing exports, Malaysia, 1960–2003*

Table 5.13   *Sector share elasticities of small primary-oriented countries*

Sector	Cross-section elasticity	Median from time series elasticities
Primary	– 0.37	– 0.55
Secondary	0.34	0.34

Source: Chenery and Taylor, 1968.

It appears that the secondary sector elasticity of 0.34 is similar for both cross section and time series data. A 1 per cent increase in GDP per capita is linked to a 0.34 per cent contribution to GDP from the secondary sector. However, the elasticity of the primary sector differs between time series and cross-section data at –0.55 and –0.37 respectively. Chenery and Taylor did not provide any explanation for these differences but Rao (1980, p. 42) stated that:

> since the countries are primary oriented, the share of primary sector in GDP when measured at current prices declines faster due to secular decline in primary product prices and the terms of trade turning in favour of the secondary sector and against primary production. The cross-section elasticity is probably less influenced by such price variations.

An early study conducted by Rao (1980), based on Chenery and Taylor (1968) methodology, on Malaysian sectors' elasticities share on aggregate output for the period of 1959–71 reported –0.6928 for the primary sector and 0.9403 for the secondary sector.

ESTIMATION

The AR(1) approach[6] is utilized to estimate the sector share elasticity based on the following equation:

$$log \: \varepsilon_i = \alpha + \beta \: log \: y + u_t \qquad (5.1)$$

where ε_i is the percentage share of a given sector i (primary, secondary and tertiary) in GDP, α is a constant, y is GDP per capita at 1960 prices (1960 = 100), β is the sector share elasticity and $u_t = \rho u_{t-1} + \varepsilon_t$. Detailed algorithms for the estimation are found later in Chapter 7, equations (7.4) to (7.5).

The primary sector includes agriculture, livestock, forestry, fishing, mining and quarrying. The secondary sector is composed of manufacturing and construction. The tertiary sector refers to utilities, transport, storage, communication, wholesale and retail trade, banking, insurance, real estate, ownership of dwellings, general administration, security and all other services. Data for the percentage share of primary and secondary sectors are adapted from Rao (1980) and obtained from various official Malaysian government publications. They include the *Yearbook of Statistics*, *Economic Report*, and Bank Negara Malaysia *Annual Report*. The period examined is from 1957 to 2003.

RESULTS

The estimated coefficients are found to be significant for the primary and secondary sectors, as shown in Table 5.14. The estimated coefficient of the tertiary sector was however not found to be statistically significant at the 5 per cent level but significant at the 10 per cent level. The estimated coefficient of 0.06 suggests that for every 1 per cent in GDP per capita, the tertiary sector contributed 0.06 to that 1 per cent growth. The primary sector elasticity at –0.37 *(p < 0.05)* indicates that a one per cent increase in GDP per capita is associated with a reduction in the primary sector share by 0.37 per cent. The coefficient for the secondary sector is 0.44 *(p < 0.05)*, and shows that a one per cent increase in GDP per capita is associated with 0.44 per cent increase in the percentage contribution to GDP.

It is possible that the estimated coefficient of 0.06 for the tertiary sector may be biased downwards by the dominant agricultural sector, particularly during the 1957–81 period. The logic is that before 1980 the service sector was based largely on low-skilled activities servicing mainly the primary sector. As the Malaysian economy shifted towards the modern production structure from 1981 onwards, the service sector should also follow along this changing pattern, from low-skilled activities to one of higher skilled. If this is to be the case, the contribution of the service sector should increase in the later years as a result of higher productivity brought about by higher-skilled activities.

Table 5.14   Estimated coefficients for the various sectors of the Malaysian economy, 1957–2003

Primary sector
Dependent variable is log primary: 1957 to 2003

α	β	R^2	$R\text{-}Bar^2$	DW
6.35 (0.18)	− 0.37* (0.02)	0.96	0.95	1.96

Secondary (manufacturing) sector
Dependent variable is log manufacturing: 1957 to 2003

α	β	R^2	$R\text{-}Bar^2$	DW
− 0.49 (0.58)	0.44* (0.02)	0.94	0.94	1.99

Tertiary (service) sector
Dependent variable is log tertiary: 1957 to 2003

α	β	R^2	$R\text{-}Bar^2$	DW
3.31 (0.26)	0.06** (0.03)	0.73	0.72	1.81

Notes: All results have been treated for autocorrelation using the AR(1) model. Standard error in parenthesis. *Significant at 5 per cent p-value, **significant at 10 per cent p-value.

To test this, the period 1957–2003 is divided into two sub-periods. The first period covers 1957 to 1981, while the second period covers 1982 to 2003. The estimated coefficients for the tertiary sector for the period 1957–81 and 1982–2003 are found in Table 5.15. The estimated contribution for the

1957–81 period was 0.06 (statistically significant at the 5 per cent level). As for the period 1982–2003, the estimated contribution was 0.17 per cent (statistically not significant at the 5 per cent level, but significant at the 10 per cent level) to every percentage of output growth. Although the contribution from the tertiary sector in the latter period was significantly higher than the earlier period as expected, it was still considerably lower than the secondary sector, despite the fact that the tertiary sector is approximately twice the size of the secondary sector.

Table 5.15   Estimated coefficients for the tertiary sector of the Malaysian economy, 1957–81, 1982–2003

Dependent variable is log tertiary: 1957 to 1981

α	β	R^2	$R\text{-}Bar^2$	DW
3.31	0.06*	0.62	0.56	2.01
(0.20)	(0.02)			

Dependent variable is log tertiary: 1982 to 2003

α	β	R^2	$R\text{-}Bar^2$	DW
2.31	0.17**	0.81	0.77	1.91
(0.84)	(0.09)			

Notes: All results have been treated for autocorrelation using the AR(1) model. Standard error in parenthesis. *Significant at 5 per cent *p*-value, **significant at 10 per cent *p*-value.

The findings suggest that the productivity of the agricultural sector as well as that of the tertiary sector were relatively lower than that of the manufacturing sector. As more resources have been shifted from the agricultural sector towards the productive manufacturing sector, higher growth of output per capita has been possible. The findings suggest that output and productivity growth in the manufacturing sector are pivotal to Malaysia's growth performance. This is consistent with Kaldor's proposition that manufacturing is the 'engine of growth' (Chapter 3).

CONCLUSION

The state has played a pivotal role in accelerating the shifts in Malaysia's production structure. During the period 1957–2003, the agricultural sector experienced a diminishing role as a contributor to growth of per capita output relative to the manufacturing sector. The growth of per capita income during that period was largely derived from the secondary sector, particularly the manufacturing sector. This suggests that increases in Malaysia's per capita output had been associated with increasing returns in the manufacturing sector which offered more scope for increasing returns (Kaldor, 1966). If new knowledge is embodied in new equipment (Arrow, 1962; Kaldor, 1960; Kaldor and Mirrless, 1962; Salter, 1962, 1966), as well as replacement capital, and can only shift into the workforce through on-the-job training and learning-by-doing (Arrow, 1962), and if most of these activities are largely confined to the manufacturing sector, then the expansion of the manufacturing sector will increase the adoption and diffusion rates of new knowledge or technology.[7] This shift in production activities from agriculture towards manufacturing is consistent with the growth-enhancing activities proposed by the endogenous growth models. The findings also fit well with the prediction of the Solow–Swan growth model, in that when factor mobility is permitted, factor inputs (capital and labour) will flow to the highest returns, and in the Malaysian case, the manufacturing sector.

The shift in the production structure has a significant impact on the Malaysian labour market. Given the role of labour in the neoclassical and endogenous growth models, the next chapter is dedicated to analysing the development of the Malaysian labour market and its contribution to economic growth.

NOTES

[1] Prior to independence in 1957, the planning process was under the control of post-colonial political executives (British bureaucrats). They were given the authority (usually from Britain) to set goals, assign priorities and lay down broad policy guidelines. During this phase, economic planning was initiated primarily to serve the British interests (British plantations and mining). Public development expenditure was heavily skewed in favour of export and urban sectors, with priority going to the provision of economic infrastructure such as railways, roads, electricity, telecommunications and port facilities to service the primary commodity export economy.

[2] Recently, Arunatilake et al. (2001) estimated that the total cost of the ethnic conflict in Sri Lanka up to 1996 was 'at least Rs. 1135 billion at 1996 prices (168.5% of the 1996 GDP, equivalent to US$ 20.6 billion)' (p. 1495).

[3] The justification for using their analysis is that the propositions set out in the model are consistent with both the neoclassical and endogenous growth models in that factor inputs would shift to activities that have higher returns.

[4] As observed by Chenery and Taylor (1968, p. 400):

The countries oriented toward primary exports have a development pattern that is notably different from the first two types. Primary production declines much more slowly and exceeds industry up to an income level of nearly US$800. The effects of rich natural resources on the productive structure are illustrated in most extreme form by Venezuela, Malaya and Iraq – the countries having the highest indices of primary orientation.

5   In order for a manufactured product to remain competitive in the international market, it has to be superior in terms of price and quality, and this can only come about by higher levels of productivity.

6   The AR(1) model is utilized to remove autocorrelation.

7   This is demonstrated by Malaysia's success in exporting sophisticated electronic and electrical products. The increase in FDI inflows which played an important role in expanding the manufacturing sector may also have accelerated the pace of technological adoption and diffusion.

6.   Structural change, labour utilization and economic growth

INTRODUCTION

The endogenous growth models of Lucas (1988), Romer (1986, 1990), Grossman and Helpman (1991) and Aghion and Howitt (1998) as discussed in Chapter 3 proposed that the rates of growth of productivity and per capita income are endogenously explained. However, these models neglect the effects of sectoral shifts in output and labour utilization. Taking into account these shifts in growth analyses is important for two reasons. First, the rate of growth per worker varies considerably from sector to sector (Kaldor, 1957; Cornwall and Cornwall, 1994; Feinstein, 1999). The findings in Chapter 5 suggest a pronounced difference in sectoral productivity growth rates in the Malaysian economy. As more resources were shifted from the agricultural sector towards the productive manufacturing sector, higher growth of output per capita was possible. Kaldor argued in many of his writings that it is impossible to understand the growth and development process without taking a sectoral approach, particularly the distinction between increasing returns activities and diminishing returns activities. According to Kaldor (1960), increasing returns is largely a characteristic of manufacturing industry, while diminishing returns characterizes the agricultural sector (land-based activities).

Second, there is a need to take a sectoral approach because the rates of productivity growth in the Solow–Swan and endogenous growth models will only be realized at a pace determined by the utilization rate of labour. Hence, by examining the patterns of labour utilization between the various sectors of the economy, a deeper understanding of the growth process and of the wide income disparity between developed and developing countries, as discussed in the convergence controversy, is possible. Solow (2000, p. 183)[1] pointed out that:

> Just about all of growth theory works on the flat assumption that the economy always achieves its potential output. This shows itself even notationally: no distinction is made between labor force and employment, or between the existing stock of capital and any sort of utilization rate. I describe this as a simple

assumption; of course some models have a facade of Walrasian equilibrium, with all markets clearing, but that too is a flat assumption.

This chapter has two aims: (1) to provide a brief overview of the Malaysian labour market and its role in facilitating the rapid transition from an agricultural base towards a modern manufacturing production structure; and (2) to estimate empirically the utilization of capital and labour on an economy-wide basis as well as between the various sectors of the economy. Kaldor's technical progress function will be employed to provide the framework for empirical analysis. The justification for using this approach is given in the later part of this chapter.

A BRIEF OVERVIEW OF THE MALAYSIAN LABOUR MARKET

The possibility of further racial tension and the deterioration in export earnings (as discussed in Chapter 4) has prompted the Malaysian government to take an active role in the development of its labour market. Malaysia's labour market policy, since the implementation of the First Malaysia Plan, has played a vital role in the overall growth policy. Labour market policy has undergone several adjustments between 1971 and 1997 in order to bring about a continuing match between the changing demand for and supply of labour. Since the beginning, the main objective of the Malaysian labour market policy has been to expand productive employment at a rate sufficient to reduce prevailing levels of unemployment. For instance, the Pioneer Industrial Ordinance was enacted in 1958 to promote a labour-intensive import-substitution economic strategy in order to generate new employment opportunities for the rapidly growing population. Several incentives were initiated to accelerate the expansion of the manufacturing sector in order to generate extra jobs. In addition to the establishment of free trade zones (implemented to attract foreign investment), labour laws were also amended to control more effectively the workers in the new labour intensive export oriented industries. During the mid-1980s, employment creations were to come from the heavy industries as the primary sector was no longer able to provide enough jobs to absorb the growing work force. The Sixth and Seventh Malaysia Plans placed strong emphasis on the development of human capital. Public expenditure on higher education was increased significantly in recognition of shortages in skilled labour.

The main strategies that have been utilized to create opportunities for productive employment have focused on the promotion of economic growth either by direct government participation in business activities or by stimulating and facilitating private sector growth, as summarized in Box 6.1.

BOX 6.1   SUMMARY OF MALAYSIAN GOVERNMENT
INITIATIVES FOR EMPLOYMENT OPPORTUNITIES

Creation of public enterprises and government companies and generally the expansion of the public service as part of the steps taken to implement the distributional programmes of the long-term plan. This not only provided new job opportunities but also enabled the Malay population to gain experience in the business sector.

Introduction of youth employment programmes, particularly in the form of public works to alleviate high youth unemployment in the early 1970s.

Revamping the structure of incentives to encourage new investments, both foreign and domestic. This included the introduction in 1971 of labour utilization relief aimed at encouraging employment creation. The labour utilization relief, in the form of tax exemption, was given to companies that employed at least 50 full-time paid workers.

In the mid-1980s, the introduction of a package of counter-cyclical strategies to overcome the recession, including:
- Implementation of a labour-intensive public works programme involving, among others, the construction of low-cost housing, roads and highways.
- Making more agricultural land available for cultivation, including allowing the conversion of ex-mining land for agricultural purposes.
- Generating more opportunities for self-employment, especially in urban areas, by relaxing the rules and regulations governing street trading.

Complementing the demand-creating strategies was another set of strategies designed to provide the necessary supply of required manpower. They included:
- Further expansion of industrial and vocational training, beginning in 1971 with a special focus on producing high-level and skilled manpower. At the same time, a stronger orientation towards science and technology was introduced into the public education curriculum.
- Strengthening the administrative machinery for the dissemination of labour market information and monitoring the labour market to ensure that labour market policies had led to the optimum utilization of manpower resources.

When there were indications in the late 1980s that the labour market was tightening up, several new strategies were introduced which included:
- Enhancing labour productivity and increasing jobs with higher skill content.
- Improving the efficiency of labour markets and increasing labour mobility in order to avoid skill mismatches and other labour market rigidities.
- Upgrading the education and training system in order to improve the quality and quantity of manpower and requiring the private sector to play a greater role in skill promotion, as well as in strengthening linkages with public sector skill institutions. The establishment of the Human Resources Development Fund aimed at encouraging a training culture in the private sector was a step towards this end.

Source: Gan, 1995, pp. 165–7.

120   *Technical Progress and Economic Growth*

In addition to the initiatives outlined in Box 6.1, the industrial relations system in Malaysia provided a conducive environment for foreign investors. This is covered in detail by several authors (Grace, 1990; Jomo and Todd, 1994; Sharma, 1996).

THE MALAYSIAN LABOUR FORCE STRUCTURE: TRENDS IN LABOUR SUPPLY AND DEMAND

The principal features of the Malaysian labour market are depicted in Table 6.1. Between 1965 and 2003, the total labour force tripled as a result of the increase in working population and the rising participation rate of female workers.

Table 6.1   Malaysian labour market ('000), 1965–2003

	1965	1970	1975	1980	1985	1990	1995	2000	2003
Total labour force	3 246	3 874	4 522	5 109	5 916	7 042	8 140	9 572	10 519
Employed	3 048	3 607	4 225	4 817	5 468	6 686	7 915	9 271	10 150
Unemployed	198	267	297	292	448	356	225	301	369
Unemployment rate (%)	6.1	6.9	6.6	5.7	7.6	5.1	2.8	3.6	3.5

Sources: Malaysia, 1971, 1976, 1986, 1996; Ministry of Finance, Malaysia, 2001, 2004.

Accordingly, employment increased from 3.048 million in 1965 to 7.915 million in 1995, and to 10.150 million in 2003. Rapid output growth has enabled the labour market to absorb most of the increase in the labour force, leading to a falling unemployment trend, from 6.1 per cent in 1965 to 3.5 per cent in 2003, apart from the recession years of the early 1970s and mid-1980s. This trend is depicted in Figure 6.1.

The decline in output had a significant impact on the employment of labour on various occasions, as shown in Figure 6.1. During the 1970s, GDP growth averaged below 6 per cent and unemployment levels averaged above 7 per cent. When GDP increased to 8 per cent in 1980 from 3.6 per cent in 1975, unemployment decreased from 7 per cent in 1975 to 5.6 per cent in 1980. From 1990 to 1997, GDP growth averaged above 8 per cent and unemployment levels dropped below 4 per cent. The relationship between GDP growth and unemployment is well established. Earlier, Okun (1962), based on the US data for 1947–60, found that an increase in unemployment by 1 percentage point would lead to a 3.3 per cent decline in the GDP growth rate. More recently, Cornwall and Cornwall (1994) argued that higher productivity growth could be achieved by implementing policy to reduce unemployment. They pointed out (p. 244) that: 'It is curious that, while more efficient resource use is stressed, the employment of unused labour has been overlooked for both have the same impact.' An important implication of Okun's analysis is that the decline in output growth will not only lead to a reduction in employment opportunities, but also to a decline in technological progress and productivity associated with unused labour.

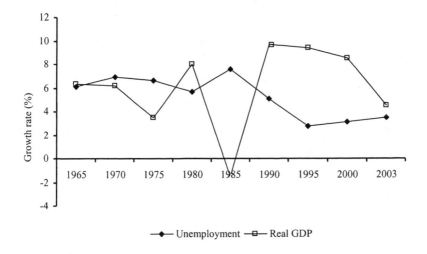

Sources: Taylor, 2004; Ministry of Finance, Malaysia, 2000, 2003.

Figure 6.1   Real GDP growth and unemployment rates, Malaysia, 1965–2003

There is also reason to expect that reducing unemployment will accelerate sectoral shifts in an economy by stimulating investment and innovation, leading to higher productivity growth rates (Ruggles, 1979; Boyer and Petit, 1981; Cornwall and Cornwall, 1992).

SUPPLY OF LABOUR

A prominent feature of Malaysia's labour force is the changing participation rates among the different age groups over the years, particularly from the early 1980s onwards, as shown in Table 6.2. It can be seen that the proportion of the total labour force who were aged between 15–24 years decreased progressively from 31.8 per cent in 1982 to 21.5 per cent in 2002. In contrast, the proportion of the 25–54 age group continued to rise from 62 per cent to 72.5 per cent over the same period. The main explanation is the rising trend in the retention of the 15–24 age group within the education system up to upper secondary education. For instance, secondary enrolment rose significantly from less than 20 per cent in 1960 to more than 60 per cent in 1992. This may suggest a growing trend towards an older, more experienced and better-educated labour force following a well-established pattern set out by the OECD countries. As the economy shifts to higher levels of productivity, the demand for experienced workers increases (Feinstein, 1999).

Table 6.2   Participation rates of Malaysian labour force by age and sex, 1982–2002 (%)

	1982	1985	1990	1995	1997	2002
Male						
15–24	29.3	28.7	27.1	23.0	23.2	19.6
25–54	63.9	64.7	66.8	70.4	70.3	73.4
55–64	6.8	6.6	6.1	6.6	6.5	6.9
Female						
15–24	36.4	34.3	32.9	29.9	28.8	24.8
25–54	58.3	60.3	62.0	65.4	66.8	70.7
55–64	5.3	5.4	5.1	4.7	4.3	4.5
Total						
15–24	31.8	30.6	29.2	25.4	25.1	21.5
25–54	62.0	63.1	65.1	68.7	69.1	72.5
55–64	6.3	6.2	5.7	5.9	5.8	6.1

Sources: Department of Statistics, Malaysia, 1992, 1995, 1999, 2003.

The period 1990–97 marked a turning point in the Malaysian labour market. Prior to this period there was an excess in the supply of labour. Since the early 1990s, the market had been experiencing labour shortage. The buoyancy of the economy during the Sixth Malaysia Plan (1991–95) period created a strong demand for labour at all levels.[2] The unemployment rate, which is an indicator of labour utilization, declined sharply from 5.1 per cent in 1990 to 2.8 per cent in 1995 (Table 6.1).[3] This rapid growth, particularly during the 1991–97 period, caused the Malaysian economy to run into capacity constraints which resulted in an increase in wage inflation and inflationary pressures as shown in Table 6.3.

In response to labour shortages from the late 1980s onwards, government policy influenced the labour market in two major ways: (1) relaxation of immigration rules relating to foreign workers; and (2) improvement in the education system to increase the supply of semi and skilled workforce (to be covered in Chapter 8). In the short term, the government relaxed immigration rules to allow employers who faced labour shortage to bring in foreign workers.[4] As a result, there was a significant increase in foreign workers in the country. For instance, in 1991 immigrant labour was estimated to comprise of 550 000 workers, or 30 per cent of Malaysia's workforce in the agricultural and forestry sectors, as shown in Table 6.4. In 1995, approximately 432 000 immigrant workers were employed in the agricultural sector, and accounted for more than 41 per cent of total immigrant labour. Despite the large inflows of foreign workers in 1995, the plantation sector experienced a shortfall of about 43 000 workers, particularly tappers, harvesters and weeders (Department of Statistics Malaysia, 1996).

Table 6.3   Average wage increase, 1993–2000 (%)

	1993	1994	1995	1996	1997	2000
Manufacturing	11.5	12.2	11.8	13.7	15.0	8.0
Commercial	8.7	11.0	12.2	10.6	n.a.	8.0
Transport	10.8	9.9	10.7	10.4	11.0	8.0
Services	10.0	6.4	10.2	8.8	13.0	7.0
Agriculture	11.6	4.4	9.1	17.6	18.0	11.0
Mining	n.a.	4.1	0.0	10.9	8.0	9.0
Construction	n.a.	n.a.	16.3	n.a.	n.a.	13.0
Other	7.3	10.0	0.0	13.7	n.a.	8.0

Sources: Ministry of Finance, Malaysia, 1995, 1996, 1997, 2000.

The data in Table 6.4 and Table 6.5 suggest that foreign workers had played a significant role in the expansion of these four sectors. This dependence increased further from approximately 21 per cent in 1991 to around 26 per cent in 2002.

The largest increase over the 1991–2002 period was in manufacturing, from a mere 3 per cent in 1991 to 22 per cent in 2002. There are two possible reasons for this rising trend. One is linked to manufacturing contribution to output growth. The findings of Chapter 5 showed that for every 1 per cent growth in GDP, manufacturing contributed 0.44 per cent. This suggests that for manufacturing to continue to grow, more labour will be needed to power that expansion. The other possible reason may be linked to the strong competition coming from Thailand and China in the form of lower wage cost. On average, Malaysia has higher labour wages than these two countries. If Malaysia is not able to contain the rising wage prices (Table 6.3), firms may move their manufacturing base to these two countries. One approach in which to release the pressure of rising wages is to utilize more foreign workers from neighbouring countries, such as Indonesia and the Philippines, as workers from these countries are more willing to work at a lower wage than their Malaysian counterparts.

Table 6.4   Number of foreign workers in various sectors in Malaysia, 1991

Sector	Employment by sector	% of foreign workers	No. of foreign workers
Agriculture & forestry	1 835 000	30	550 000
Construction	456 000	70	319 200
Non-government services	2 290 000	10	229 000
Manufacturing	1 374 000	3	41 220
Total	5 955 000	21	1 200 920

Source: Pillai, 1992, p. 43.

Table 6.5   Number of foreign workers in various sectors in Malaysia, 2002

Sector	Employment by sector	% of foreign workers	No. of foreign workers
Agriculture & Forestry	1 316 800	29	381 872
Construction	905 100	14	126 714
Non-government services	2 113 000	33	697 290
Manufacturing	2 068 900	22	455 158
Total	6 403 800	26	1 661 034

Source: Department of Statistics, Malaysia, 2003.

Although the agricultural sector experienced a falling trend in new employment opportunities, this sector continued to experience labour shortages, leading to wage increases in excess of productivity growth. On various occasions, the agricultural sector experienced higher than average wage increases compared to the manufacturing sector. For instance, in 1994, the average wage increase in the agricultural sector was 11.6 per cent compared to 11.5 per cent in the manufacturing sector; in 1996, it was 17.6 per cent and 13.7 per cent respectively (Table 6.3).

The usual consequence of an economy which is in transition is an increase in rural–urban migration. In the Malaysian case, such a migration pattern created an imbalance in labour supply in the agricultural sector, particularly for large plantations. Under the directions of the NEP, the rural–urban migration pattern was exacerbated because of the establishment of labour-intensive factories where wage and working conditions were better than those in the plantations. Compared to wages earned by workers in non-agricultural sectors, wages in the agricultural sector were low. For instance, in 1994, monthly salaries for a foreman or supervisor and a female sprayer were RM513 and RM246 respectively, relative to RM1 470 for a supervisor and RM510 for an unskilled production worker in the manufacturing sector (Department of Statistics Malaysia, 1996).

The rural–urban migration pattern contributed to the depletion of labour in plantations and in turn badly affected the agricultural sector. A survey conducted by the Rubber Research Institute of Malaysia between 1978 and 1984 found that the industry faced a massive labour shortage during this period which resulted in the production loss of 72 000 tonnes of rubber and 600 000 tonnes of palm oil (Nayagam, 1991). Another survey conducted by the United Planting Association of Malaysia reported that in 1985, member estates lost an average of 21.8 per cent of their workforce, and that about 24 000 additional workers were needed between 1988 and 1992. In response to these shortages, many big plantations, particularly rubber and oil palm, began to rely more on low-cost foreign workers (also illegal immigrant labour), as they did during the colonial era.

DEMAND FOR LABOUR

The composition of employment by sector in the Malaysian economy has undergone significant changes since 1947. In 1947, the agricultural, forestry and fishing sectors employed 65.1 per cent of the labour force (Rao, 1980). This figure fell to 56.9 per cent in 1957, 55.4 per cent in 1962 and 52.1 per cent in 1965. On the other hand, the proportion employed by the mining sector remained more or less constant between 1947 and 1965. This sector employed 2.5 per cent of the workforce in 1947, which increased marginally to 2.8 per cent in 1957, declined to 2.3 per cent in 1962 and then increased slightly to 2.5 per cent in 1965. Employment in the manufacturing sector constituted 7.1 per cent of the labour force in 1947, 7.4 per cent in 1957, 7.7 per cent in 1962 and 8.4 per cent in 1965. The construction sector employed 2.1 per cent of the labour force in 1947, 3.2 per cent in 1957, 3.5 in 1962 and

3.5 per cent in 1965 (Rao, 1980). The demand for labour by industry in 1965–2003 is shown in Table 6.6.

Table 6.6   Employment by industry, 1965–2003 (% of total labour force)

	1965	1975	1985	1990	2000	2003
Agriculture, forestry, livestock & fishing	52.1	47.1	30.1	26.2	15.2	13.8
Mining & quarrying	2.5	2.2	0.8	0.6	0.4	0.4
Manufacturing	8.4	11.1	15.2	19.9	27.6	27.7
Construction	3.5	4.2	7.4	6.2	8.1	7.8
Utilities	0.6	0.6	0.6	0.7	0.8	0.9
Transport, storage & communication	3.9	4.4	4.3	4.5	5.0	5.2
Finance & insurance	n.a.	0.9	3.9	3.9	5.5	6.3
Wholesale & retail trade	11.1	12.2	17.6	18.1	17.1	17.1
Services	17.9	17.3	20.1	19.9	20.2	20.8

Sources: Malaysia, 1971, 1976, 1981, 1986, 1991, 1996; Department of Statistics, Malaysia, 2000, 2004.

Table 6.6 shows that agriculture was the largest employer of labour in the 1960s, 1970s and early 1980s. However, during the mid-1980s, the proportion of total employment provided by this sector began to decline, and in 1990 it fell to 15.2 per cent, and then to 13.8 per cent in 2003. The declining trend in employment can be attributed to a rise in agricultural productivity, and the wage difference between the rural and urban sectors, which contributed to mass migration of the rural labour force to large towns and cities in search of higher wages.

The most significant growth in employment over the 1985–2003 period was generated by the manufacturing sector. Its contribution to employment was 7.4 per cent in 1957 compared to 19.9 per cent in 1990. From 2000 onwards, the manufacturing sector became the largest employer compared to other sectors as shown in Table 6.6. In 1991–95, the manufacturing sector generated almost 60 per cent of total employment creation (Department of Statistics Malaysia, 1996). The mining sector, on the other hand, experienced a declining employment trend as a result of depletion in resources and decrease in commodity prices. The construction sector, in contrast, showed a steady increase in employment which peaked in 2000 at around 8.1 per cent from 3.5 per cent in 1965.

WOMEN AND THE LABOUR MARKET

Female labour has played a profound role in the expansion of Malaysia's manufacturing sector. The rise in female participation in the workforce could be explained in part by the initiatives introduced by the state in order to rectify the labour shortages which Malaysia has experienced since the early 1980s, and in part by the growing educational opportunities for women. The Sixth Malaysia Plan emphasized the importance of female labour to the growth of the nation's economy. In 1989, the National Policy for Women was announced to promote the role and position of women in economic development. The government provided tax exemptions to employers for the establishment of child-care centres near or at workplaces to enable working mothers to look after their children during rest periods or breaks. Institutions such as the Women's Institute of Management provided training in small business and entrepreneurial activities. Other assistance provided by the public and private sectors included the provision of job training, better career prospects, and improved recreation, transport and welfare facilities. Employers were urged to provide proper housing and hostel facilities, particularly for rural migrants, many of whom were women.

Table 6.7   Employment of women by industry, 1970–2002

Industry	1970	1980	1985	1990	1998	2002
Agriculture & forestry	67.9	49.3	33.7	28.2	14.6	11.3
Mining & quarrying	0.7	0.3	0.2	0.2	0.1	0.1
Manufacturing	8.1	16.3	18.9	24.3	27.2	25.7
Utilities	0.1	0.1	0.5	0.1	0.2	0.2
Wholesale & retail trade, hotels & restaurants	5.8	11.2	19.1	19.7	22.4	25.2
Transport, storage & communications	0.5	0.7	1.3	1.5	2.1	2.2
Finance, insurance, business services	n.a.	1.6	3.9	3.9	6.7	3.5
Community, social & personal services	16.4	19.5	21.2	21.4	25.0	27.5

Sources: Department of Statistics, Malaysia, 2000, 2003; Malaysia, 1991, 1996.

Employment distribution of female workers varies with industry. Table 6.7 shows the employment distribution by industry of women workers between 1970 and 2002. Over the period 1970–98, there was a decline in the proportion of women working in the agricultural sectors, and a progressive increase in their participation in the manufacturing and services sectors, particularly in the distributive trade and financial sectors. Overall, the manufacturing sector absorbed a large share of employed women, accounting for about 24.3 per cent in 1990 and 27.2 per cent in 1998.

The female contribution to the manufacturing sector was significant. In 1992–98, the share of women employed in manufacturing averaged 42.6 per cent. Women also made up a large proportion of the labour force in Malaysia's major export industries during the 1980s. In 1984, they represented 63.7 per cent of the labour force in textile production for export, 89.4 per cent in the clothing industry and 73.7 per cent in the electronics sector. The proportions for 1990 were 57.8, 85.3 and 75.3 respectively (Malaysia, 1996).

The employment trends of males and females in the manufacturing sector are displayed in Figure 6.2.

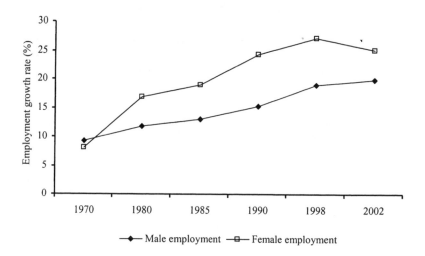

Sources: Department of Statistics, Malaysia, 2000, 2003; Malaysia, 1991, 1996.

Figure 6.2   Annual employment growth by sex in manufacturing, Malaysia, 1970–2002

Figure 6.2 shows that during 1970–2002, women experienced higher employment growth in the manufacturing sector than their male counterparts. This employment distribution was largely due to a similar pattern observed in the electronic industry, which constituted a large proportion of the manufacturing sector during this period. Elson and Pearson (1981) and Fuentes and Ehrenreich (1982) argued that multinational electronics firms have a strong preference for female workers because of the general perception that women possess unique qualities such as patience, dexterity, deference to authority and acceptance of low pay. Their arguments are supported by trends in the semiconductor industry in Penang (Malaysia) during the 1970s and 1980s. The data in Table 6.8 indicate that women formed the bulk of the labour force from the early 1970s when the semiconductor industry was established, largely by US companies. In 1972, the total employed by the semiconductor industry was 2 655, out of which 84.3 per cent or 2 239 were females. In 1986, 10 334 out of 13 098 employed in the industry were females. Although women were largely confined to low-skilled, labour-intensive jobs in the agricultural sector and to low-paying, semi-skilled, assembly-type production operations in the manufacturing sector, there seems to be an emerging trend in which women are making significant progress in the professional and technical occupational category, as shown in Table 6.9.

Table 6.8   Male and female employment in the semiconductor industry, Penang, Malaysia, 1972, 1977–86

Year	Male	% of total	Female	% of total	Total
1972	416	15.7	2 239	84.3	2 655
1977	1 924	17.2	9 241	82.8	11 165
1978	2 355	17.3	11 226	82.7	13 581
1979	2 202	19.7	8 960	80.3	11 162
1980	2 308	19.6	9 471	80.4	11 779
1981	4 339	21.2	16 159	78.8	20 498
1982	3 913	21.7	14 153	78.3	18 066
1983	4 094	21.5	14 982	78.5	19 076
1984	3 900	21.4	14 326	78.6	18 226
1985	3 181	21.0	11 966	79.0	15 147
1986	2 764	21.1	10 334	78.9	13 098

Source: Rasiah, 1988, p. 31.[5]

The proportion of women in the professional and technical, and administrative and managerial occupation categories significantly increased from 5.3 per cent and 0.1 per cent in 1970 to 19 per cent and 5.1 per cent respectively in 2002. The share of women employed as agricultural workers declined from 66.8 per cent in 1970 to 10.9 per cent in 2002, in line with the expectations of higher wages found in the manufacturing sector. Figure 6.3 shows that women experienced higher growth rates than their male counterparts in the professional and technical occupations.

Table 6.9   Women employed by occupation, 1970–2002

Occupation	1970	1980	1985	1990	1998	2002
Professional & technical	5.3	8.5	9.1	9.4	15.0	19.0
Administrative & managerial	0.1	0.3	0.6	0.6	2.5	5.1
Clerical	4.1	11.1	14.2	14.1	20.3	17.3
Sales & service related	13.3	16.2	24.7	25.1	25.0	17.1
Agriculture	66.8	46.3	33.7	28.1	14.6	10.9
Production related	10.4	17.6	17.7	22.3	22.5	25.1

Sources: Malaysia, 1991, 1996; Department of Statistics, Malaysia, 2000, 2003.

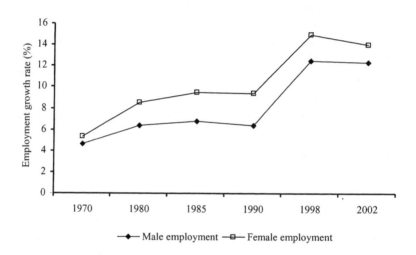

Sources: Department of Statistics, Malaysia, 2000, 2003; Malaysia, 1991, 1996.

*Figure 6.3   Annual employment growth in professional and technical
occupations by sex, Malaysia, 1970–2002*

Given the large representation of female labour in Malaysia's major export industries (which constituted more than 70 per cent of GDP in 1997), it can be inferred that the evolution of technological progress in Malaysia is largely associated with female labour. For example, technological progress may be through Arrow's (1962) learning-by-doing process and accelerated by international trade in a manner suggested by Grossman and Helpman (1991).This will be investigated empirically in Chapter 9.

In summary, the thrust of the Malaysian labour market policy, since the implementation of the First Malaysia Plan, was to bring about a continuing match between the changing demand and supply of labour. This was achieved by expanding productive employment at a rate sufficient to reduce prevailing levels of unemployment. On the basis of the declining unemployment trend from 6.1 per cent in 1961 to 3.5 per cent in 2003, the labour market policy appeared to have achieved its aim. Whether the Malaysia labour force is utilized in a productive manner has yet to be determined. This is the subject of the following sections.

TECHNICAL PROGRESS, OUTPUT AND EMPLOYMENT GROWTH IN MALAYSIA

Technological progress can have a significant impact on the growth rates of output and the utilization of the labour force. One approach is through additional demand for labour generated by higher growth rates (Okun, 1962) driven by technological progress (Solow, 1956; Swan, 1956; Arrow, 1962; Romer, 1986). The other possibility, and perhaps of more importance, is through the embodied technical progress (found in new capital equipment) that affects labour utilization. As workers learn how to use the embodied technical progress more efficiently, advances are made in the existing methods of production, which in turn increase productivity, leading to an expansion in output and employment (Kaldor, 1960; Kaldor and Mirrlees, 1962; Salter, 1962; 1966).

The following sections provide empirical estimates of the impact of technical progress on output growth and labour utilization in Malaysia. Kaldor's technical progress function is used for the empirical analysis. Although Kaldor's technical progress function has been subjected to numerous criticisms (Rothschild, 1959; Harcourt, 1963; Hahn and Matthews, 1964; McCallum, 1969), and has been 'out of favour' (Hahn, 1989), there are reasons to suggest that this approach is still appropriate for estimating Malaysia's growth process. Turner (1993, p. 153) commented that 'Mark Blaug may criticize Kaldor, as he did, for asking the "Big Questions" and trying to answer them in a "Big Way". Yet, judging by this prophetic issue of the *Economic Journal*, it is Kaldor's questions and answers which will be of interest to economists of the twenty-first century.'[5] Stern (1991b) predicted a resurgence of Kaldor's works on the dynamics of increasing returns. Most importantly, the recent endogenous growth models (Romer, 1986, 1990; Lucas, 1988; Aghion and Howitt, 1992) and Kaldor's technical progress function share an imperative feature: technological progress relates to investment activities. The relationship between technological progress and investment has been discussed in Chapter 3. Briefly, Kaldor (1960) proposed that the rate of growth of output per worker is a function of the rate of growth of capital per worker, as depicted by equation (6.1):

$$\dot{Y} = F\,(K/L), \qquad F' > 0; \, F'' < 0 \qquad (6.1)$$

Technological progress is then expressed as:

$$\psi = \dot{K}/L \qquad (6.2)$$

where ψ is the rate of technological progress.

Accordingly, technological progress requires investment and investment normally embodies new knowledge that will increase labour productivity. A similar view is also proposed in the assimilation analysis in Chapter 2. Thus, the shape of the curve in Kaldor's technical progress function (Figure 3.2) is dependent upon the degree to which capital accumulation embodies new techniques which improve labour productivity. In the reworked version of Kaldor's (1960) technical progress function, Kaldor and Mirrlees (1962) showed that technological progress is driven by the rate of improvement in the design of a newly produced capital good.[6] The rate of productivity growth or technological progress is primarily determined by the capital–output ratio on new capital.

A distinction between the Kaldor approach and the recent endogenous growth models is that the latter models provide a micro structure (a detailed account of a market mechanism) in allocating resources to generate endogenous growth. Kaldor, however, confined his analysis to the aggregate level (1957). Since this thesis is only concerned with the aggregate level, Kaldor's approach is chosen for this study.

Another reason for applying Kaldor's technical progress function for empirical testing is based on the fact that not many studies have been conducted since the model was introduced in the late 1950s. Earlier, Rothschild (1959, p. 572) stated that:

> the existence of the said functional relationship has not yet been 'recognised', if we mean by 'recognised' empirically tested. This relationship is a very ingenious assumption, but it is at present not more than an assumption, and a highly simplified one at that.

An extensive search of the growth literature failed to reveal any study conducted on Malaysia based on this approach. The only empirical study based on the Kaldor approach to explain the growth experiences of some of the East Asia countries may be found in Chen (1979). It should be pointed out that Chen's (1979) empirical analysis was based on a regression model that incorporated Eltis's model into Kaldor's technical progress function. Chen (1979) reported that technical progress in Japan was related to investment activities, while the technological progress for Hong Kong, Singapore and Taiwan was related to the importation of foreign technology rather than investment activities. South Korea, on the other hand, did not conform to either investment activities or importation of foreign technology. Here, Kaldor's technical progress function is tested in its original form. According to Hahn (1989), it was pointed out to Kaldor that his technical progress function could be rewritten as $Y = Ae^{\alpha t} K^{\beta}$ but this was rejected by Kaldor.

Furthermore, a large proportion of growth analyses used to explain Malaysia's growth performance over the 1960–90 period were executed in the neoclassical growth framework. If we are to shed further light on the growth process, it would be useful to provide an alternative perspective. Otherwise, our understanding of the growth process will be confined to a narrow view.

ESTIMATIONS

In testing Kaldor's technical progress function, the AR(2) error specification is employed to estimate the following equation:

$$log \, y = \alpha + \beta \, log \, k + u_t \qquad (6.3)$$

where $u_t = \rho_1 \, u_{t-1} + \rho_2 \, u_{t-2} + \varepsilon_t,$[7] $y = Y/L$, and Y is the real domestic product, deflated by the price level (1960 = 100). Labour, L, is the number employed in the Malaysian economy. $k = K/L$, and K is the capital stock which is derived from:

$$\int_{i=1}^{t} I_i - \delta_i / P_i \qquad (6.4)$$

where I denotes gross domestic investment, t represents the age of the oldest vintage, δ is depreciation, and P is the price level, weighted by the 1960 price index, and is derived from the sum of public and private investments (see equation 9.2 in Chapter 9 for a detail account of the construction of capital stock).

Data for output, capital and labour were obtained from various Malaysian official government publications. They include *Yearbook of Statistics, Economic Report* (Ministry of Finance, various years), Bank Negara Malaysia *Annual Report*, and the *Labour Force Survey Report*. The results are shown in Table 6.10. The Durbin–Watson (DW) statistic revealed no indication of serial correlation.

Table 6.10   Estimated Kaldor's coefficient for Malaysia, 1961–2003

Dependent variable is log per worker output *(y)*: 1961 to 2003			
Constant (α)	*β*	*R-Bar²*	*DW*
– 0.95	0.34*	0.98	2.0
(0.62)	(0.06)		

Notes: All results have been treated for autocorrelation using the AR(2) error specification. Standard error in parenthesis. *Significant at 5 per cent *p*-value.

The estimated coefficient shows the expected sign in which the endogenous technical progress hypothesis strongly holds with reference to the proposition that technical progress is positively related to investment activities. The coefficient of *k* is 0.34, which is statistically significant (*p* < *0.005*). This implies that for every 1 per cent growth in per worker output, capital contributed 0.34 to that 1 per cent growth. The strong correlation (*R-Bar²* = 0.98) between capital and output per worker is consistent with the rapid rise in investment activities in the manufacturing sector as discussed in Chapter 5.

However, there is a possibility that four events – the lagged effects of the 1997 financial crisis, September 11, the Severe Acute Respiratory Syndrome (SARS) epidemic and the Iraq War – may in one form or another impact upon the production of output and capital investment decisions in Malaysia.[8] If this is the case, there should be significant differences in the contribution of capital to output per worker prior to the happening of these events. To test this, the period 1999–2003 is isolated from the regression analysis. The period 1961 to 1998 is regressed with the same procedure. The results for the period 1961–98 are summarized in Table 6.11.

Table 6.11   Estimated Kaldor's coefficient for Malaysia, 1961–98

Dependent variable is log per worker output *(y)*: 1961 to 1998			
Constant (α)	*β*	*R-Bar²*	*DW*
1.11	0.72*	0.99	2.0
(0.15)	(0.03)		

Notes: All results have been treated for autocorrelation using the AR(2) error specification. Standard error in parenthesis. *Significant at 5 per cent *p*-value.

The results show that for the period 1961–98, capital contributed 0.72 to every 1 per cent of per worker output. This is significantly larger than the previous finding encompassing the period 1961–2003. The higher estimated value of 0.72 during the period 1961–98 compared to 0.34 of the 1961–2003 period could be linked to the cumulative impacts of the four major events, and this may have impact upon the investment decisions and activities in Malaysia, particularly during the late 1990s and early 2000s. Despite these estimated differences, both results suggest that technical progress is positively related to investment activities.

With reference to policy implications, the introduction of the 'Pioneer status' initiatives (Chapter 5) has played an important role in encouraging the employment of capital-intensive production techniques. Preference is usually given to firms that use new or up-to-date equipment. According to Lim (1975) there have been many cases where applications for Pioneer status have been rejected on the grounds that the equipment employed by the applicants was not the latest available. The Malaysian experience is not unique: Minami (1986), in his comprehensive account of the economic development of Japan, found that 'the real engine of economic growth is capital formation and that Japan's economic growth has been investment-led' (p. 180).

An important implication of Kaldor's technical progress function for output growth is that technological progress depends not only on investment activities but also on the division of capital and labour. This division is the key to increasing returns:

> The recognition of the existence of a functional relationship between the proportionate growth in capital and the annual proportionate growth in productivity shows the futility of regarding the movements in capital–output ratio as dependent upon the technical character of the stream of inventions – according as they are predominantly 'labour-saving' or 'capital-saving' in character. (Kaldor, 1960, p. 264)

In short, technological progress is associated with labour-saving production techniques.[9] The relationship between labour-saving production techniques and output growth is empirically determined for Malaysia. This relationship is captured by the elasticity of employment. The logic is that as the Malaysian economy matures, its employment elasticity should decline, reflecting the shift in production techniques. One of the reasons for the rate of growth of employment lagging behind the rate of growth of output is in the nature of technological progress, which generally takes the form of an increase in productivity of labour. This has the effect of economizing on the use of labour, that is reducing the employment associated with a given increase in output. The pattern of economic growth may tend to assume capital-intensive and labour-saving forms.

The AR(2) error specification is employed to estimate the following equation:

$$Log\ Y_{GDP} = \alpha + \beta\ log\ e + u_t \qquad (6.5)$$

where $u_t = \rho_1 u_{t-1} + \rho_2 u_{t-2} + \varepsilon_t$, Y_{GDP} is GDP at 1960 prices (1960 = 100) and e denotes total employment. The estimate β is the employment elasticity of output.

Although there are a large number of studies which have analysed the employment elasticity of output in both the developed and developing countries, studies on Malaysia are rare. Rao (1980) estimated an employment elasticity of 2.22 per cent for Malaysia covering the period of 1947 to 1970.[10] More recently, Huq (1994) reported that the employment elasticity for the 1975–85 period was 2.13 per cent.

The period examined, 1959 to 1998, is divided into two sub-periods. The first period covers 1959–80, while the second period covers 1981–98. The purpose of this approach is to trace labour utilization with respect to output growth between these two periods. Given the changing characteristics of the Malaysian economy between these periods, it is likely that the utilization of labour would reflect this change. The choice of these two sub-periods is based on the growth trends of output and employment, and the structural transformation of the Malaysian economy. The plots of the natural logarithm of the variables (output and employment) are illustrated in Figure 6.4. Both the output and employment variables displayed rising trends. However from 1981 onwards, the required percentage rise in output in order to increase employment was higher than in the 1959–80 period as shown in Figure 6.4.

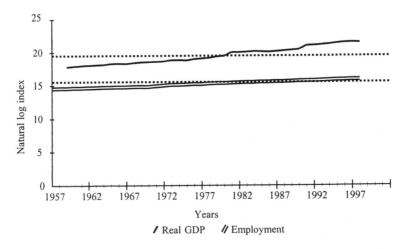

Figure 6.4   Natural logarithms of real GDP and employment, Malaysia, 1959–98

The findings in Chapter 5 suggest that the shift in production structure (that is, from agriculture to manufacturing) can be in part explained by this trend. As more resources were shifted from the agricultural sector towards the manufacturing sector, higher growth of output was possible.

The year 1981 also marked the beginning of a new industrialization epoch in Malaysia. Heavy industrialization was pursued as the engine of economic growth (Chapter 5). Soon after becoming Prime Minister in 1981, Dr Mahathir implemented a series of initiatives:[11]

> to accelerate the pace of industrialization even further because he viewed industrialization as a vital component of government policies designed to restructure Malaysian society ... In effect, Dr Mahathir subscribed to the 'big push' theory of industrial economic growth that had been popular in the 1960s among development economists. And in Malaysia, the 'push' would have to come from the government. (Means, 1991, p. 94)

Throughout the 1981–98 period, the manufacturing sector expanded rapidly while the agricultural sector continued to decline significantly in terms of output contribution to GDP and employment generation (Chapter 5). In broad terms, the Malaysian economy during 1959–80 could be characterized as a labour-intensive production structure, dominated by the agricultural sector (Chapter 5). From 1981 onwards, the economy shifted towards a more capital-intensive mode of production with the expansion of the manufacturing sector. Since the first period (1959–80) is associated with a labour-intensive production structure, while the second (1981–98) is associated with a capital-intensive structure, the employment coefficient is expected to be lower in the first period and higher in the second period.

RESULTS AND DISCUSSION

The estimated employment elasticity with respect to output for the 1959–80 period was 1.91 ($p < 0.05$), and 3.29 ($p < 0.05$) for the 1991–98 period, as shown in Table 6.12. The results show that during the period 1959–80, a 1.9 per cent increase in GDP contributed to a rise in employment by 1 per cent, while for the 1981–98 period, the Malaysian economy needed 3.3 per cent of GDP growth in order to attain 1 per cent growth in employment.[12] This is expected, because as the Malaysian economy shifted towards a higher level of productivity, the usage of labour declined with a given level of output. This pattern of output growth tends to be associated with labour-saving production techniques. In order to absorb extra labour into the production process, a higher level of output is needed. The rising trends of the coefficient of employment elasticity in the second period suggest that a trend towards substituting capital for labour occurred from 1981 onwards.

Table 6.12   Employment elasticity of output: exact AR(2) Newton–Raphson interactive method converged after four iterations

Dependent variable is real GDP: 1959–80			
Constant (α)	β	R-Bar²	DW
– 10.01	1.91*	0.98	1.89
(– 1.84)	(0.12)		

Dependent variable is real GDP: 1981–98			
Constant (α)	β	R-Bar²	DW
– 30.92	3.29*	0.96	1.94
(5.34)	(0.35)		

Notes: All results have been treated for autocorrelation. Standard error in parenthesis. *Significant at 5 per cent *p*-value.

The sectoral employment elasticity with respect to output growth for the period of 1947–98 is shown in Table 6.13.

Table 6.13   Sectoral Employment Elasticity of Output and Productivity, Malaysia, 1947–98

Sector	1947–70[#]	1970–85[^]	1980–98
Agriculture	4.40 (0.96)	3.75 (0.63)	– 1.18 (0.88)[a]
Mining	3.09 (0.88)	– 1.58 (0.71)	– 0.93 (0.99)[b]
Manufacturing	2.46 (0.99)	1.26 (0.96)	0.50 (0.89)[c]
Transport & communications	n.a.	n.a.	1.04 (0.93)[d]
Finance, insurance, real estate & business services	n.a.	n.a.	– 0.99 (0.97)[e]
Construction	2.72 (0.99)	0.93 (0.98)	0.17* (0.46)[f]
Government services	n.a.	n.a.	– 0.64 (0.97)[g]
Other services	0.93 (0.97)	1.62 (0.99)	– 0.29* (0.82)[h]

Notes: The results for the period 1980–1988 have been treated for autocorrelation using the AR(2) error specification. Figures in parentheses are correlation values.
* Not significant at 5 per cent.
[a] DW 1.81, [b] DW 1.41, [c] DW 2.14, [d] DW 1.96, [e] DW 2.36, [f] DW 2.01, [g] DW, 2.55, [h] DW 1,87.
[#] Rao, 1980, p. 189. Elasticity based on 6 years: 1947, 1957, 1962, 1965, 1967 & 1970.
[^] Huq, 1994, p. 32. Elasticity based on 16 years: 1970–1985.

Source: Taylor, 2004, p. 520.

Changing elasticities suggest a shift in labour utilization. Between the periods 1947–70, 1970–85 and 1980–98 (Table 6.13), the agricultural sector experienced a declining employment elasticity trend, from 4.4 per cent to 3.75 per cent, and to –1.177 per cent respectively.[13] This suggests that the productivity of the agricultural sector increased over time, with fewer workers needed to produce the same level of output. According to Kaldor, land-saving in agriculture is technical progress. Kaldor (1967) believed that the key to development in the less-developed economies was technical progress linked with 'labour-saving innovations' (p. 56). An implication of this rise in productivity within the agricultural sector is that more labour is made available to the non-agricultural sectors.

This switch to labour-saving methods of production largely accounted for the declining demand for agricultural workers. In 1965, the agricultural sector employed 52.1 per cent of the total labour force. By 1998, that figure had dropped to 18.8 per cent. In the 1965–98 period, employment in the agricultural sector increased by approximately 765 000.[14] This increase was however modest given the fact that the cultivated areas and tonnages more than doubled over the 33-year period.[15] This clearly points to the adoption of labour-saving production techniques.[16] This fits well with Kaldor's technological progress function which suggests that labour will flow to sectors with higher returns.

The declining coefficient of employment in the manufacturing sector provides a measure of an increase in productivity. In the Malaysian case, declining elasticity of employment in relation to output was most pronounced during the 1980–98 period. As the Malaysian economy matured, capital stock shifted or transformed from a stock which was appropriate to labour-intensive production into that appropriate for less labour-intensive production. With reference to the relationship between employment and technological progress, neoclassical wisdom holds the view that utilizing capital-intensive and labour-saving production techniques during periods of high labour force growth may lead to higher unemployment rates. A concern raised by several authors (International Labour Organization, 1970; Turnham and Jaeger, 1971) is the increase in the unemployment rates in most of the developing countries as a result of following an industrialization process that utilizes capital-intensive production techniques. Accordingly, it is more appropriate to utilize a lower K/L ratio when an economy is experiencing a surplus in labour supply. Utilizing higher K/L production techniques would lead to higher unemployment. This was not the case for Malaysia. Although the K/L ratio for the period 1961 to 1998 was high (as indicated by the regression results found in Table 6.11), the underlying trend in unemployment rates was declining (Figure 6.1).

Accordingly, unemployment rates significantly dropped. Despite taking into account the economic recession of the mid-1980s (when unemployment peaked at a record level of 7.6 per cent in 1985), the unemployment rate averaged approximately 3.8 per cent during the 1981–2000 period. In fact,

Malaysia experienced on average higher unemployment rates during 1959–80. In general, production in this period was labour-intensive and dominated by agricultural activities. Unemployment rates during this period averaged above 5 per cent compared to an average of 3.8 per cent in the 1980–2000 (capital-intensive) period. Minami (1986, p. 198) asserted that: 'there is no theoretical reason to believe that K/L will decrease when there is a labour surplus or increase when there is a labour shortage. K/L can increase even if there is a labour surplus'. Following Kaldor's (1968) reasoning, the K/L ratio can increase even when there is a labour surplus because the utilization of labour is primarily demand driven, particularly in a dual economy. As pointed out by Kaldor (1968, p. 386):

> In fact the size of the labour force in the non-industrial sector is a residual – entirely determined by the total supply of labour on the one hand and the requirements for labour in the industrial sector on the other hand. The best definition I could suggest for the existence of 'labour surplus' in this sense is one which is analogous to Keynes' definition of 'involuntary unemployment': a situation of 'labour surplus' exists when a faster rate of increase in the demand for labour in the high-productivity sectors induces a faster rate of labour-transference even when it is attended by *a reduction, and not an increase, in the earnings-differential between the different sectors.*

Hence, the high K/L ratio for Malaysia did not lead to a decline in employment as would be predicted under a neoclassical framework. Although less labour is needed to produce a given output (as indicated by the declining employment elasticity in the manufacturing sector), during 1988–98 the Malaysian manufacturing sector on average generated more than 50 per cent of total employment. The rapid growth rate in the Malaysian manufacturing sector accelerated the transference of labour from the surplus agricultural sector to the productive manufacturing sector. This led to higher manufacturing output growth rates and therefore GDP growth.

CONCLUSION

This chapter has traced the evolution of productivity through the shift in labour utilization from a predominantly agricultural production structure towards a modern manufacturing base. The Malaysian development experience is consistent with that of the OECD countries during their early stages of development in that the utilization of labour was largely driven by the evolution of the production structure (Feinstein, 1999). During the early stages of economic development in Malaysia (1950–75), employment was concentrated in the agricultural sector. The labour force during this period was largely unskilled, male and engaged in agriculture. There were relatively few opportunities for women. By the early 1980s, all these features had changed profoundly. The expansion of the modern sectors required a higher proportion of semi-skilled and skilled workers. The demand for a more skilled labour force as a result of the expansion of the modern sector impacted upon the labour market and output growth rates.

During this period of transformation of the Malaysian economy, there were also substantial social consequences, most notably the expansion of Malaysia's education system (discussed in Chapter 8) and the traditional role of women in Malaysian society. As education opportunities for Malaysian women increased, their expectations changed, leading them to question their social status as reflected by religious and cultural values. The subsequent 'revolution of rising expectations' (Ariffin, 1992) among educated Malaysian women prompted a larger proportion of women to seek paid employment. The significant rise in women's participation in the labour force occurred in the modern sectors.

In summary, the changes in output (Chapter 5) and employment structures have played important roles in the economic development of Malaysia. Technological progress driven by capital investment facilitated Malaysia's rapid structural change. The positive and significant coefficient of K/L during the 1961–98 period shows that economic growth in Malaysia is capital (investment) driven. The pivotal role of investment in economic growth has also been verified by Levine and Renelt (1992). They utilized a number of variables that are commonly used in econometric analysis of growth and regressed them in thousands of growth regressions with different conditioning sets of other variables, in order to establish whether the test variables remained significantly related to growth. In all of the variables they tested (which Levine and Renelt defined as robust), only investment survived as a robust variable. This led Kenny and Williams (2001, p. 8) to comment that: 'This might suggest that all variables but investment have, at best, a relationship with growth dependent on a range of other conditions or, at worst, they are only correlated with growth while the causal variable lies elsewhere.' The sector share elasticities (Chapter 5) and the employment elasticity of output estimated earlier suggest that for the period 1961–98 growth in Malaysia was positively related to the expansion of the manufacturing sector. In the next chapter, this expansion of the manufacturing sector will be linked to productivity-driven growth in the Malaysian economy. Kaldor's three propositions of growth will be employed to analyse this link.

NOTES

[1] From Robert M. Solow, *Growth Theory: An Exposition*, 2000 Oxford University

Press, New York. By permission of Oxford University Press, Inc.

[2] There was also a high turnover in several categories of skilled and professional workers (Ministry of Finance, 1998). The education and training system could not respond adequately to meet all the requirements for skilled workers. Given Malaysia's relatively small labour supply base, rapid economic growth and its corresponding employment growth translated into skill shortages.

[3] Based on Table 6.1, it was during the period 1990–2000 that Malaysia experienced the lowest levels of unemployment which averaged around 3.6 (taking into account the 1997 financial crisis), compared to the average of 5.6 per cent for 1970–79, and 6.1 per cent for the average of the period 1980–89.

[4] Importing temporary foreign workers to meet labour shortages offers many advantages. A country tapping a big regional pool of potential workers can impose various requirements on foreign workers. It does not have to pay for their upbringing and schooling. As most foreign workers are young and motivated, they can be trained to be highly productive. They can also be repatriated when economic conditions deteriorate, sparing a country the trauma of high unemployment. However, there are also disadvantages associated with the import of foreign workers. One disadvantage is that the country may become too dependent on foreign workers to do the hard, dirty and unpleasant jobs that its citizens do not want to perform. In the Malaysian context, this has been the case for employment in the service industry, particularly in restaurants, hotels and coffee shops. Another drawback is that structural adjustments needed to improve labour market efficiency are postponed or slowed. Wages in some sectors remain low because of the supply of foreign workers, so locals stay away. Additional workers are imported, thus perpetuating a cycle of dependence. The construction and agricultural sectors in Malaysia in addition to parts of the service sector, in many instances, have experienced this phenomenon.

[5] From The Semiconductor Industry in Penang: Implication for the New International Division of Labour Theories, Rasiah, R., Journal of Contemporary Asia, 18 (1), p. 31, 1988, reprinted by permission Taylor & Francis Ltd.

[6] In the hundredth anniversary (1991) of the *Economic Journal*, 20 prominent economists were asked to predict what economics might be like in the 21st century.

[7] Here, the driver of technical progress is more specific in that it is driven by the desire to replace outmoded capital equipment. The rationale for doing so is linked to the obsolescence of capital equipment. Not only will the profitability of older plant and equipment continue to diminish over time, but more importantly, equipment and plant of subsequent dates are likely to be superior. In the framework proposed by Kaldor and Mirrlees (1962) the operative life span of equipment or plant is not determined by physical wear and tear but by obsolescence.

[8] Where $\varepsilon t \sim N(0, \sigma 2\varepsilon)$, $t = 1, 2, ..., n$. For the AR(2) process, $u1$ and $u2$ are normally distributed with zero means and a constant variance for given by:

$$V(u_1) = V(u_2) = \sigma^2_\varepsilon (1 - \rho_2) / (1 + \rho_2)^3 - \rho^2_1 (1 + \rho_2)$$

$$Cov(u_1, u_2) = \sigma^2_\varepsilon \rho_1 / (1 + \rho_2)^3 - \rho^2_1 (1 + \rho_2)$$

[9] During the period 1992–97, total industrial production growth averaged above 10 per cent per year. That figure declined to –4.1 per cent in 1998 as a consequence of the financial crisis which began in mid-1997. Although the total industrial

production index rebounded and grew by 9 per cent in 1999 and 19.1 per cent in 2000, this rise, however, did not last. The industrial production index plummeted from a peak of 19.1 per cent in 2000 to –4.1 in 2001, as shown in the figure below. Even as the industrial production index rose in 2002 and 2003, the index did not grew as spectacular as the pre September 11 era. A possible explanation could be linked the uncertainty generated by the events leading up to the Iraq War. The manufacturing output index also followed a similar trend as shown in the figure below.

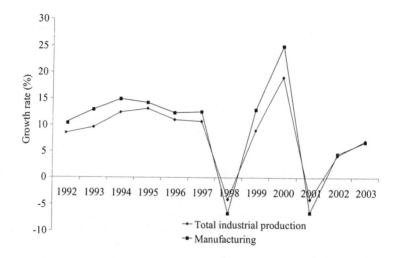

Source: Ministry of Finance, 1998, 2003.

Total industrial production and manufacturing output, Malaysia, 1992–2003

Furthermore, FDI, which is an important component of investment in Malaysia's manufacturing sector, experienced a gradual decline from the early 2000s onwards (see Table 5.8 in Chapter Five), which in turn could have affected the production activities of the Malaysian manufacturing sector.

[10] The notion that technological progress and output growth are associated with labour saving or capital intensity can be illustrated by the growth experience of several countries as shown in Table 2.7 (Chapter 2). This table shows that a higher ratio of capital per worker is associated with higher output per person as well as higher TFP growth. This may be explained by embodied technological progress in new capital investment which is expected to raise output per worker as suggested by the assimilation theories (Chapter 2). With reference to Table 2.7, the high growth rates of Singapore and Thailand could be explained by their high rates of capital accumulation which embodied technological progress. The low growth rates of per capita output and TFP as in the Philippines and US could be linked to lower capital ratio per person.

[11] Based on six years: 1947, 1957, 1962, 1965, 1967 and 1970.

[12] As discussed in Chapter 5, under the direction of the Prime Minister, an Industrial Master Plan was implemented to emulate the South Korean pattern of development (Means, 1991). The Heavy Industries Corporation of Malaysia became the instrument through which to channel large capital investments into industries that were identified as suitable for national development.

[13] The estimated coefficient for the elasticity of employment with respect to output for the period 1981–2003 was 2.63 as shown in the table below.

Employment elasticity of output: exact AR(2) Newton–Raphson interactive method converged after four iterations

Dependent variable is real GDP: 1981–2003			
Constant (α)	β	R-Bar²	DW
– 27.4	2.63*	0.96	1.94
(5.43)	(0.34)		

Notes: All results have been treated for autocorrelation. Standard error in parenthesis. *Significant at 5 per cent *p*-value.

This may suggest that productivity was higher in the 1981–98 period than in the 1981–2003 period. It could well be that the four events (as discussed earlier) had had an impact on the Malaysian production structure. In either case, output growth seems to be driven by productivity.

[14] There is the possibility that the comparison of the current estimates with those of Rao (1980) and Huq (1994) may be inappropriate due to different time periods and methodologies. The intention of this chapter is to provide an update, and some indication of the trend in labour usage between the different sectors of the economy.

[15] Annual employment growth for the agricultural sector was 0.5 per cent in 1970–80 and –0.4 per cent in 1980–90, compared to 5.8 per cent and 4.7 per cent for the manufacturing sector over the same periods.

[16] During the 1966–70 period, areas under cultivation totalled approximately 450 000 hectares (Malaysia, 1971). That figure rose to 1.8 million hectares in 1995 (Malaysia, 1996).

[17] Tractors in use per hectare of arable and permanently cropped land rose from 1 unit in 1970 to around 5.7 units in 1998 (World Bank, 2000).

7.   The role of manufacturing in economic growth: a Kaldorian perspective

INTRODUCTION

This aim of this chapter is to provide an empirical analysis of the economic growth in Malaysia based on Kaldor's growth propositions. Three reasons are given for using Kaldor's growth propositions. The first is to link the expansion of the manufacturing sector (as discussed in Chapters 5 and 6) to productivity-driven growth. Second, the exogenous and endogenous components of technological progress (such as human capital accumulation, R&D and international trade) do not provide the whole story of knowledge creation and the growth process. The rate at which technology advances is dependent upon or is facilitated by the speed or capacity at which an economy is able to restructure its production techniques. According to Kaldor (1966), the faster the rate of growth in the manufacturing sector, the faster would be the growth of aggregate output. This is because the manufacturing sector offers more opportunities for increasing returns than other sectors. Furthermore, a large proportion of the components of growth suggested by Romer (1986, 1990), Lucas (1988) and Aghion and Howitt (1992) that are thought to drive technological progress are usually found in activities that are associated with the manufacturing, that is the modern sector. As pointed out by Kaldor (1960, p. 293):

> The historical emergence of capitalist enterprise involved a tremendous increase in the 'technical dynamism' of the economic system. The most important characteristic of capital business enterprise is the continuous change and improvement in the methods of production, as against the relatively unchanging techniques of peasant cultivation and artisan production.

Hence, the type of sector in which growth takes place is important, as it will have a profound impact upon the evolution of technological progress. Following this line of reasoning may shed further light on the wide divergence in income as discussed in the convergence controversy. Third, the bulk of Kaldor's empirical analysis has been conducted on developed economies. Empirical evidence on developing countries is rare. The most recent estimates conducted on a group of South-East Asian countries only took Kaldor's first proposition into account (Felipe, 1998).

As covered in Chapter 2, several studies (Baumol, 1986; Barro, 1991; Mankiw et al., 1992) found that the convergence hypothesis holds in the OECD countries. However, when carried out on a larger sample or on a worldwide sample, evidence on convergence is less conclusive. The standard explanations given were that poor countries lacked the necessary technology and they experienced high population growth rates and low education completion rates.

An alternative explanation emphasizes that those countries that have converged or are in the 'convergence club' are economies that have 'matured'. Mature economies are those in which a large proportion of their GDP is contributed by the manufacturing sector. Kaldor (1967, p. 7) said that:

> The contention that I intend to examine is that fast rates of economic growth are almost invariably associated with the fast rate of growth of the secondary sector, mainly, manufacturing, and that this is an intermediate stage of development; it is a characteristic of the transition from 'immaturity' to 'maturity'.

Abramovitz (1986) indicated that the pace at which a lagging country is able to catch up with the leading country in a particular period is dependent upon the rate of structural change, the accumulation of capital and the expansion of demand. An important implication of such a proposition is that new investments channelled to expand the manufacturing sector will increase the productivity and aggregate output of a backward country. This in turn will reduce the gap between the lagging country and leading country in the catching up process.

The findings in Chapter 6, in which per capita output growth in Malaysia was linked to capital investment, provided some empirical evidence to explain the catching-up rate of Malaysia relative to the OECD countries, which averaged between 1 and 3 per cent (Table 2.3). Targetti and Foti (1997) using a modified Kaldor–Verdoorn Coefficient,[1] reported that for the period 1950–88, productivity in the OECD countries showed a clear tendency to catch up with the leading country, the US. Furthermore, they argued that:

> The stronger the cumulative growth process and the higher the share of investment, the faster the catching-up process has been. As far as LDC countries are concerned, convergence may or may not take place. We have focused our attention on two groups of countries: one group of the main Latin American countries and one group of the fastest growing East Asian countries. The latter has shown clear signs of convergence, while the former has not. ... Our interpretation is that an economic area which is growing rapidly because of dynamic economies to scale is more apt to introduce frontier technologies than a stagnant one. (p. 41)

Consequently, those countries that have successfully converged (such as the OECD countries and those located in East Asia) tended to have their production structures concentrated in activities that were subjected to increasing returns (mainly manufacturing). Those countries that were considered to be less successful by the United Nations (1997) and, as a result, have not converged (such as India, Bangladesh, Peru, Pakistan, Turkey, Honduras and Namibia), tended to concentrate their production structures primarily on activities (mainly agricultural) that were associated with diminishing returns. In short, countries that are in the 'convergence club' are matured economies[2] while countries that have not matured will only converge provided that they have made the transition to manufacturing. Thus, establishing the link to productivity-driven manufacturing growth is an important step to understand the wide disparity in per capita income in the world today.

In addition, it may help to explain why capital does not flow from the rich to the poor countries, as postulated by the Solow–Swan growth model, as the production of output in poorer economies is often associated with activities that are subjected to diminishing returns. Under such circumstances, there will be little incentive for capital to flow into activities that are associated with the agricultural sector. Prices for agricultural products have on average not only declined, but also have been subject to large price fluctuations (United Nations, 1997; World Bank, 2002), making investment particularly risky.[3]

KALDOR'S PROPOSITIONS AND MALAYSIA'S ECONOMIC DEVELOPMENT, 1980–98[4]

The shift towards a manufacturing export-led production structure had a significant impact on the economic development of Malaysia. The estimated coefficient of elasticity of output in the secondary sector (Table 5.14) shows that a 1 per cent increase in GDP per capita for the period 1957–2003 was associated with a 0.44 per cent increase in GDP per capita contribution compared to a negative contribution of − 0.37 per cent in the primary sector. Both Verdoorn (1949) and Kaldor (1966) stressed that there is a strong and positive relationship between growth in the manufacturing sector and total output. Although Verdoon's and Kaldor's expositions were subjected to numerous criticisms (Cripps and Tarling, 1973; Rowthorn, 1975), their analysis provided an important insight into the growth process in that a large part of productivity growth is endogenous to economic growth. This, according to McCombie (1998, p. 353), 'does shed light on the growth process'.

It is also important to note that various authors (see King, 1994) have pointed out the econometric problems associated with Kaldor's growth propositions.[5] It is not the purpose of this chapter to provide an analysis of the misspecifications of Kaldor's growth propositions but rather to test whether the growth experience in Malaysia is consistent with Kaldor's propositions. The aim here is to establish whether there is a linkage between economic growth and the manufacturing sector. Cornwall (1976, p. 308) commented that:

> it should be stressed, that even if Kaldor and others are quite wrong ... in their models, this does not mean that rapid growth of manufacturing output is not the key to rapid growth of total output.

The rate of output growth is substantially determined by the impact of economies of scale, leading to increasing returns through the division and specialization of labour. The findings in Chapter 6 suggest this is to be the case for Malaysia. Since the manufacturing sector offers more scope for increasing returns, it constitutes the main determinant of productivity growth. Kaldor (1966) proposed that the faster the rate of growth in the manufacturing sector, the faster would be the growth of total output. The faster the growth of labour productivity in the manufacturing sector, the faster would be the growth of manufacturing output. Taking a cross-section of 12 developed economies,[6] Kaldor (1966) provided empirical evidence in support of his three propositions (Appendix 7.1). The results have been largely confirmed by other findings (Bernate, 1996; Fingleton and McCombie, 1998; McCombie and de Ridder, 1983). Briefly, Kaldor's three growth propositions[7] are as follows:

1. There is a strong correlation between the growth of manufacturing output and rate of growth of GDP.
2. Growth of labour productivity in the manufacturing sector, p_m, is positively related to growth of manufacturing output, g_m. Kaldor (1966) also assumed that growth rate of manufacturing output is equal to the sum of productivity growth, p_m, and employment growth, e_m, which can be expressed as

$$g_m = p_m + e_m \qquad (7.1)$$

where
$$p_m = \alpha + \beta\, g_m \qquad (7.2)$$

$$e_m = -\alpha + (1-\beta)g_m \qquad (7.3)$$

Only if equations (7.2) and (7.3) are equal will the estimates be the same. The sum of the constants of equations (7.2) and (7.3) should be zero, and the sum of the regression coefficients unity, irrespective of the correlations involved.

3. Overall productivity growth is positively correlated with employment growth in the manufacturing sector and negatively related with growth of employment in the non-manufacturing sector.

MANUFACTURING, TECHNICAL PROGRESS AND ECONOMIC GROWTH

In refining the technical progress function, Kaldor and Mirrlees (1962) showed the unlimited potential of the manufacturing sector in generating new technology. Accordingly, technological progress is driven by the rate of improvement in the design of a newly produced capital good. Hence, technical progress can be specifically defined, in that it is driven by the desire to replace outmoded capital equipment. The profitability of old plant and equipment continues to diminish over time, but more importantly, subsequent plant and equipment is likely to be superior. In this type of operating environment, the operative life span of equipment or plant is not determined by physical wear and tear but by obsolescence. With reference to development policy, initiatives put in place to accelerate the retirement of old equipment will accelerate technological progress. This is because 'every change in the rate of investment per worker implies a change in the extent to which new ideas ("innovations") are actually exploited' (Kaldor and Mirrlees, 1962, p. 189). In short, adding a layer of new capital equipment to the existing stock of equipment will accelerate the effects of technological progress which is embodied in the machines. Kaldor and Mirrlees (1962) also suggested that it is not possible to increase the productivity of labour by reducing the number of workers in relation to the existing capital equipment. Rather, productivity of labour is governed by the amount of capital equipment available for workers to operate, that is, 'by the amount of investments per operative' (Kaldor and Mirrlees, 1962, p. 175). In this context, employment, income and output growth are primarily dependent upon the expansion and the dynamic characteristics of the manufacturing sector.

METHODOLOGY OF ESTIMATIONS

Kaldor's propositions are estimated with the AR(1) error specification, given that this is a more statistically robust and therefore preferred method of estimating time series data. The following estimations are considered:

$$y = \alpha + \beta y + u$$

where $u_t = \rho u_{t-1} + \varepsilon_t, \quad \varepsilon_t \sim N(0, \sigma^2_\varepsilon), \quad t = 1, 2, ..., n$ (7.4)

The initial value, u_1, is normally distributed with zero mean.[8] The constant variance for u_1 is given by:

$$V(u_1) = \sigma^2_\varepsilon / 1 - \rho^2 \qquad (7.5)$$

ESTIMATION OF KALDOR'S FIRST PROPOSITION

In order to estimate the relationship between the growth of manufacturing output and the growth rate of GDP, the following estimation is considered:

$$Log\ Y_{GDP} = \alpha + \beta log\ M + u \quad 1 > \beta > 0 \qquad (7.6)$$

where Y_{GDP} is real GDP (1978 = 100), M denotes real manufacturing output (1978 = 100), and $u_t = \rho u_{t-1} + \varepsilon_t$.

Results of Kaldor's Proposition 1

Table 7.1 shows the results of the estimation. The coefficient of manufacturing output is found to be 1.08 ($p < 0.005$).

Table 7.1   Kaldor's Proposition 1: Exact AR(1) inverse interpolation method converged after six iterations

Dependent variable is Y_{GDP}: 1980 to 1998			
Constant (α)	*M*	*R^2*	*DW*
9.94	1.08*	0.94	1.83
(0.90)	(0.09)		

Notes: All results have been treated for autocorrelation. Standard error in parenthesis. *Significant at 5 per cent *p*-value.

This indicates that for the period 1980–98, Malaysian manufacturing output growth rate exceeded GDP growth rate. Given that the coefficient of manufacturing output is above unity, it does not conform to Kaldor's specification. However, a coefficient that is greater than unity should not be taken to imply that Kaldor's first proposition should be rejected, particularly when a strong and positive correlation ($R^2 = 0.94$) is found between the two variables. The estimated coefficient is not significantly larger than one.

A possible reason for the value above unity in the estimated coefficient is that the manufacturing processes for the production of output in the 1950s and 1960s bear little resemblance to those of the 1980s and 1990s. In the later years, the production capacity and productivity levels were significantly higher due to technological progress.[9] The integration and globalization of the world economies, particularly since the late 1980s, also meant that derived demand for Malaysian manufacturing output would be expected to be higher, given the size of the international market.[10] A larger export sector will increase scope of economies of scale, leading to increasing returns and therefore output expansion.

Nonetheless, there is a high possibility that the specification (equation 7.6) derived by Kaldor in order to estimate his first proposition may be subject to spurious correlations in that a large component of total output is composed of manufacturing output. McCombie and de Ridder (1983) noted that even if a close statistical relationship existed between the growth of aggregate output and the growth of manufacturing output, it is by no means clear that the results can only be those proposed by Kaldor (1966). Instead, it could be that 'In the case of the advanced countries, the observed association could be the result of income or growth elasticities of demand that differed between countries' (p. 374).

Kaldor was well aware of this problem[11] and added an improvisation to his first growth proposition. Non-manufacturing output is used as the dependent variable rather than aggregate output. If there is a strong relationship between the rate of growth of total output and the rate of growth of manufacturing output, there should also be a correlation between non-manufacturing output growth and manufacturing output growth. The following estimation is shown below.

$$Log\ NM = \alpha + \beta log\ M + u \quad 1 > \beta > 0 \qquad (7.7)$$

where *NM* denotes the growth rate of real output of non-manufacturing (1978 = 100).

Results of Kaldor's Proposition 1a

Table 7.2 shows the results of the estimations.

Table 7.2 Kaldor's proposition 1a: Exact AR(1) inverse interpolation method converged after six iterations

Dependent variable is *NM*: 1980 to 1998			
Constant (α)	*M*	*R^2*	*DW*
6.90	0.39*	0.96	1.42
(0.37)	(0.03)		

Notes: All results have been treated for autocorrelation. Standard error in parenthesis. *Significant at 5 per cent *p*-value.

The coefficient for manufacturing output is found to be 0.39 ($p < 0.005$). Since the coefficient is significantly less than unity, it can be interpreted that the greater the excess of the growth rate in manufacturing output over the growth rate in aggregate output, the faster will be the aggregate growth rate.[12] By regressing non-manufacturing output growth rate on manufacturing output growth rate, the coefficient of manufacturing output for Malaysia is consistent with Kaldor's first proposition.

ESTIMATION OF KALDOR'S SECOND PROPOSITION

The coefficient for the growth of labour productivity with respect to manufacturing output can be derived as follows:

$$Log\ p = \alpha + \beta log\ M + u \quad \beta > 0 \tag{7.8}$$

where $p = (M/e_m)$ and e_m denotes employment in the manufacturing sector.

Results of Kaldor's Proposition 2

Results of the estimation are given in Table 7.3. The estimated coefficient for manufacturing output is found to be 0.43 ($p < 0.005$).

Table 7.3   Kaldor's proposition 2: Exact AR(1) inverse interpolation method converged after five iterations

Dependent variable is p: 1980 to 1998			
Constant (α)	M	R^2	DW
– 1.38	0.43*	0.95	1.57
(0.55)	(0.05)		

Notes: All results have been treated for autocorrelation. Standard error in parenthesis. *Significant at 5 per cent p-value.

This indicates that there is a strong correlation ($R^2 = 0.95$) between labour productivity growth and growth of manufacturing output.

In order to test whether output in the manufacturing sector is equal to the productivity of labour and the volume of employment, the volume of employment in the manufacturing sector is regressed on the growth rate of the manufacturing sector:

$$Log\ e_m = \varepsilon + \lambda log\ M + u \quad \lambda > 0 \tag{7.9}$$

where e_m is number of persons employed in the manufacturing sector, and M is real manufacturing output (1978 = 100) generated from the manufacturing sector.

Results of Kaldor's Proposition 2a

Table 7.4 displays the results. The coefficient of manufacturing output is estimated to be 0.57 ($p < 0.005$). The sum of estimated constants for equations (7.2) and (7.3) is zero, while their sum of regression coefficients comes to unity.[13] Since the coefficients of both estimates approximate 0.5, it can be interpreted that a 1 per cent increase in growth rate of manufacturing output would result in a 0.5 per cent increase in productivity of labour and a 0.5 per cent increase in manufacturing employment. It appears that the Malaysian experience conforms to Kaldor's first and second laws.

Table 7.4   Kaldor's proposition 2a: Exact AR(1) inverse interpolation method converged after five iterations

Dependent variable is *em*: 1980 to 1998			
Constant (α)	*M*	R^2	*DW*
1.38	0.57*	0.97	1.57
(0.55)	(0.05)		

Notes: All results have been treated for autocorrelation. Standard error in parenthesis. *Significant at 5 per cent *p*-value.

Results for all the sectors of the Malaysian economy are summarized in Table 7.5.

Table 7.5   Annual growth rates of productivity, employment and output of selected sectors, Malaysia, 1980–98

Manufacturing	
$p = -1.38 + 0.43i$	$R^2 = 0.95$
(0.05)	DW = 1.57
$e = 1.38 + 0.57i$	$R^2 = 0.98$
(0.05)	DW = 1.57
Agricultural sector	
$p = -9.07 + 1.17i$	$R^2 = 0.84$
(0.24)	DW = 1.81
$e = 9.07 - 0.17i$	$R^2 = 0.55$
(0.24)	DW = 1.82
Mining sector	
$p = -12.06 + 1.95i$	$R^2 = 0.91$

Table 7.5 (continued)

(0.15)	DW = 1.72
$e = 12.06 - 0.95i$	$R^2 = 0.69$
(0.15)	DW = 1.72
Transport and communication sector	
$p = -1.62 + 0.53i$	$R^2 = 0.98$
(0.02)	DW = 1.97
$e = 1.62 + 0.47i$	$R^2 = 0.98$
(0.02)	DW = 1.97
Service sector	
$p = -6.63 + 1.02i*$	$R^2 = 0.82$
(1.02)	DW = 1.31
$e = 4.54 + 2.11i$	$R^2 = 0.92$
(0.23)	DW = 1.53
Government service	
$p = -5.49 + 0.86i$	$R^2 = 0.95$
(0.07)	DW = 1.75
$e = 5.49 + 0.14i$	$R^2 = 0.19$
(0.06)	DW = 1.75
Finance Sector	
$p = 0.63 + 0.31i*$	$R^2 = 0.09$
(0.22)	DW = 1.81
$e = -0.63 + 0.69i$	$R^2 = 0.36$
(0.22)	DW = 1.80
Construction sector	
$p = -0.003 + 0.24i$	$R^2 = 0.62$
(0.07)	DW = 1.62
$e = 0.003 + 0.75i$	$R^2 = 0.94$
(0.07)	DW = 1.62

Notes: All results have been treated for autocorrelation using the AR(1) model. Annual rates of growth of productivity, p, and of employment, e, on the rates of growth of output, i, sector.   Standard errors are provided in parentheses. * Not significant at 5 per cent level.

The regression results in Table 7.5 show some interesting patterns. The estimation for the transport and communication sector appears to be similar to that for the manufacturing sector. The estimated productivity coefficient of the government service sector is higher than for manufacturing, while the estimation for the construction sector produced a lower coefficient value than manufacturing. This indicates that the effects of economies of scale on growth in productivity are significant not only for manufacturing but also for the government service sector, construction sector, and transport and communication sector. Agricultural and mining, however, deviated from this trend in that productivity growth exceeded growth in production, and thus is independent of growth in output. This finding is consistent with Kaldor's earlier findings on 12 OECD countries:

Agriculture and mining reveal a different picture ... In both of these cases productivity growth has exceeded the growth of production for every single country; and the growth in productivity has owed nothing to increasing returns to scale. (Kaldor, 1966, p. 39)

In the case of the service sector, estimated results are not consistent with Kaldor's specification. The productivity coefficient was found to be statistically insignificant at the 5 per cent level. Although estimations for the finance sector were quite similar to those for manufacturing, no correlation was found between productivity growth and output growth.

ESTIMATION OF KALDOR'S THIRD PROPOSITION

The following equation is employed to estimate the relationship between output growth and employment in the manufacturing sector and non-manufacturing sectors:

$$Log\ p_{GDP} = \alpha + \beta\ log\ e_m + \gamma\ log\ e_{nm} + u \quad \beta > 0\ \gamma < 0 \quad (7.10)$$

where p_{GDP} is total productivity of the aggregate economy and e_{nm} is employment in the non-manufacturing sector.

Results of Kaldor's Proposition 3

Results of the regression are shown in Table 7.6. The coefficient of manufacturing employment is found to be 0.52 ($p < 0.005$). The coefficient of the non-manufacturing sector employment is found to be –0.88 ($p < 0.005$). The results are consistent with Kaldor (1966) in that overall productivity is positively correlated with employment growth in the manufacturing sector and negatively related to employment in the non-manufacturing sector.

Table 7.6   Kaldor's proposition 3: Exact AR(1) inverse interpolation method converged after 14 iterations

Dependent variable is p_{GDP}: 1980 to 1998				
Constant (α)	e_m	e_{nm}	R^2	*DW*
6.22	0.52*	– 0.88*	0.87	1.46
(1.41)	(0.16)	(0.17)		

Notes: All results have been treated for autocorrelation. Standard error in parenthesis.
*Significant at 5 per cent *p*-value.

These results can be interpreted as showing that the growth in Malaysia's manufacturing sector is not constrained by a shortage of labour, despite the fact that from 1990 to 1995 Malaysia experienced a severe labour shortage, leading to the importation of large numbers of foreign workers. If labour shortage is not a constraint, then what is? According to Kaldor (1966), the fundamental constraint on growth of output in an open economy is the level of exports. Kaldor's argument is essentially based on the proposition that the long-run growth rate of an economy depends on the growth of exogenous export demand. However, the empirical evidence provided by the third proposition is difficult to assess because the statistical evidence is entirely confined to the proposition that growth of productivity depends on growth in manufacturing output with no relevant statistical reference to exports. If the growth rate of manufacturing is not constrained by labour shortage but by derived export demand, then the rate of growth in manufacturing exports can have a significant impact on the growth rate of employment in the manufacturing sector. There should be a positive relationship between employment and exports growth, ex_m, in the manufacturing sector. In order to test whether such a positive relationship exists, the following estimation is considered:

$$Log\ e_m = \alpha + \beta log\ ex_m + u \quad 1 > \beta > 0 \qquad (7.11)$$

where ex_m denotes real exports of the manufacturing sector (1978 = 100).

Results of Manufacturing, Employment and Exports

Estimated results of equation (7.11) are presented in Table 7.7. The results show a strong relationship ($R^2 = 0.95$) between employment growth and export growth.

*Table 7.7   Manufacturing, employment and exports: exact AR(1) inverse
            interpolation method converged after eight iterations*

Dependent variable is *em*: 1980 to 1998			
Constant (α)	e_{xm}	R^2	DW
− 1.57	0.43*	0.95	1.48
(0.55)	(0.02)		

Notes: All results have been treated for autocorrelation. Standard error in parenthesis.
*Significant at 5 per cent *p*-value.

If β is interpreted as the elasticity with respect to employment and export, a 1 per cent growth in manufacturing export is associated with a 0.43 per cent growth in employment in the manufacturing sector. An estimated coefficient of manufacturing that is positive and less than unity would suggest that economies of scale are being generated through exports.

CONCLUSION

The results indicate that Malaysia's growth experience in 1980–98 was positively related to manufacturing productivity growth. The importance of the manufacturing sector in the generation of the nation's economic growth and employment is confirmed for Malaysia. The findings also show a relationship between rate of growth in the manufacturing sector and rate of growth in productivity and employment in the sector. This is supported by the estimated results in equations (7.2) and (7.3). The findings, which support Kaldor's analysis, show that a 1 per cent growth in output leads to approximately 0.5 per cent growth in employment and 0.5 per cent in productivity of the manufacturing sector. Overall productivity growth in the Malaysian economy was found to be positively correlated with employment growth in the manufacturing sector and negatively correlated with employment growth outside the manufacturing sector. This seems to support the declining trend in employment opportunities in the agricultural sector. In 1980, the agricultural sector employed more than 40 per cent of the total labour force. That figure declined in 1989 to 18.8 per cent of a larger labour force, in relative terms a reduction of more than half compared to 1980. From a policy perspective, the key role assigned to the manufacturing sector through a series of industrial plans initiated by the Malaysian government, particularly from the late 1970s onwards, was crucial to the development of its manufacturing sector (Chapter 5).

An important lesson that may be learnt from Malaysia's experience is that a developing economy that neglects its manufacturing sector is more likely to experience a slower growth rate. The comment made by Kenny and Williams (2001, p. 12) is appropriate here: 'It is a near-universal phenomenon that the proportion of labour in agriculture declines as countries become richer and that manufacturing and services contribute more to GDP.'

Although the Kaldorian growth perspective emphasizes increasing returns to scale, the mechanism driving such returns is not well specified nor is it explained in great detail. In many instances, a positive coefficient of manufacturing output is interpreted as evidence of substantial increasing returns to scale. Kaldor (1966) proposed that exports through cumulative causation could be the mechanism that is driving productivity growth. However, Kaldor did not provide a systematic analysis of the role of exports in productivity growth, nor did he provide any statistical evidence to substantiate his claim.

The strong correlation between employment and export growth in manufacturing may provide a basis on which to explore the directions of such causation. It is plausible that the drive for technological diffusion could lead to higher labour productivity and competitiveness in international markets, which in turn could yield higher employment and exports. It is also likely that international trade, through technological spillovers, is an important source for harnessing technological progress (Thirlwall, 1983; Grossman and Helpman, 1991; Obstfeld and Rogoff, 1996; Aghion and Howitt, 1998; Gapinski, 1998) for the attainment of higher productivity.

Before the linkages between international trade and productivity growth are explored (in Chapter 9), it is essential to provide a brief overview of the development of human capital in Malaysia. This is important because the ability of a nation to absorb and diffuse new technology depends substantially on its social capacity. Similarly, whether technological progress is transferred through embodied new capital or knowledge that is imported, or discovered through research and development, or learning-by-doing, is dependent upon its social capacity. In order to employ the knowledge content of spillovers, a minimal amount of understanding of foreign technology is necessary and this is dependent upon the quality of the labour force or human capital. There has been an expansion in the growth literature emphasizing the importance of human capital development (Lucas, 1988; Romer, 1986, 1990; Barro, 1989, 1997; Mankiw et al., 1992; Grammy and Assane, 1996; Solow, 2000). Ranis et al. (2000, p. 197) stated that: 'Human development has recently advanced as the ultimate objective of human activity in place of economic growth.' Devoting the next chapter to tracing the role of the state in the development of Malaysia's human capital reflects a recognition of this proposition.

NOTES

[1]   Defined as: $pr = \alpha + \beta q + \gamma\ (GAP) + \delta\ I/Q$
where the lower case letters denote the rates of growth of the following variables: Q = real output, PR = productivity, I/Q = investment-output ratio, and GAP = leader–follower productivity ratio.

[2]   According to De Long (1988), the countries that have converged are those that are most industrialized.

[3]   In addition, Martin and Mitra (2001) estimated the difference in TFP growth between   agriculture and manufacturing for 50 countries for the period 1967–92. The range of TFP estimates was found to be 1.4 to 2 per cent for agriculture and 0.2 to 0.9 per cent for manufacturing. An important implication of their findings is that higher TFP in agriculture (compared to manufacturing) largely accounts for the falling agricultural prices relative to manufacturing. If this trend continues, prices for agricultural products will decline further.

[4]   There are two primary reasons for choosing this period (1980–98). First, 1980–98 saw the rapid expansion of the manufacturing sector (as discussed in the previous

chapters). Prior to 1980, its contribution to output growth was significantly lower than that of the agricultural and service sectors, and as such, would not make a meaningful analysis. Second, the 1999–2003 period saw the occurrence of the September 11 crisis, the SARS epidemic and the Iraq War. All of these events may in one form or another have impacted upon the manufacturing sector as discussed in Chapter 6.

5   Econometric problems are not confined to Kaldor's models, but are also in other growth models. According to several authors (Levine and Renelt, 1991; Blaug, 1992; Mayer, 1992; Caselli et al., 1996; Evans, 1996; Pritchett, 1998), it is not always clear what the appropriate techniques are.

6   The countries were Austria, Belgium, Canada, Denmark, France, Italy, Japan, the Netherlands, Norway, the United Kingdom, the United States of America, and West Germany.

7   See Chapter 3 for a discussion of Kaldor's growth propositions.

8   This estimation technique 'allows for the effect of initial values on the parameter by adding the logarithm of the density function of the initial values to the log-density function of the remaining observations obtained conditional on the initial values' (Pesaran and Pesaran, 1997, p. 336). For instance, the log-density function of $(u_2, u_3, ..., u_n)$ conditional on the initial value, u_1, is given by:

$$log\{f(u_2,u_3,...,u_n|u_1)\} = -(n-1)/2 \; log(2\pi\sigma^2\varepsilon) - 1/2\sigma^2\varepsilon \; (\sum_{t=2}^{n} \sigma^2 t)$$

and:

$$log \; \{f(u_1)\} = -1/2 \; log \; (2\pi\sigma^2\varepsilon) + 1/2log \; (1-\rho^2) - (1-\rho^2)/2\sigma^2_\varepsilon \; u^2_1$$

combining the above yields:

$$log\{f(u_1, u_2, ..., u_n)\} = -n/2 \; log \; (2\pi\sigma^2_\varepsilon) + \frac{1}{2} \; log \; (1-\rho^2) - 1/2\sigma^2_\varepsilon \; (\sum_{t=2}^{n} (u_t - \rho u_{t-1})^2 + (1-\rho^2)u^2_1)$$

9   In the Malaysian case, technological advancement is primarily initiated by foreign investments.

10 Over the 1990s, Malaysian manufacturing exports constituted around 75 per cent of total exports.

11 Since manufacturing is an important component of GDP, a good fit is expected.

12 Cripps and Tarling (1973) provided support for Kaldor's first growth proposition on a sample of 12 countries covering the period 1951–70. Felipe (1998) reported a coefficient of 0.36 for Malaysia when regressing non-manufacturing output on manufacturing output covering the period of 1967–92. However, the Durbin–Watson (DW) statistic is rather low; it lay below the critical values.

13 Kaldor (1966) estimated that for the period 1953/54 to 1963/64 (12 OECD countries), β was approximately 0.5. This result has been largely confirmed by other data sets (McCombie and de Ridder, 1983; Bernate, 1996; Fingleton and McCombie, 1998). According to Casillas (1993), the conclusion and method employed in the estimation became so important in the literature of growth in advanced economies that it warranted the publication of a book by Cripps and Tarling (1973).

8. Human capital accumulation: education development in Malaysia

INTRODUCTION

This chapter has two objectives. Its first objective is to provide a background to Chapter 9, which focuses on the importance of human capital development for TFP growth. In the Malaysian case, human capital development (through formal education) has always been an important component of Malaysia's national economic policies, as outlined in the various five-year development plans. During the early 1970s, formal education was the mechanism to fulfil the two objectives of the NEP: the eradication of poverty, and the correction of economic imbalance between the Malays and non-Malays. In the mid-1980s, high priority was given to the expansion of the higher education sector in response to the increasing demand for higher-quality labour from the rapidly expanding modern sectors of the economy. In addition, the initiatives put in place by the Malaysian government are consistent with the model predictions of Lucas (1988) and Romer (1990). Human capital is crucial in driving the evolution of technological progress: the more effort and resources allocated to the development of human capital, the higher will be the capacity of workers in absorbing and diffusing new technology.

The second objective of this chapter is to provide estimates of the private and social rates of return to higher education. Private and social rates of return are common forms of accounting for the contribution of education to economic development. In addition to the spillover effects generated by higher education, like any other investments, decisions must be made with reference to the returns (both private and social) from higher education. This is important because scarce resources need to be distributed and allocated efficiently. Data on rates of return provide decision-makers with a guide to the optimum level of human capital accumulation, which in turn is crucial for technological progress. Furthermore, human capital accumulation must be profitable to be effective (Lucas, 1988), and rates of return to education provide some measure of the profitability of education.

ECONOMIC IMPACT OF EDUCATION: A BRIEF OVERVIEW

It has been extensively documented that formal education is important to economic development. Alfred Marshall (1922)[1] stated that education is the most valuable of all capital in the contribution to economic growth:

> We may then conclude that the wisdom of expending public and private funds on education is not to be measured by its direct fruits alone. It will be profitable as a mere investment, to give the masses of the people much greater opportunities than they can generally avail themselves ... And the economic value of one great industrial genius is sufficient to cover the expenses of the education of a whole town ... All that is spent during many years in opening the means of higher education to the masses would be well paid for if it called out one more Newton or Darwin, Shakespeare or Beethoven. (p. 216)

The World Bank (1999) also reported that education is the key to competing successfully in world markets.

With reference to the Solow–Swan growth model, education can affect the labour variable in that the higher the effectiveness of labour input (which can be improved by an increase in schooling years), the higher will be the value A, and therefore the greater the level of output. Increasing ordinary labour, L, will only have a level effect but not a growth effect. This is supported by the empirical findings of Mankiw et al. (1992), who found that more investment in human capital is conducive to growth but a swift expansion in population is not.

The rapid expansion of the endogenous growth literature can be partly attributed to the consideration given to the role played by formal education. Investment in people makes it possible to take advantage of technological progress as well as ensure a continuation of that progress (Aghion and Howitt, 1998; Lucas, 1988; Romer, 1986, 1990), and investment in education is seen to expand and extend knowledge. The rationale is that new technology in itself does not guarantee the emergence of a modern economy, nor an increase in labour effectiveness. Knowledge by itself is useless or unproductive if labour or society as a whole is unable to absorb and diffuse it into economic output. A sophisticated mathematical or technical statement which cannot be understood by more than two mathematicians or technicians in the society will have little economic value. Modern technology is a blueprint, which can only be applied successfully to developing economies provided that the society has the capacity to interpret and implement the blueprint. The enhancement of the capability of an economy will increase its capacity to absorb and diffuse new technology (Kuznets, 1957). The successful introduction of Western technology to Japan has been attributed to its people's capabilities. As indicated by Minami (1986, p. 143):

educational improvements meant that Japan's social capability to adopt new technology increased during industrialization. The number and quality of engineers increased as a result of the development of higher education. As a result the level of R&D activities increased a great deal ... present-day developing countries can learn from Japan's experience. Those countries which have a large 'backlog' of unexploited technology must strive to increase their social capability to adopt it.

Based on the propositions of Aghion and Howitt (1998), Lucas (1988) and Romer (1986, 1990), as discussed in Chapter 3, policy implications of human capital accumulation can be summarized in Figure 8.1.

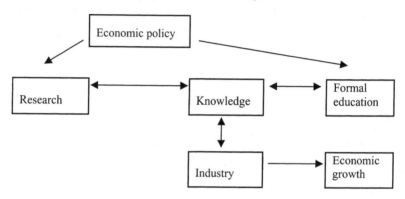

Figure 8.1   Education, knowledge accumulation and economic growth

Figure 8.1 shows that initiatives put in place to expand the research and the formal education sectors can increase the rate of knowledge accumulation which is then utilized by the industrial sector to produce output more efficiently. In short, increasing knowledge will increase the effectiveness of labour, which in turn will slow the falling marginal product of labour as output increases. When labour accumulates new knowledge, this also contributes simultaneously to the productivity of physical capital (Arrow, 1962; Kaldor, 1960; Lucas, 1988; Romer, 1990).

Empirical findings tend to reinforce the importance of education in the growth of aggregate output. In the US, Denison (1964) reported that improvements in the quality of the labour force through additional education contributed 23 per cent to the nation's growth rates in 1929–57, as shown in Table 8.1. Barro (1991, 1997) and Benhabib and Spiegel (1994) found education to be correlated with the growth rate of per capita GDP across different countries. In their regression estimations of 52 developed and developing countries, Bils and Klenow (2000, p. 1160) reported that: 'greater schooling enrolment in 1960 consistent with one more year of attainment is associated with 0.30 per cent faster annual growth over 1960–1990'. Lau et al. (1991) estimated that one additional year of education in East Asia contributed over 3 per cent to real GDP. In the context of the convergence debate, Mankiw et al. (1992) incorporated a human capital variable proxied by secondary schooling, and reported that poorer countries appear to approach their own steady states at a fairly uniform rate of 2 per cent per year.

Table 8.1   Additional education and economic growth in the US, 1909–56

	Period	
	1909–29	1929–56
Growth rate of total real national income	2.82	2.93
Amount of growth rate ascribed to education	0.35	0.67
Percent of growth rate ascribed to education	12.0	23.0
Growth rate of real national income per person employed	1.22	1.6
Amount of growth rate ascribed to education	0.35	0.67
Percent of growth rate ascribed to education	29.0	42.0

Source: Denison, 1964.

DEVELOPMENT OF MALAYSIA'S EDUCATION SYSTEM

Prior to independence in 1957, the education system primarily served the British interests.[2] The education policy during that period was that of the guardian of native rights and customs. Economic development was not a major priority. In British Malaya, education was commonly valued for its humanistic qualities and for its role in elite formation. Colonial officialdom tended to see education as a purely social service, something good and desirable but offering few direct economic returns. Education was treated as a consumption item in public accounts, which depleted the financial resources available for investment in economic growth. This created a complicated financial treatment of the education system, with private, state and central sources participating in its provision, each according to its own priorities and perceptions of needs.

With the transition to the newly elected government in 1957, the national school policy was initiated. Public expenditure on education now came to be redefined as 'investment' in the country's political future. At this stage, conventional economic philosophy had not yet conceived education as being functionally related to economic, as distinct from social or political, development objectives. This was to come later, after it became increasingly apparent during the early 1960s that inadequate human resources constituted a limiting factor for economic progress.

As such, there was a revision of education policy, from a mere social (or political) service to one that places high priority on human capital formation for economic development.[3] All of the Five-Year Plans treated education as a factor of human capital formation. The main emphasis of the various Five-Year Plans focused on skill accumulation to meet the demand of a changing economic production structure, in the context of employment restructuring, poverty alleviation and skill formation. In the First Malaysia Plan (1966–70), emphasis was given to the mobilization of investable resources for accelerating economic growth, and in doing so, treated education as a factor for human capital development. Under the Second Malaysia Plan (1971–75), references were made to the restructuring of the Malaysian society (a direct result of the race riot in 1969), along a more balanced line of economic attainment between Malays and non-Malays in which education served as a strategy for overcoming poverty among all races. Objectives of employment, social mobility as a strategy and economic nationalism rendered education an integral component of planning for economic development.

It was during the Fourth Malaysia Plan period (1981–85) that education began to expand more rapidly as a result of a shift in the development policy towards the focus on an export-oriented and modern industrialization production structure. The launching of the Fourth Malaysia Plan in 1981 initiated an export-led growth economic structure, with foreign direct investment together with a heavy industrialization programme as the engine for restructuring the economy. The adoption of such a strategy would require a more skilled and productive labour force, which Malaysia did not possess at that time. This led to the rapid expansion of the educational system, particularly tertiary education.

The Fifth, Sixth and Seventh Malaysia Plans highlighted the role of education in increasing the contribution of the manufacturing sector by addressing significant skills gaps at all levels. It was envisioned that improving formal education and occupational training programmes as initiated in the plans would contribute towards relaxing the constraints on the supply of skills, which was seen as essential for Malaysia to maintain its rapid economic growth momentum. The Eighth Malaysia Plan (2001–05) continued to support the importance of education in human capital formation:

> During the plan period, human resource development continued to be given priority in support of the implementation of a productivity-driven growth, which required highly skilled, trainable and knowledgeable manpower. Emphasis continued to be given to increase accessibility to education at all levels in line with the democratization of the education policy. (Malaysia, 2001, p. 98)

The role of education in the industrialization of the Malaysian economic structure is summarized in Figure 8.2.

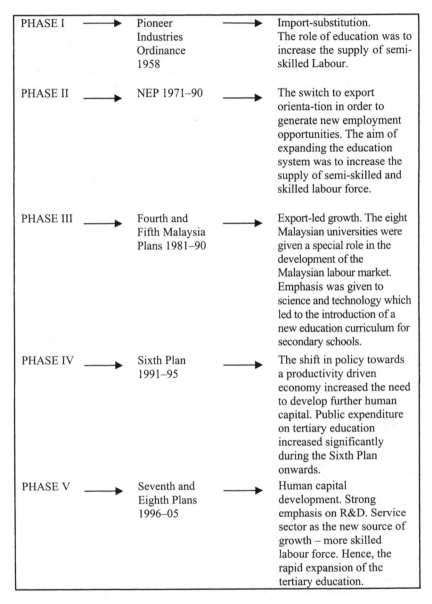

Sources: Malaysia, 1971, 1981, 1986, 1991, 1996, 2001

Figure 8.2 Industrialization and education development (1958–2005)

EXPENDITURE ON EDUCATION IN MALAYSIA

Since the mid-1960s, education expenditure has increased significantly in order to increase access to primary, secondary and tertiary education for the growing population. Figure 8.3 gives an indication of that trend. Public expenditure on total education increased from RM470.8 million in the 1966–70 period to RM17 948 million during 1995–2000. For the 2001–05 period, public expenditure allocation further increased, totalling RM18 660 million.

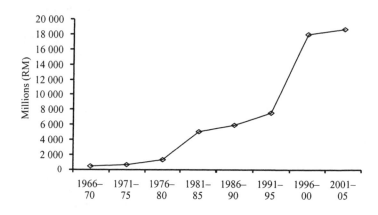

Sources: Malaysia, 1971, 1976, 1981, 1986, 1991, 1996, 2001.

Figure 8.3   Total government education allocation, 1966–2005

Allocation for education has been consistently high and has ranged between 13 and 25 per cent of total government expenditure,[4] and between 4 and 6 per cent of GDP, as shown in Table 8.2.

In comparison to primary and secondary education, higher education experienced a larger increase in allocation, particularly from the Fourth Malaysia Plan period (1981–85), reflecting the changing economic structure and the skills demand of the labour force. This is shown in Table 8.3.

In summary, the importance of human capital development in Malaysia is evident by the initiatives put forward by the various Malaysian Plans. If technological progress is associated with 'anything' that raises labour effectiveness (the Solow–Swan production function, equation 2.1, Chapter 2), and if education is one such factor (Barro, 1991; Benhabib and Spiegel, 1994; Lucas, 1988; Mankiw et al., 1992), the growth performance of the Malaysian economy could be partly explained by the expansion of its education sector. From a policy perspective, Malaysia's education policy has provided an avenue in which skills could be constantly upgraded in accordance with the structural transformation of the economy as well as the absorption of the new technology in the production process. In short, education policy has played an important role in increasing the effectiveness of the Malaysian labour force. The following section is an attempt to account for the rise in labour effectiveness based on earnings differentials.

Table 8.2   Education expenditure, Malaysia, 1965–2003

Year	% of government total expenditure	% of education expenditure to GDP
1965	18.9	4.6
1970	18.1	4.3
1975	19.4	6.3
1980	13.2	5.4
1985	15.2	6.3
1990	17.9	5.9
1995	14.5	5.3
2000	22.8	3.7
2003	25.2	5.0

Sources: Malaysia, 1971, 1981, 1996; Ministry of Finance, Malaysia, 1998, 2003.

Table 8.3   Shares in public expenditure for the various education sectors, 1966–2005 (%)

	1966 –70	1971 –75	1976 –80	1981 –85	1986 –90	1991 –95	1996 –00	2001 –05
Primary	14.8	14.8	19.6	16.9	14.9	16.2	16.8	15.5
Secondary	51.5	41.8	18.8	24.6	14.1	22.3	25.7	17.5
Technical	8.5	11.6	4.1	6.5	13.2	5.7	3.6	8.6
University	8.2	23.5	43.9	45.7	49.3	42.8	35.6	47.7
Teacher training	7.7	0.8	7.2	3.4	5.4	2.4	5.6	1.6
Other programmes	9.3	7.5	6.4	2.9	3.1	10.6	12.7	9.1
Total	100	100	100	100	100	100	100	100

Sources: Malaysia, 1965, 1971, 1976, 1981, 1986, 1991, 1996, 2001.

EARNINGS AND PER CAPITA GROWTH: EMPIRICAL EVIDENCE

The effectiveness of labour in the form of effort being devoted to schooling can be captured by the difference in wages found in the labour market (Layard and Psacharopoulos, 1974). Although skills embodied in an individual are a function of initial endowments such as genetic inheritance, abilities, personality drives and motivation, it is through education that human capital is augmented. Hence, the amount of human capital an individual accumulates, which in turn leads to higher wages, is linked to the number of years that he or she spends in education.[5]

Denison (1979) demonstrated that additional education accounted for between 15 to 25 per cent of growth in the US national income per worker, and this contribution tended to increase over time. His findings were supported by Pencavel (1993). Psacharopoulos (1973, 1981, 1985) found that in almost every country for which data on average earnings and level of education achievements are available, higher earnings tend to be associated with higher education. In a review of more than 20 American studies, Psacharopoulos (1975) reported that education is responsible for more than three-quarters (0.77) of the observed earnings differential between educational groups. This led Psacharopoulos (1975, p. 58) to comment that: 'the greatest part of the observed earnings differentials by educational level is due to education. When all available studies are taken into account, this part is greater than it was thought before'. Blaug (1972, p. 54) noted that: 'the universality of this positive association between education and earnings is one of the most striking findings of modern social science'. Murphy et al. (1998) reported that during the 1980s and 1990s in the US, the ratio of earnings between the university graduates and high school graduates rose sharply.

In addition, differences in wages can lead to an increase in the supply of more educated workers. A study conducted by Beaudry and Green (1998) over 25 years on the US and Canada showed that both relative prices and quantities moved in favour of higher-skilled workers. Einarsson and Marquis (1999, p. 428) reported that: 'those patterns in earning profiles appear to be robust across market economies that may differ significantly in many other respects'. Huang (1996) found that entry-level earnings of young cohorts in Taiwan had risen sharply as a result of higher education qualifications. This also seems to be the case for Singapore. Chan (1996, p. 83) reported that: '55% of workers with a university degree earned $3 000 (per month) or more while only 7% of those with secondary qualifications enjoyed similar incomes'. The earnings profiles of Malaysians also support the proposition that individuals with higher levels of education earned higher wages, as shown in Figure 8.4.

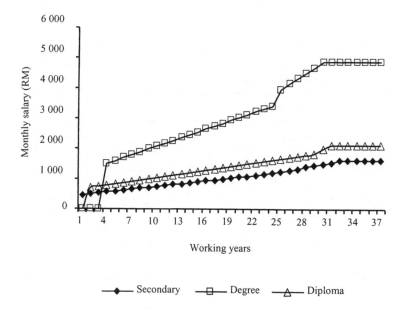

Figure 8.4 Earning profiles of Malaysians with different education levels, 2000

As shown in Figure 8.4, individuals with only secondary-level education earned the least in comparison to those with diploma and degree qualifications, based on the monthly averages of the public sector salary scales. The starting salary for secondary school graduates on the administered public sector salary scales averaged RM470 per month and peaked on average at RM1 609 per month after 37 years of employment. Individuals with a diploma certificate attracted salaries on average between RM724 and RM2 108 after 35 years of employment. Degree graduates were administered on average starting salaries of RM1 498 which peaked at RM4 869 after 34 years of employment. It appeared that the average salary difference between secondary graduates and university graduates in Malaysia was large. As indicated, the starting average salary for secondary graduates was RM470 compared to an average of RM1 498 for university graduates, a ratio of 3.2. What was even more profound was that after 37 years of employment, an individual with a secondary qualification earned only RM111 more than the average starting salary of new university graduates. The ratio between the earnings of secondary graduates and university graduates at the end of their working lives (after 38 years for secondary graduates and 35 years for university graduates) was about 3.1.

The view that higher education would lead to higher wages in the Malaysian context can also be reinforced by the wage difference between the rural and urban regions. The economic structure of the rural regions is dominated by agriculture, while manufacturing and services dominated the urban region. Entry into modern-sector employment depends initially on the level of completed education, whereas income-earning opportunities in the traditional sector have no fixed educational requirements. The greater the income differential between the modern and traditional sectors, the higher the demand for education. In general, the agricultural sector employs mostly unskilled labour with minimum levels of education compared to the manufacturing and services sectors which required semi-skilled and skilled labour with higher education qualifications, and therefore paying higher wages (as discussed in Chapter 6). For instance, the 1993 annual salary of an agricultural worker (factory) averaged RM4 680 relative to RM9 980 for a manufacturing worker (factory worker). In addition, wages in the manufacturing sector on average show an increasing trend as presented in Figure 8.5.

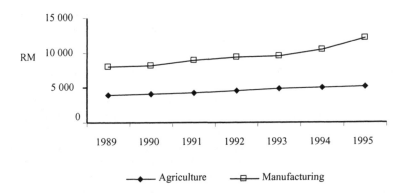

Source: Ministry of Finance, Malaysia, 1996.

Figure 8.5   Differences in wages between manufacturing and agricultural sectors, Malaysia, 1989–95

Wages in the manufacturing sector were not only relatively high during 1989–95, but they also increased from less than RM8 000 in 1989 to around RM12 000 by 1995. Wages in the agricultural sector, on the other hand, were significantly lower (a difference of around RM4 000 in 1989, and around

RM7 000 in 1995, which is about half), and the rate of increase throughout the period of 1989–95 was small.

The higher earnings received by workers in the manufacturing sector is consistent with the findings in Chapter 7 in that expansion of the manufacturing sector is linked to productivity-driven growth in the Malaysian economy. An increase in the growth rate of real wages can raise labour effectiveness in several ways. The higher the growth of real wages, the lower will be the relative price of new capital (relative to the level that it will otherwise have been). This will encourage firms to employ relatively more capital and less labour, and therefore raise their capital–labour ratios. In fact, Solow (2000) pointed out that wages must rise if capital accumulation is to occur.

A higher capital to labour ratio will lead to a higher accumulation of knowledge through greater learning-by-doing and spillover of knowledge (Arrow, 1962; Kaldor, 1960; Romer, 1986, 1990). Romer (1987, p. 166) commented that: 'an increase in the rate of growth of the labor force, with the implied decrease in the rate of growth of wages, could cause a decrease in innovation, and hence a decrease in knowledge spillovers from innovation'. Following this type of technological progress, a higher K/L ratio will not increase unemployment (as indicated by the findings in Chapter 6). Instead, a higher K/L will accelerate technological progress, which in turn increases the rate of output growth. Conversely, a lower K/L ratio will increase unemployment because it will lead to lower technological progress (compared to that of a higher K/L ratio) due to a decline in learning-by-doing activities and the transference of embodied technology in capital to the production process. Hence, a lower K/L usually decreases technological progress and, therefore, output growth, leading to higher unemployment rates.

In summary, the wage differentials between the manufacturing and agricultural sectors suggest that Malaysia's economic growth is productivity driven, and this growth is generated by the expansion of the manufacturing sector (which is consistent with the findings in Chapters 5, 6 and 7). This demonstrates that factor inputs do flow to sectors with increasing returns, as postulated by the Solow–Swan growth model. The initiatives implemented by the state to expand the Malaysian education system have helped to accelerate this flow.

Since the wage differentials in the Malaysian labour market are, to a large extent, influenced by the levels of schooling (which in turn impact upon the demand and supply of labour), it is appropriate to measure the patterns of investment in the different schooling levels. Since education competes with other economic functions for scarce resources, it must be justified in terms of its contribution to national output. The following section will quantify the returns to investing in higher education by comparing the mean earning profiles of degree-holders and high school leavers.

RATES OF RETURN TO EDUCATION: EMPIRICAL FINDINGS

On a worldwide basis, the rates of return to all levels of education (primary, secondary and tertiary) have been found to be positive. Psacharopoulos (1994) found both private and social rates of return to be large and positive, as shown in Table 8.4.

Table 8.4   Returns on education by continent and level of per capita income

Country	Social			Private		
	Primary	Secondary	Tertiary	Primary	Secondary	Tertiary
Sub-Saharan Africa	24.3	18.2	11.2	41.3	26.6	27.8
Asia	19.9	13.3	11.7	39.0	18.9	19.9
Europe/Middle East/North Africa	15.5	11.2	10.6	17.4	15.9	21.7
Latin America/Caribbean	17.9	12.8	12.3	26.2	16.8	19.7
OECD	14.4	10.2	8.7	21.7	12.4	12.3
World	18.4	13.1	10.9	29.1	18.1	20.3

Country	Social			Private		
	Primary	Secondary	Tertiary	Primary	Secondary	Tertiary
Low income (US$610 or less	23.4	15.2	10.6	35.2	19.3	23.5
Lower middle income (to US$2449)	18.2	13.4	11.4	29.9	18.7	18.9
Upper middle income (to US$7619)	14.3	10.6	9.5	21.3	12.7	14.8
High income (US$7620 or more)	n.a.	10.3	8.2	n.a.	12.8	7.7
World	20.0	13.5	10.7	30.7	17.7	19.0

Source: Psacharopoulos, 1994, p. 1328.[6]

Based on the data found in Table 8.4, four stylized facts emerge:

1. Private rates of return are usually higher than social rates of returns.
2. Returns to primary school are higher than those of secondary and tertiary.
3. Patterns of rates of return remain stable as countries develop with only relatively minor drop.

4. Rates of return in advanced economies are lower than those in developing economies.

In the following section the return to higher education for Malaysia will be calculated. University education is not only more costly than other levels of education, but undergraduates who made up less than 8 per cent of total student population accounted for more than 35 per cent of total education expenditure in 1995.[6] In 1995, the average cost (by dividing the total public expenditure with the number of students enrolled in the different levels of education) per university student was RM9 498 compared to RM272 for a secondary student and RM101 for a primary student. Moreover, it is often perceived that university education is by and large the most important contributor of technological progress, particularly in its contribution to the development of a domestic R&D structure to propel technological progress (Romer, 1990; Grossman and Helpman, 1991; Aghion and Howitt, 1992; Nelson, 1996).

PRIVATE AND SOCIAL RATES OF RETURN TO HIGHER EDUCATION IN MALAYSIA

Although a substantial literature has analysed the rates of return to education of various countries, studies on Malaysia are rare. One such study was conducted by Mehmet and Hoong (1986). They reported that the private rate of return of graduates (for a three-year undergraduate degree) was 12.2 per cent in the 1982–83 period, while the social rate of return was estimated to be 7.6 per cent during the same period. Mehmet and Hoong (1986) concluded that university education was particularly attractive from an individual point of view although it could be viewed from a social standpoint as 'a very poor public investment' (p. 141).

The profitability of higher education from the viewpoint of private individuals and the society as a whole is estimated by utilizing the net present value (NPV) technique. The rate of return was calculated on net cost–benefit streams of income associated with undertaking a three-year university degree as an alternative to leaving school at sixth form, the minimum entry qualification for a degree course. Investment in education is considered to be profitable if NPV is greater than 0, and otherwise if NPV is less than 0. This is also the case for the society as a whole.

DATA

Income data for this study were drawn from the Malaysian public service salary scales (by averaging the administered public service salary scales). Two reasons are given for the use of these data. First, it is well documented that the public sector employed a large proportion of graduates from the Malaysian universities. The figures obtained from various issues of the *Economic Report* published by the Malaysian Ministry of Finance, *Yearbook of Statistics*, and the *Labour Force Survey*, ranged from more than 70 per cent (Mehmet and Hoong, 1986) to more than 80 per cent. In an earlier study on the rates of return on education in Malaysia, Mehmet and Hoong (1986, p. 127) stated that: 'Since only 15% of the employed graduates worked for the private sector, the numbers were considered too small to permit meaningful rates of return calculations on human capital utilised in the private sector'.

The public sector wages can also have a profound influence on the general wages of the economy. The pay revision in the public sector during the 1970s and 1980s had prompted the private sector to undertake wage adjustments. Osman Rani and Salleh (1994, pp. 221–2) commented that:

> the public sector acts as a 'wage setter'. Par revisions in the public sector have a strong impact on wages in the private sector, especially in the middle and lower level occupational categories ... What is important here is that prevailing labour market conditions are not important in adjusting public wages ... As a result of these, public sector wages have become 'downwardly rigid' and have proven almost totally insensitive to prevailing labour market conditions.

Second, there is no consistent official publication categorizing the different levels of income earned, either by education or by age. Mehmet and Hoong (1986) surveyed graduates in deriving their estimates for income earned. Due to resource constraints, a survey could not be undertaken in this study.

PRIVATE RATE OF RETURN

Estimates of the private rates of return to a given level of education are calculated by comparing the discounted benefits over the lifetime earnings of secondary and degree education. Thus, private rates of return to three years of university[7] are estimated by taking the difference between post-tax earnings of university graduates by age and those secondary school graduates. A secondary school leaver is defined as anyone who has completed the highest year in secondary school (sixth form), but did not possess any post-secondary qualifications. A degree-holder is defined as anyone with a Bachelor's (Pass) degree. The earnings of the latter also represent the opportunity costs of staying at university. Direct costs are obtained from statistics on a student's out-of-pocket expenditure that are strictly related to the costs of university attendance. This amount, which was estimated to be approximately RM2 800 per year, is derived from the averaged costs associated with university attendance from the major Malaysian public universities.[8]

A simplified estimation for private rates of return is specified as:

$$NPV = \sum_{i=1}^{n} [(eg_i - es_i) / (1+r)_i] - \sum_{j=1}^{3} [(es_j + c_j) / (1 + r)_j] \quad (8.1)$$

where:

NPV is the net present value of a university degree,

i denotes first year of employment,

eg_i is the mean annual after tax earnings of university graduates per year,

es_i is the mean after tax earnings of secondary school graduates per year,

n is the number of earnings years, which is assumed to be 35, before retiring at 55,

c_j is the mean private direct cost of study,

r is the private rate of return, the interest rate which makes $NPV = 0$.

SOCIAL RATE OF RETURN

A social rate of return to university education is estimated in a similar way to the private rate of return. The only difference is that university graduates' earnings are pre-tax and the private direct cost is substituted with the full amount of resources committed per student for the university. Full social cost is estimated from the total public expenditure spent on the Malaysian universities divided by the number of students.[9] The equation for the social rate of return is:

$$SNPV = \sum_{i=1}^{n} [(eg_i - es'_i) / (1+r)_i] - \sum_{j=1}^{3} [(es'_j + c'_j) / (1 + r) \quad (8.2)$$

where :

$SNPV$ is the net present value for society of a university education,

eg'_i is the mean annual pretax earnings of university graduates,

es'_j is the mean pretax earnings of secondary school graduates,

n is the number of years of university study,

c'_j is the mean of the full cost of study.

Table 8.5 gives some indication of the internal rates of return to education over a range of periods. The estimated private rate of return for a university graduate in 2000 was found to be 18.4 per cent and is within the range of the Asia and world average of 19.9 and 20.3 per cent respectively (Psacharopoulos, 1994).

Table 8.5   Internal rates of return to education, Malaysia, 1967–68, 1982–
83, 1990, 2000

	1967–68[a]		1982–83[b]		1990[c]		2000	
	Social	Private	Social	Private	Social	Private	Social	Private
Primary	8.2	12.9	-	-	25.5	33.5	27.1	35.4
Secondary	13.2	17.1	-	-	14.6	18.2	12.0	16.8
University	9.5	16.0	7.6	12.2	7.2	11.7	13.1	18.4

Notes:
[a] Hoerr (in Lim, 1975).
[b] Mehmet and Hoong, 1986.
[c] The earnings profile for the 1990–91 estimation was derived from the 1990 Malaysia public service salary scale. The direct costs of university were estimated based on 1990 admission figures. The individual income tax rates were also based on the 1990 rates. The full costs of each level of education (primary, secondary and university) were estimated by dividing the total public expenditure spent on each level of education with the number of students enrolled in that level. For the 2000 period, the earnings profiles were derived from the 2000 public service salary scales.

The social rate of return was estimated to be 13.1 per cent. This is slightly higher than the world average of 10.9 per cent (Psacharopoulos, 1994). One explanation is that the Malaysian public sector wages are set through a system of administrative procedures that reflects the employment, distributional and political goals of the government (as discussed in Chapters 4 and 5):

> Between 1970 and 1990, Malaysian educational policy was dominated by affirmative action considerations, especially at the tertiary level. Success in achieving most of the goals of the NEP, plus full employment, led to changes both in economic strategy and in educational policy. The National Development Policy (NDP), which replaced the NEP in 1991, stressed the 2020 target and downplayed ethnic quotas, yet did not forswear *Bumiputera* preferences. (Snodgrass in Rowan, 1998, p. 176)

As such, the Malaysian public sector pay policy may bias upward the estimates of social rates of return to investment in higher education. In order to close the gap of income inequality between the Malays and non-Malays, the government increased employment opportunities for Malays in the public sector (Rasiah and Shari, 2001) and remunerated them in accordance with schooling qualifications (Figure 8.4).[10] This form of institutional arrangement resulted in a rise in demand for public sector employment, which in turn propelled the expansion of the university education.

Based solely on high private and social rates of return, the large increase in public expenditure that is allocated for education expansion, particularly in

2000, was justifiable.[11] In addition to economic gains, such as higher earnings and linkages associated with technological progress (Lucas, 1988; Romer, 1986, 1990), there are also the spillover effects associated with political stability (Chapter 4). In Malaysia, education is an important mechanism for minimizing and stabilizing ethnic tensions. It is through the expansion of the education system that the reduction of the wide disparities in income between the Malays and the non-Malays was made possible. In doing so, political stability was achieved. In short, the expansion of the education system provided a path for the Malays to economic prosperity.

CONCLUSION

This chapter has examined the role of education in the economic development of Malaysia. The initiatives put in place by the state to expand Malaysia's education system are consistent with the predictions of the Solow–Swan growth framework and the endogenous growth models in that an increase in labour productivity (through education) is the key to technological progress. The wide earning differentials, of about three times, between secondary and tertiary educated workers give an indication of the productivity of the Malaysian labour. If higher education contributes to productivity as indicated by the human capital approach, then this productivity gain should be reflected in the returns. Both the private and social rates of return to higher education in Malaysia demonstrated this to be the case. However, it is possible that the high returns do not accurately capture the marginal product of labour given that public sector wages are administered independently of the market.

If this is the case, labour productivity may not be due to the expansion of university education. Instead, the increase in labour productivity as suggested by the findings in Chapters 5 and 6 may lie elsewhere. There is also a strong possibility that education is not the sole contributor to salary increments and productivity growth (Arrow, 1973; Lang and Kropp, 1986; Riley, 1976, 1978; Spence, 1974; Stiglitz, 1975; Taubman and Wales, 1973). The results in Chapter 7 suggest that international trade could be that source. These issues will be examined in the next chapter.

NOTES

[1]   First published in 1890.
[2]   The British administration was mainly interested in trade and extraction of economic resources, mainly tin and rubber. Little attention was given to education.
[3]   The race riots of 1969 accelerated the expansion of the education sector.

3   The race riots of 1969 accelerated the expansion of the education sector.
4   The OECD average allocation for education averaged 5.2 per cent of total government expenditure for the period 1965–99, compared to 17.9 per cent for Malaysia over the same period.
5   The benefits of education for a decision-maker can be captured by the discounted value of future income.
6   Reprinted from World Development, 22 (9), Psacharopoulos. G., Returns to investment in education: A global update, p. 1328, © Elsevier 1994, with permission from Elsevier.
7   During the period 1986–2000, public expenditure on higher education averaged 42.5 per cent (of total education expenditure) compared to 20.7 per cent for secondary, 15.9 per cent for primary, and 20.7 per cent for other programmes (that is, technical and vocational training and teacher training).
8   Although a number of courses require more than three years to complete (medicine, dentistry, architecture, law, engineering, and so on), in this analysis, a period of three years is assumed to be the time taken to complete a degree. This is because a large proportion of Malaysian university graduates are from the arts and commerce streams, which take three years to complete. The small number of graduates in medicine, dentistry, architecture, law and engineering is likely to have little impact on the average rates of return to total university education.
9   University of Malaya, Universiti Kebangsaan Malaysia, Universiti Sains Malaysia, Universiti Pertanian Malaysia, and Universiti Tecknologi Malaysia.
10   Various issues of Malaysia's *Yearbook of Statistics*.
11   University places are allocated based on a quota system. Approximately 80 per cent of the places are allocated to Malays with the remainder distributed among the non-Malays. Public sector employment is biased towards the Malays with more than 70 per cent of public sector employment taken up by them. Mehmet and Hoong (1986, p. 140) reported: 'more than four out of every five employed graduates with a scholarship worked for the public sector'.
12   The high returns are made even more attractive when compared with commercial interest rates that averaged around 7 per cent in 2000.

9. Effects of human capital and international trade on total factor productivity and economic growth

INTRODUCTION

The purpose of this chapter is to measure TFP growth in Malaysia for the period 1963–98,[1] with particular emphasis on the role of human capital and openness, and the estimation of α, the capital's share of output. It has been argued in the previous chapters that Malaysia's growth rate, which averaged above 7 per cent per annum between 1963 and 1998, was attributable to productivity growth in the manufacturing sector, export-oriented industrialization and high human capital formation. On the other hand, the accumulationist school of thought (as discussed in Chapter 2) maintained that the growth in Malaysia and its neighbours was largely due to growth in inputs rather than productivity. Several studies (Drysdale and Huang, 1995; Tham, 1995; Alavi, 1996) reported that minimal or negative TFP growth estimated for Malaysia could be taken as evidence supporting Krugman's propositions as discussed in Chapter 2. Tham (1995), for instance, reported that TFP growth for Malaysia covering the period 1971–87 was −1.44 per cent and TFP contribution to growth was −0.23 per cent. However, there are also others who found TFP growth for Malaysia to be significant and positive (Harberger, 1996; Dowling and Summers, 1998). How can such divergences be explained?

According to Collins and Bosworth (1996), Dowling and Summers (1998), Harberger (1996) and Sarel (1996), TFP is highly sensitive to the sampling period, the assumed size of the capital share of output, α, and the overall rate of output growth during the survey period. Rao and Lee (1995) reported a positive TFP growth for Singapore when growth was decomposed into three sub-periods (1966–73, 1976–84 and 1987–94) despite a near universal finding that the contribution to TFP growth for Singapore was negative or minimal. These findings suggest that care must be taken in the estimation of TFP growth.

Traditionally, TFP growth is estimated either by the standard Cobb–Douglas production function or by the growth accounting approach (Solow, 1957). A major limitation of these approaches lies with the difficulties in the construction of capital stock (Chapter 2). This approach is made more difficult when estimating TFP growth in many East Asian countries due to the unavailability of reliable data on capital stocks. Above all, a large proportion of TFP studies on developing countries are conducted on cross-country regressions with a predetermined value of α, which in most cases is a reflection of the production structure of the developed countries. Given the problems of heterogeneity associated with parameters which vary across countries that could render the estimates to be unreliable (Levine and Renelt, 1992; Levine and Zervos, 1993; Quah, 1993; Pack, 1994; Solow, 2000), caution must therefore be exercised when interpreting such TFP estimates.

There is also the view that the decomposition of growth in output is difficult because technical progress is embodied in new capital (Kaldor, 1960; Arrow, 1962; Kaldor and Mirrlees, 1962; Salter, 1966; Singh, 1998; Nelson and Pack, 1999). Accordingly, the effects of technical progress cannot be separated from the expansion of capital inputs. Technological progress can only take place through the introduction of new capital investments. Even replacement is associated, in this view, with technical progress. The rationale is that when a machine is being replaced by a new one, the latter is likely to be technologically more advanced and not simply a new copy of the old one (Kaldor and Mirrlees, 1962; Salter, 1966; Singh, 1998). The findings in Chapter 6 show that output per worker in Malaysia is linked to capital expansion, suggesting that the growth process is driven by embodied technical progress.

In addition, all of the TFP studies on Malaysia (Table 2.9 in Chapter 2) were conducted in a closed-economy framework.[2] Given that trade makes a major contribution to Malaysia's GDP (Table 4.9 and Table 4.10 in Chapter 4), estimating TFP growth in a closed economy may not be appropriate.[3] Taking these limitations into account, an alternative approach is developed to estimate TFP growth for Malaysia. Here, the value of α, the capital share in output, is empirically determined by taking into account the impact of human capital and international trade.[4] The logic is that the value of α will be lower due to the improvement in labour quality brought about by technological progress embodied in physical capital. This form of progress is driven by on-the-job training or learning-by-doing and accelerated by new capital investments and/or knowledge imported from abroad.

Using a cointegrating error correction mechanism framework, a model of growth is estimated which allows TFP to be measured and the effects of human capital accumulation and openness to be tested. The chapter is structured as follows. First, a review of the role of human capital and trade in the determination of productivity growth is undertaken. The model and data are then specified. Finally, the results are presented and discussed.

THE ROLE OF HUMAN CAPITAL ACCUMULATION AND TRADE

The recent resurgence of the importance of human capital accumulation in the determination of economic growth (Lucas, 1988; Romer, 1986, 1990; Barro, 1989, 1997; Mankiw et al., 1992; Grammy and Assane, 1996) reflects the increasing recognition of its importance in the growth framework. Solow (2000), for instance, pointed out that research on the role of human capital in economic growth 'should have high priority' (p. 154). In fact, human capital accumulation has long been stressed as a prerequisite and/or concomitant for economic growth (Nelson and Phelps, 1966).

In the Malaysian case, human capital accumulation has often been given a high priority in the quest for economic development. As outlined in the previous chapter, the government has taken many initiatives[5] to upgrade the quality of its human capital in a move to make Malaysia a productivity-driven economy. By 1990, 93 per cent of Malaysian children who were aged six to seven years were enrolled in Primary One (first grade). Out of the total school enrolment, 96 per cent managed to complete at least six years of primary education. Within the 10–15 age group, secondary enrolment increased significantly from less than 20 per cent in 1960 to more than 60 per cent in 1992. However, enrolment rates for tertiary education increased only marginally from less than 2 per cent in 1960 to about 6 per cent in 1992 for the 20–24 age group (Asian Development Bank, 1998) and 9.4 per cent in 1998 (Department of Statistics Malaysia, 1998). This is surprising in view of the massive increase in the allocation of government expenditure on this sector.

The findings of the previous chapter suggest that output growth in Malaysia is driven in part by the accumulation of human capital brought about by the expansion of the education system. This is consistent with the Lucas model (1988) as discussed in Chapter 3. Briefly, output growth, g, is driven by the efficiency or productivity of human capital, ψ. The latter, in turn, is dependent upon the term $1 - u^*$, which is the share of labour being utilized between the production of consumer goods and human capital accumulation, and u^* is the optimal allocation of individuals' time between production and education. Hence, output growth is expressed as $g = \psi \ (1 - u^*)$. In this type of framework, the decision to change u, that is, by expanding the education system, would increase the growth rate of human capital accumulation and therefore output growth.

The optimal allocation or choice between the production of intermediate goods and education can only be effective if human capital accumulation is an economically motivated activity (Lucas, 1988). The wide wage and salary differentials between the higher-educated and the lower-educated labour force, and the high rates of return to higher education suggest this is the case for Malaysia. Thus, the profitability of education in Malaysia acted as a catalyst in shifting resources and effort toward education. However, there is no indication to suggest that the expansion of public expenditure to develop Malaysia's education system has been provided in an efficient manner. Whether the resources that were allocated to the education system have actually increased the effectiveness or efficiency of the Malaysian workers is yet to be determined. Knowing this will shed further light on the role of human capital in economic development. This will be attempted in the next section.

In this analysis, human capital is assumed to be accumulated via two primary channels: formal education and a combination of work experience and training provided by the employers. It is not known *a prior* which is the most significant factor. Although workers with higher education received significantly higher wages relative to those with minimum amounts of education, there is a strong possibility that all the increments to earnings may not be entirely due to education. A substantial proportion of incremental earnings enjoyed by university graduates may be attributed to ability, not education. According to the screening hypothesis,[6] the main role of education is not so much to train people but rather to select those individuals who will do best in the job market (Taubman and Wales, 1973; Riley, 1978; Lang and Kropp, 1986). Even if education is found to increase earnings, there is yet another question which needs to be addressed: what is the mechanism at work? Gills et al. (1996, p. 267) expressed this view:

> Do schools teach skills that turn out to have economic value, or do they only socialize people to work better – to be punctual in their attendance and conscientious in completing their assignments?

If higher education is linked to higher productivity of an individual (Schultz, 1961), then surely the quality of education matters. An obvious reason is that the capability of an individual in accumulating and dissipating new knowledge into the society is by and large determined by the quality of education. This is also the case for the R&D sector.

Despite all the initiatives implemented by the Malaysian government to improve the education system, some authors have maintained that the quality of general education is low, as reflected by rising skills shortages (Malaysia, 1996). According to past studies (Malaysia, 1991, 1996; Narayanan and Lai, 1993; Guyton, 1994; Goh, 1999), skills shortages are the primary reason that Malaysia was unable to make the transition from being dependent upon foreign technology to being able to produce the technology locally. Furthermore, Snodgrass (in Rowan, 1998, p. 179) commented that: 'enrollment ratios in Malaysia are not outstanding and student learning is probably not outstanding by international standards'. This concern was raised by others (Mehmet and Hoong, 1986; Osman Rani and Salleh, 1994). Mehmet and Hoong (1986, p. 142) remarked that: 'university education is not doing an efficient job of producing technical and professional manpower needed by the economy'. Since the public sector employs a large proportion of university graduates, the public sector can determine the demand (through its role as an employer) and supply (through education policy) of the educated labour force. The affirmative education policy initiated between 1970 and 1990 (Snodgrass, 1998) had placed greater emphasis and demand on the applicants with academic qualifications over those with skills but no academic qualifications. This has influenced potential job-seekers to seek paper qualifications instead of skills acquisition. This will in turn affect the quality of the labour force in general.[7]

If the observed fact of low-quality education holds,[8] the capability of Malaysia to absorb and diffuse technological advancement through the education system will be low. This is because higher levels of human capital facilitate the absorption of higher technology from leading economies. This is likely to be particularly important for schooling at the higher levels. An important aspect of higher levels of schooling is in the contribution to the development of a domestic R&D structure to propel technological advancement, which is vital for long-run growth (Romer, 1990; Grossman and Helpman, 1991; Aghion and Howitt, 1992; Nelson, 1996). This is certainly not the case for Malaysia if tertiary education and R&D statistics are taken as indicators of indigenous technological capabilities. Table 9.1 provides a comparison of tertiary enrolment levels between Malaysia and a selected group of countries. It shows that Malaysia lagged behind all the other countries selected.

Table 9.1   Percentage of 20–24-year-olds enrolled in tertiary education in selected countries, 1980 and 1993

Country	Enrolments (%)	
	1980	1993
USA	56	81
Japan	31	30
South Korea	15	38
Australia	25	42
Singapore	8	38
Hong Kong	10	18
Malaysia	4	7

Source: World Bank, 1997.

Given the low enrolments in tertiary education, it is not surprising to see

184   *Technical Progress and Economic Growth*

that Malaysia has a smaller supply of scientists and engineers engaged in
R&D as shown in Table 9.2.

*Table 9.2   Scientists and engineers engaged in R&D per million people
1981–95 in selected countries*

Country	Numbers
US	3 732
Japan	5 677
South Korea	2 636
Singapore	2 512
Malaysia	87

Source: World Bank, 1999.

Similarly, the data in Table 9.3 show that R&D development in terms of
R&D expenditure, share of world scientific papers and share of US patents in
Malaysia lagged behind those in other countries. A study conducted by
Narayanan and Lai (1993) found that most of the R&D activities in Malaysia,
which were carried out by foreign-owned or controlled firms, tend to draw
personnel from parent plants abroad. R&D activities, when present, are
largely confined to low-end design matters and usually do not require highly
trained personnel. A recent study on Malaysian manufacturing industry
conducted by Narayanan and Lai (2000, p. 453) concluded that:

> R&D levels in Malaysian manufacturing are far below those consistent with its
> maturing industrial structure. The concomitant technological maturity requires
> mastery of both production and product technology. While important gains have
> been made towards attaining the former, there has been negligible progress in
> terms of the latter. In particular, Malaysian manufacturing has not yet developed
> the self-sustaining innovative impulse that drives industrialized economies.

Since indigenous technological capabilities play little role in the
development of the manufacturing sector, particularly in the generation of
new knowledge or technology, how does one then explain the evolution of
the manufacturing sector from the manufacturing of basic foodstuffs and
textiles to an exporter of high-technology electronic products[9] in a time span
of less than two decades? Perhaps the relationship between R&D activities
and productivity growth is not as clear-cut as postulated by Romer (1990),
Grossman and Helpman (1991) and Aghion and Howitt (1992). A time series
study conducted by Jones (1995) on the impact of R&D on TFP growth from
1960 to 1988 for France, Germany, Japan and the US found no clear evidence

to suggest that an increase in R&D activities will lead to an increase in TFP growth. Despite the significant increase in the number of scientists and engineers engaged in R&D,[10] France and Japan show negative trends in TFP growth. There was no distinct trend in TFP growth for Germany and the US. The results are similar when the number of scientists and engineers was substituted by R&D expenditure. This led Jones (1995, p. 519) to state that:

> The models of Romer (1990), Grossman and Helpman (1991a, 1991b) and Aghion and Howitt (1992) are rejected easily ... The models posit that the growth rates of per capita output and total factor productivity should be increasing with the level of resources devoted to R&D, which is wildly at odds with empirical evidence.

Table 9.3   Selected research and development data from various countries

Country	R&D expenditure (million ECU)	R&D (%) of GDP (1992)	Share (%) of US patents (1981–1984)	Share (%) of world scientific Papers (1993)	High-technology trade Imports (1992)	Exports (1992) (million ECU)
USA	112 503	2.67	34.6	50.1	192 243	172 066
Canada	5 658 (1993)	1.45	4.5	2.2	49 029	41 360
Mexico	776 (1989)	0.31	0.3	0.1	17 850	7 209
Chile	434 (1992)	0.78	0.2	0	3 143	285
Australia	2 811 (1990)	1.56	2.1	0.4	14 361	2 565
New Zealand	280 (1992)	0.98	0.4	0	3 231	387
Japan	44 237 (1993)	2.92	7.3	24.2	37 269	180 778
South Korea	5 176 (1991)	2.33	0.2	0.9	22 857	22 760
Taiwan	2 331 (1992)	1.82	0.4	1.4	n.a.	n.a.
Singapore	401 (1993)	1.12	0.1	0	26 387	27 139
Hong Kong	n.a.	0.08	0.2	0.1	36 711	8 282
Malaysia	73 (1989)	0.37	0.1	0	15 731	11 095
Thailand	342 (1991)	0.16	0.1	0	13 492	5 420
Philippines	110 (1984)	0.21	0	0	3 907	1 408
Indonesia	980 (1993)	0.26	0	0	8 566	1 296
China	16 917 (1993)	0.6	0.9	0.1	29 158	12 064

Source: Baker and Goto in Thompson, 1998, p. 256.

If R&D plays a small role in productivity growth, then what is a significant factor? One such factor could be on-the-job training offered by the employers. According to Helpman and Rangel (1999), human capital could be accumulated either through general knowledge, which is acquired through formal education and training, or technology-specific experience that individuals acquire through working with a technology. Solow (2000, p. 101)[11] remarked that: 'there are more important sources of technological progress that have no relation to research and development. Arrow's 'learning by doing' is an example of just such a source or process.'

Technical progress, which is embodied in new capital goods as well as replacement capital (Kaldor, 1960; Kaldor and Mirrlees, 1962; Salter, 1966; Singh, 1998), could only shift into the workforce through on-the-job training and learning-by-doing (Arrow, 1962). It is highly possible that learning-by-doing or on-the-job training plays a more significant role than formal education in improving the quality of human capital in Malaysia.

It is also likely that the extent to which on-the-job training is able to improve the quality of human capital depends on the openness of the economy. The reason is that firms competing in the international markets have to sell products that are comparatively superior to those of their competitors. This will require them to employ state-of-the-art equipment and production techniques. Advances in production techniques are consistently acquired and upgraded through international trade. This is particularly the case for Malaysia where international trade is the only avenue for technology accumulation because it does not have the capacity to generate better production techniques and to develop technologies internally (Goh, 1999; Narayanan and Lai, 2000).

The justification for including openness into the growth framework is twofold. First, as suggested by the discussion in Chapter 3, it is through trade that exchange of ideas is facilitated. This increases the rate of adoption and diffusion of new ideas into the production process (Grossman and Helpman, 1991). Accordingly, *A* can be driven by the diffusion of new knowledge, which is linked to international trade. This means that high productivity growth is possible in initially poor countries as a result of the diffusion of knowledge already available in the industrialized countries. Developing countries could take advantage of their relative backwardness to accelerate their growth performance as postulated by the neoclassical growth analysis. This may explain why developing countries with high trade barriers often linked to import-substitution strategies are showing few signs of convergence to the per capita income levels of the industrialized countries.

International trade could also affect the saving variable, *s*, in the Solow–Swan growth model by changing the allocation of investment in the production of output between domestic consumption and exports. In order to compete successfully in the international market, it is necessary for firms to utilize cutting-edge production technology. Investment allowances must therefore be made to encourage new technology or to update existing technology.[12] The increase in capital investment will also lead to additional investment in human capital accumulation as suggested by Kaldor's technical progress function. This is because additional human capital is required to absorb and diffuse new technology.[13] Thus, as technology evolves, so does human capital and both of these evolutionary processes must be augmented by additional investment. The findings of Chapters 6 and 7 suggest that this is the case for Malaysia's growth experience. The regression results in Table 7.7 (Chapter 7) show a strong relationship (R^2 = 0.95) between employment growth and export growth. This suggests that labour productivity in the manufacturing sector during the period 1980–98 was driven by manufacturing exports.

The average growth rate in the Aghion and Howitt (1998) model is stipulated in equation (3.11) in Chapter 3. The model predicts that a variety of factors which could help to increase $\tilde{n}$ will increase the rate of growth. International trade is one such factor. Since international trade is an important source of new knowledge (Grossman and Helpman, 1991), it can be further stipulated that domestic R&D and innovations can be further enhanced by the interactions between the international communities, thereby increasing $\tilde{n}$ in the process. This is also the case for Kaldor's (1960) technical progress function in that the evolution of A could be driven by economies of scale (leading to increasing returns) through export demand.

Furthermore, despite the large amount of literature on the role of international trade in determining productivity gains and economic growth, empirical evidence on the superiority of free international trade (outward-oriented policies) is scarce. The surveys carried out by Edwards (1993) and Maurer (1994) found no strong evidence to link trade to growth. Recently, Rodriguez and Rodrik (1999) reported that there is considerable weakness in the econometric literature on trade and growth. They concluded that there is little evidence that open trade policies (lower tariff and non-tariff barriers) are linked to economic growth.

When based on historical facts, many capitalist economies, such as the US and Japan, experienced rapid growth under early conditions of protection. This is also true for many East Asia economies. The inclusion of international trade would test the significance of its contribution to gains in efficiency and productivity as captured by TFP growth. Gapinski (1998) found that openness is a major determinant of economic growth in Hong Kong and Singapore. Gapinski (1998, p. 90) concluded that: 'international trade is the main cause of growth in Hong Kong and Singapore. It is also the main determinant of TFP growth and the dominant component of the residual.'

Second, as indicated earlier, Malaysia is one of the world's most open economies. During the period 1963–98, exports averaged around 64 per cent of GDP[14] (Bank Negara Malaysia, 1994, 1999). Given these magnitudes, leaving trade out of the growth equation could bias α, capital's share estimation upwards which in turn would bias TFP growth downwards. This may explain why a large number of studies have reported low TFP for Malaysia and its neighbours.

THE MODEL

The estimation of TFP growth takes the following production relationship:

$$Y_t = A_t K_t^{\alpha} L_t^{1-\alpha} \qquad (9.1)$$

where Y is the aggregate real output, K is capital stock, L is labour and A indicates productivity or TFP. α, is a parameter with a value between 0 and 1, equal to capital's share of the value of output. K denotes real aggregate capital stock.

As stressed by the capital theory controversy of the 1960s and 1970s (Chapter 2), the treatment of capital as homogenous in the neoclassical growth model so that it could be aggregated in a production function (like equation 9.1) is a proposition that defies reality.[15] Granger (1997) pointed out that the actual economy is a constitution of heterogeneous factors of productions and consumptions. If capitals are heterogeneous (Granger, 1997; Hunt, 1979; Robinson, 1978), how should they be aggregated? Kaldor and Mirrlees (1962) attempted to depart from these difficulties by taking obsolescence into account. This makes the measurement of capital stock irrelevant. Instead, 'it operates solely with the value of gross investment (gross (fixed) capital expenditure per unit of time) and its rate of change in time' (p. 174). This view was shared by Salter (1962, 1966) who argued that new knowledge would lead to continuous change in the production function for each commodity. The common characteristics of all such advances are that they lead to a new production function that is superior to its predecessor. If investment is required to utilize new methods of production, then the higher the rate of investment, the more rapidly will new techniques be brought into general use. In this type of technical progress, the life of investment is not determined by the marginal rates of substitutions between capital and labour or the marginal rates of returns to capital. Rather, it is imposed directly by expectations of obsolescence. Since only new equipment is involved, capital stocks could be made homogenous by summing capital across vintages. Earlier, Keynes (1936) remarked that heterogeneous capital could be made homogeneous by assuming that technical progress is embodied in capital: 'The output from equipment produced today will have to compare, in the course of its life, with output from equipment produced subsequently, perhaps at a lower labour cost, perhaps by an imported technique' (p. 141).

Since, each vintage of capital produces a stream of output, it is possible to aggregate heterogeneous capital by summing output across vintages.[16] In addition, summing capital across vintages bring to mind that productivity change is embodied into the production process. Following the definitions of capital by Gapinski (1997, 1998), Kaldor and Mirrlees (1962), Keynes (1936), Salter (1962, 1966) and Solow (1960), the measurement of capital in this framework takes into account the sum of capital stock from all existing vintages:

$$\int_{i=1}^{t} I_i - \delta_i / P_i \qquad (9.2)$$

where I denotes gross domestic investment, t represents the age of the oldest vintage, δ is depreciation, and P is the price level.

By taking logs and differentiating with respect to time, output growth can be derived from equation (9.1) as shown below:

$$\dot{y}_t = \dot{a}_t + \alpha \dot{k}_t + (1 - \alpha)\dot{l}_t \qquad (9.3)$$

Once an estimate of α is provided, $\hat{\alpha}$, then TFP, $\hat{a}_t$, is estimated as follows:

$$\hat{a}_t = \dot{y}_t - \hat{\alpha}\dot{k}_t - (1 - \hat{\alpha})\dot{l}_t \qquad (9.4)$$

This function is extended to include human capital and openness.[17] The hypothesis advanced in this section can be written as:

$$Y_t = A_t K_t^{\alpha} L_t^{1-\alpha} H_t^{\beta} O_t^{\gamma} \qquad (9.5)$$

where H is human capital and O is openness.

It follows that the technological progress term A_t captures the impact of human capital development, H_t, international trade, O_t, and an exogenous component proxied by time, t. The time trend t is included as a proxy for Hicks-neutral technological progress. In this model, both H_t and O_t do not impact directly upon A_t, but through α, the coefficient of capital. It is possible that the value of α will be lowered due to improvements in labour quality being brought about by technological progress embodied in new foreign equipments via international trade. If this is to be the case, diminishing returns to capital will not occur because the higher the rate of capital investment, the greater will be the turnover of machines and the greater will be the learning-by-doing process, thereby increasing labour quality leading to a lower value of α and therefore higher TFP growth.

In order to estimate the impact of human capital development and international trade on TFP growth, the labour and capital coefficients are constrained to sum to unity ($\alpha_k + \alpha_l = 1$), and the equation used to estimate α is:

$$(y - 1)_t = a + \alpha(k - 1)_t + \beta e_t + \gamma o_t + \delta t + u_t \qquad (9.6)$$

where u_t is the independent, identically distributed error term.

Sources of Data

Data for output, capital, labour, education and trade were obtained from various Malaysian official government publications. They include the *Yearbook of Statistics*, *Economic Report* (Ministry of Finance, Malaysia, various years), Bank Negara Malaysia *Annual Report* and the *Labour Force Survey Report*.

The aggregate output, Y, is the real gross domestic product, deflated by the price level ($1960 = 100$). Labour, L, is the number employed in the Malaysian economy. Ideally, the number of hours worked is a better proxy for L. However, the unavailability of reliable data for Malaysia renders this exercise difficult. Capital, K, in this context is derived from equation (9.2) using real gross domestic investment, weighted by the 1960 price index, and is derived from the sum of public and private investments. An annual depreciation rate of 5 per cent[18] is applied to take into account the depreciation of physical capital. Education is defined by three measures – e_1, e_2 and e_3 – the proportions of employed persons with, respectively, primary, secondary and higher education. O is the sum of imports plus exports as a proportion of GDP.

Estimation

The Autoregressive-Distributed Lag (ARDL) method of Pesaran et al. (1996) was employed to estimate the parameters based on the following specification:

$$\phi (L, p) \, y_t = \sum_{i=1}^{k} \beta(L_i q_i) \, x_{it} + w_t + e_t \qquad (9.7)$$

where:

$$\phi (L, p) = 1 - \phi L - \phi_2 L^2 - \dots - \phi_p L^p$$
$$\beta (L_1, q_i) = 1 - \beta_{i1} L - \beta_{i2} L^2 - \dots - \beta_{iqi} L^{qi} \text{ for } i = 1, 2, \dots, k$$

The lag operator is L, whereby $Ly_t = y_{t-1}$ and w_t is a vector of intercept and time trends, y is the dependent variable and the x_i's are the independent variables. The ARDL approach involves two stages. In the first stage, the long-run relationship between the selected variables is tested by computing the F-statistic for the significance of the lagged levels of the variables in the error correction form of the underlying model. The asymptotic distribution of the F-statistic is non-standard and is compared to critical values tabulated in Pesaran et al. (1996). Two bounds are calculated: one assuming all the variables are $I(1)$ and one assuming all variables are $I(0)$. If the F-statistic value falls above the upper bound, then the lagged terms are significant and, therefore, it can be inferred that there exists a long-run relationship between the selected variables. If the F-test value lies below the lower bound, then the long-run relationship can be rejected. If the computed statistic falls between the two bounds, then standard techniques for testing for unit roots must be applied.

The second stage involves the estimation of the coefficients of the long-run relationship using the ARDL where the optimal lag structure is determined by the Akaike information criterion. In addition, the estimation of the long-run coefficients and their asymptotic standard errors are provided by the error correction model (ECM). Given that real output does not instantaneously adjust to its long-run determinants, the ECM reflects how the system converges to the long-run equilibrium.

Prior to the commencement of the estimation of the structural parameters, it is first necessary to establish the existence of a long-run relationship between the selected variables. This is to establish that the long-run relationship between the variables to be estimated later is not spurious. The long-run equilibrium model is specified as:

$$(y_t - l_t) = a + \alpha\,(k_t - l_t) + \delta_1 e_{1t} + \delta_2 e_{2t} + \delta_3 e_{3t} + \lambda o_t \quad (9.8)$$

where e_1 is employed persons with primary education, e_2 is employed persons with secondary education, e_3 denotes employed persons with tertiary education as a proportion of workforce.

The two most commonly used proxies for human capital are secondary school enrolment rates (Levine and Renelt, 1992; World Bank, 1993), and the stock of educational attainment (Barro and Lee, 1993). Due to the unavailability of reliable data required to construct mean years of schooling, human capital in this analysis is constructed by the distribution of employed persons by level of education. O signifies openness of the economy, defined as imports plus exports as a proportion of gross domestic product (Grossman and Helpman, 1991). Traditionally, imports are used as a measure to capture embodied technological progress. Here, exports are included to provide some insight into the effectiveness in the absorption of embodied technology. For instance, importing new equipment to produce goods for exports does not guarantee that the goods will be successfully sold in the global markets. It depends on the competitiveness of the goods (in terms of pricing and quality). The competitiveness of the goods is, to a large extent, dependent upon the productivity of factor inputs. The higher the rates of absorption of the embodied technology, the higher will be the level of competitiveness. By learning how to utilize more efficiently the equipment used in the production process, the higher will be the quality of output, which in turn would lead to higher demand and lower production costs, and therefore prices. Kaldor (in Filippini et al., 1996, p. 69) stated that:

> The growth of a country's exports thus appears to be the most important factor in determining its rate of progress, and this depends on the outcome of the efforts of its producers to seek out potential markets and to adapt their product structure accordingly.

The error correction mechanism (ECM) of the ARDL is given by:

$$DLY_t = a + \sum b_i\, DLY_{t-i} + \sum c_i\, DLK_{t-i} + \sum e_i\, De_{1t-i} +$$
$$\sum f_i\, De_{2t-i} + \sum g_i\, De_{3t-i} + \sum h_i\, Do_{t-i} + \lambda_1\, LY_{t-1} +$$
$$\lambda_2 LK_{t-1} + \lambda_3 e_{1t-1} + \lambda_4\, e_{2t-1} + \lambda_5\, e_{3t-1} + \lambda_6\, o_{t-1} + u_t \quad (9.9)$$

where:
LY is the logarithm of real GDP minus log of employment;
LK is the logarithm of real capital investment minus log of employment;
e_1 is the logarithm of the proportion of employed persons with primary education;
e_2 is the logarithm of the proportion of employed persons with secondary education;
e_3 is the logarithm of the proportion of employed persons with tertiary education;
o is the logarithm of import plus exports as a proportion of GDP; and
D denotes the first difference of a variable.

RESULTS

The above equation was estimated using ordinary least squares with and without the lagged levels variables. The regression is of no significance other than to test the existence of a long-run relationship between the selected variables. From the tables provided by Pesaran et al. (1996), the lower bounds and the upper bounds, at the 5 per cent level, are 2.752 and 3.883 respectively, and at the 10 per cent level are 2.410 and 3.492 respectively. Since the F-value from the regression was found to be 3.929, which is above the upper bound, it suggests that there is a long-run relationship between the variables in this model.

Having established the existence of a long-run relationship between the variables, the next step is to estimate capital's share of output by the ARDL method on the standard production function. This model is first tested to find out whether it satisfies the regression diagnostics. This is followed by an estimation of the long-run coefficients of the variables in the model and the ECM adjustment coefficient. The ARDL method is repeated with the different forms of production function.

Result 1: Estimation of Parameters in the Standard Production Function

The estimated coefficients of equation (9.3) are displayed in Appendix 9.1. The results satisfy all the standard diagnostics except for functional form. Of greater interest is the long-run coefficient of α, which is presented in Table 9.4.

Table 9.4   ARDL estimates of long-run coefficients of the standard production function

Regressor	Coefficient	Standard error	T-ratio (Prob)
LK	0.55147	0.21649	2.5473 (0.016)
Constant	1.4234	0.46924	3.0335 (0.005)
Time	0.01854	0.021196	0.87471 (0.389)

Notes: ARDL (2, 2) selected based on Akaike information criterion. Dependent variable is *LY*. 36 observations used for estimation from 1963 to 1998.

The results in Table 9.4 show four prominent features. First, all the coefficients show the expected signs, with the exception of time trend, which is positive but statistically insignificant (at the 0.05 level). Second, the long-run coefficient of α with respect to capital's share of output is found to be 0.55. Third, the error correction mechanism (ECM) coefficient estimated from a separate ECM equation,[19] which is –0.23426 with a t-statistic of –2.3526 (p < 0.05), as shown in Appendix 9.2, suggests that adjustment to long-run equilibrium is relatively slow. Fourth, the low coefficient in the estimated time trend indicates that the dominating growth factor for Malaysia is capital accumulation rather than productivity growth.

One of the major methodological difficulties associated with the calculation of TFP growth is linked to the estimation of the value α, which is capital's share of output. This is due to the unavailability of reliable capital stock data, particularly in the developing economies, as well as difficulties associated with the construction of capital stock (as highlighted in the capital controversy). Thus, TFP growth estimations are often conducted with α being determined *a priori*. Estimates in the literature have found a value for α of 0.3 for industrialized economies (Maddison, 1987), and 0.4 for the newly industrialized economies in East Asia (Kim and Lau, 1995; Collins and Bosworth, 1996; Harrison, 1996). The justification for a higher α for the developing economies is the argument that the capital stock is much smaller in these economies so the output elasticity should be higher as postulated by the hypothesis of diminishing returns. Past studies on TFP reveal that the value of α employed for different countries ranged from 0.29 to 0.69. These estimates are presented in Table 9.5.

Table 9.5   Different α values for selected countries

OECD Countries, 1947–73			
France	0.40	Canada	0.44
Germany	0.39	Italy	0.39
Japan	0.39	Netherlands	0.45
UK	0.38	US	0.40
G-7 Countries, 1960–90			
Canada	0.45	France	0.42
Germany	0.40	Italy	0.38
Japan	0.42	UK	0.39
US	0.41		
Latin American Countries, 1940–80			
Argentina	0.54	Brazil	0.45
Chile	0.52	Colombia	0.63
Mexico	0.69	Peru	0.66
Venezuela	0.55		
East Asian Countries, 1966–90			
Hong Kong	0.37	Singapore	0.53
Korea	0.32	Taiwan	0.29

Sources: Christensen et al. (1980); Dougherty (1991); Elias (1990); Young (1994).

The α value of 0.55 for Malaysia in Table 9.4 is similar to that found in the Latin American countries and Singapore shown in Table 9.5, and is consistent with prior estimations. However, there is a possibility that the value of 0.55 may be high based on more recent studies of TFP growth in East Asia conducted by several authors (Kim and Lau, 1994; Collins and Bosworth, 1996; Harberger, 1996; Sarel, 1996; Dowling and Summers, 1998).

One possible implication of estimating TFP with a high α value is that it can bias TFP growth estimation. This is because TFP estimation is highly sensitive to the value of α. According to Chen (1997), the inappropriate choice of α would explain why many studies reported a small TFP value in East Asia. In fact, several authors (Sarel, 1994; Collins and Bosworth, 1996; Harberger, 1996) reported that TFP is highly sensitive to the sampling period, the size of α, and the overall rate of output growth during the survey period. Sarel (1996) carried out a sensitivity exercise of TFP for Hong Kong, Korea, Taiwan and Singapore by applying the α values of 0.25 and 0.45. He found that the productivity growth in these countries was estimated to be 3.7 per cent based on a capital share, α, of 0.25 in comparison to a productivity growth of 2 per cent based on a capital share of 0.45. Recently, Dowling and Summers (1998) reinforced the view that TFP estimation is highly sensitive to the size of α. Employing Summers–Heston (1961–95) data, with a capital share of 0.4, TFP growth for Korea was estimated to be 2.6 per cent, 2.8 per cent for Singapore and 2.5 per cent for Taiwan, while a capital share of 0.3 produced TFP growth of 3.5 per cent, 3.5 per cent and 3.3 per cent respectively. Their findings are presented in Table 9.6.

Table 9.6   TFP growth estimates

Nehru-Dhareshwar capital stock, World Bank output							
Capital share	Sample period	China	Korea	Malaysia	Singapore	Taiwan	Thailand
0.4	1961–95	1.4	1.9	1.5	1.6	2.0	1.3
0.35	1961–95	1.6	2.4	1.9	2.1	2.4	1.7
0.3	1961–95	1.9	2.9	2.3	2.6	2.9	2.2
King-Levine capital stock, Summers-Heston output							
Capital share	Sample period	China	Korea	Malaysia	Singapore	Taiwan	Thailand
0.4	1961–95	n.a.	2.6	1.9	2.8	2.5	1.6
0.35	1961–95	n.a.	3.1	2.2	3.1	2.9	2.0
0.3	1961–95	n.a.	3.5	2.5	3.5	3.3	2.4

Source: Dowling and Summers, 1998, pp. 180–81.

These findings suggest that care must be taken in the selection of independent variables. Most studies of TFP growth in the East Asia economies tend to focus on parameter estimations of the size of α, resulting in enormous effort being devoted to the achievement of a spurious accuracy which in the first place is problematic due to difficulties in the construction of capital stock (Robinson, 1962; Hunt, 1979).

The momentum that has been generated by the endogenous growth models reinforces the need to include other independent variables in the analysis of economic growth. Failure to do so would bias the estimate of α. In this analysis, human capital and openness of the economy are included in the production function.

Results 2: Estimation of Production Function Incorporating Human Capital

Primary, secondary and tertiary levels were first regressed simultaneously using the ARDL approach. In addition, different combinations of education levels, such as primary and secondary, secondary and tertiary, and so on, were also carried out. The results were roughly similar, indicating secondary and tertiary levels to be insignificant to the contribution of the growth in output. For these reasons, only primary education is included in the production function. The overall estimation results in Appendix 9.3 show that all the regression diagnostics are satisfied in the equation except for normality. Table 9.7 reports on the long-run coefficient of the selected variables.

Table 9.7   ARDL estimates of long-run coefficients of the production function with education

Regressor	Coefficient	Standard error	T-ratio (Prob)
LK	0.39815	0.14179	2.8080 (0.009)
e_1	1.4757	0.58027	2.5431 (0.016)
Constant	2.3218	0.41883	5.5436 (0.000)
Time	0.057580	0.018407	3.1281 (0.004)

Notes: ARDL (1,1,0) selected based on Akaike information criterion. Dependent variable is LY. 36 observations used for estimation from 1963 to 1998.

The data show that the coefficients of the variables are significant at the standard 0.05 level. The coefficient of primary level education shows a positive sign. The ECM coefficient (with primary education from a separate ECM equation as shown in Appendix 9.4) estimate of -0.34863 with a t-statistic of -3.4242 ($p = 0.002$) show that adjustment to long-run equilibrium is somewhat faster than the ECM coefficient of the standard production function of -0.23426, as shown earlier.

It appears that secondary and tertiary levels of education in Malaysia during the 1963–98 period were not significant to the nation's growth in output; primary education was more important in contributing to the growth in output.[20] These findings are consistent with the results published by the World Bank (1993), particularly with reference to the significant contribution by primary education. According to the World Bank (1993, p. 52):

> Primary education is by far the largest single contributor to the HPAEs' predicted growth rates. Between 58 percent (Japan) and 87 percent (Thailand) of predicted growth is due to primary school enrollment. Physical investment comes second (between 35 and 49 percent), followed by secondary school enrolment … while the laggards in secondary enrollment rates, Indonesia, Malaysia, and Thailand, have the smallest proportion of their predicted growth attributed to secondary enrollments (less than 15 percent).

The long-run coefficient of α is estimated to be 0.39 with the inclusion of primary education. This is lower than the first estimation in the standard production function of 0.55. The lower α points to a significant role for embodied technical progress (Kaldor, 1960) due to the improvement in labour quality through a learning-by-doing process (Arrow, 1962). Workers with a basic education (primary) can absorb and diffuse the embodied technological progress at a faster rate than their counterparts who lack a basic education. As workers learn how to operate machinery more effectively, their productivity level will increase, leading to higher labour wages and a higher share of output. Accordingly, capital will become cheaper (thereby lowering the value α), which in turn will stimulate additional capital accumulation, leading to additional employment and learning-by-doing activities and hence a higher labour share of output.

The next phase in the development of the growth framework is the incorporation of openness of the economy. The inclusion of openness of the economy into the growth framework involves two different stages. The first stage utilizes only openness in order to examine its sole impact on α. In the second stage, education and openness are simultaneously included in the production function.

Results 3: Estimation of Production Function with the Effect of International Trade

Appendix 9.5 presents the overall regression results which satisfy all the regression diagnostics. The next step is estimation of the long-run coefficient of α. The results in Table 9.8 show that the coefficients of the variables are significant ($p < 0.05$). It appears that openness played a significant role in Malaysia's growth in output from 1963 to 1998. In addition, the α value is found to be somewhat lower when openness is included.

Table 9.8   ARDL estimates of long-run coefficients including openness

Regressor	Coefficient	Standard error	T-ratio (Prob)
LK	0.42413	0.13361	3.1744 (0.004)
O	0.58553	0.21642	2.7055 (0.012)
Constant	2.0326	0.35631	5.7044 (0.000)
Time	0.017468	0.01227	1.4236 (0.166)

Notes: ARDL (2, 2, 2) selected based on Akaike information criterion. Dependent variable is *LY*. 36 observations used for estimation from 1963 to 1998.

The value of α (0.42) is lower than that of the standard production function (0.55), but marginally higher in comparison to the production function that includes human capital (0.39). The ECM adjustment (Appendix 9.6) coefficient of −0.40638 with a t-statistic of −2.9294 ($p = 0.007$) implies adjustment is faster when openness is included. The decline in the α value is consistent with the proposition that international trade increases the effectiveness of both labour and capital. The importation of new equipment will increase learning-by-doing activities, which in turn will increase the productivity of labour. The results are also consistent with the proposition put forward by Grossman and Helpman (1991) that international trade is important to output growth as a result of spillover effects. Outputs that are exported stimulate additional capital investment which in the process increases further learning-by-doing activities, thereby increasing the productivity of labour and hence labour's shares of output. The results are also consistent with the findings in Chapter 7 in that trade is an avenue for productivity growth.

Primary education is now included together with openness into the production function.

Results 4: Estimation of Production Function with International Trade and Human Capital

The data in Appendix 9.7 indicate that the model satisfies all the regression diagnostics. Of much greater interest are the long-run coefficients of openness and primary education. The results are presented in Table 9.9. The coefficients of both openness and primary education are found to be positive and significant, indicating that openness and primary education have a positive long-run effect on output growth. The estimated ECM coefficient is −0.53654 with a t-statistic of −3.7647 ($p = 0.001$), which indicates that adjustment is significantly faster than in all the previous versions as shown in Appendix 9.8.

Table 9.9 ARDL estimates of long-run coefficients with openness and human capital

Regressor	Coefficient	Standard error	T-ratio (Prob)
LK	0.43369	0.094145	4.6066 (0.000)
e_l	0.87124	0.36722	2.3725 (0.026)
O	0.49258	0.16037	3.0715 (0.005)
Constant	2.3095	0.28317	8.1559 (0.000)
Time	0.032833	0.011749	2.7946 (0.010)

Notes: ARDL (2, 2, 0, 2) selected based on Akaike information criterion. Dependent variable is *LY*. 36 observations used for estimation from 1963 to 1998.

The coefficient of time, which is found to be statistically significant ($p <$ 0.05), is 0.033, indicating a productivity growth of 3.3 per cent per year. The next stage is to estimate TFP growth for Malaysia.

TOTAL FACTOR PRODUCTIVITY ESTIMATES

The determination of TFP would, in the first instance, require the coefficients of α and $1 - \alpha$. By substituting these estimated coefficients together with the logarithms of growth of output *Y*, capital *K* and labour *L*, TFP growth for Malaysia can be estimated. It should be noted that the four different forms of production function presented earlier (standard, standard with human capital, standard with openness, and standard with openness and human capital) have produced different α values. They are shown in Table 9.10.

Table 9.10 Coefficient of α and $1 - \alpha$

Method	α	$1 - \alpha$
Standard production function	0.55	0.45
Production function with human capital	0.39	0.61
Production function with openness	0.42	0.58
Production function with openness & human capital	0.43	0.57

The results in Table 9.10 indicate that the addition of openness and human capital into the standard production function appears to have decreased the value of α from 0.55 to 0.43. The findings suggest that in addition to capital and labour, openness and human capital are important factors in the determination of Malaysia's growth. Compared to the α value of 0.55 in the standard production function, the inclusion of human capital saw the α value dropped to 0.39 but the inclusion of openness was followed by a rise to 0.42. The best estimate of α, given that both significant variables are included, is 0.43. Table 9.11 summarizes TFP growth for Malaysia based on the different forms of production function.

Table 9.11   TFP growth for Malaysia, 1963–98

Method	TFP growth
Standard production function	0.025
Production function with human capital	0.035
Production function with openness	0.034
Production function with openness & human capital	0.033

The results in Table 9.11 show that openness and human capital are important factors to take into account in the determination of Malaysia's growth, as shown by the higher TFP value when openness and human capital are included than that estimated from the standard production function. The above results suggest that the best estimate of TFP growth for Malaysia is 3.3 per cent per year.

CONCLUSION

The findings in this chapter have highlighted the sensitivity of TFP estimates to the value of α. In general, the lower the value of α, the higher is the estimate of TFP growth. In the Malaysian case, the declining value of α is driven by the quality of the labour force brought about by international trade. This helps to explain why enormous effort has been devoted to the achievement of accuracy in estimating α. On the one hand, the traditional approach focuses on the construction of capital stock by augmenting capital with a quality component. This has not been an easy task, as indicated by the 'capital controversy' of the late 1960s and early 1970s. On the other hand, the endogenous growth proponents argued for the need to incorporate other variables into the standard Solow (1957) production function. One such variable is human capital, particularly with reference to the quality component of labour. Perhaps the time is ripe to revisit the accumulationists' view on the 'East Asian miracle' with the incorporation of international trade. Since trade constitutes a large proportion of GDP in many of the East Asian economies, leaving trade out of the analysis would bias α, which in turn would bias TFP estimation downwards.

This study found higher education to be insignificant in the Malaysian growth experience during 1963–98. This does not imply that higher education is unimportant to Malaysia's economic development. What is suggested is that Malaysia's economic structure over the period of 1963–98 had not, on average, the capacity to utilize a highly educated labour force effectively.[21] In such circumstances, primary education appears to be far more important than secondary and tertiary education for economic growth.[22] If manufacturing is taken as the engine of growth and knowledge is its driver, then it would be natural to expect that the accumulation of knowledge is, to a great extent, brought about by a highly trained and educated labour force. This is not the case for Malaysia,[23] despite the fact that the manufacturing sector contributed more than 50 per cent of GDP and 76.2 per cent of exports in 1998 (Ministry of Finance, Malaysia, 1999). It is, in fact, the lower-educated proportion of the labour force which largely propelled the growth of the manufacturing sector. Although Malaysia's industrialization initiatives were implemented in the early 1970s, its contribution to the nation's GDP remained relatively small compared to other sectors until the early 1990s. It could well be, however, that in the latter years of the sample, Malaysia had reached a level where higher education became important. However, a sufficiently long time series does not yet exist to test this.

Perhaps of more importance for long-run growth is the significant role played by openness in the economy. In the early stages of development, opening the economy up could generate enormous benefits, as witnessed in Malaysia's growth in TFP. Despite the fact that both openness of the economy and education are found to be significant to Malaysia's growth (in addition to capital and labour) between 1963 and 1998, the state of technological advancement of TFP in Malaysia appears to have been brought about more by openness of the economy than by domestic education. Although the establishment of an R&D-based structure of production is important for a nation's long-run economic growth (Romer, 1990; Grossman and Helpman, 1991; Aghion and Howitt, 1992; Nelson, 1996), it is time-consuming and, in most cases, is beyond the capacity of developing economies in terms of resources and labour power. However, through openness, less-developed economies with appropriate trade policies could harness new technology minus the R&D establishment costs. It may not be the latest technology, but nonetheless, it is often superior to that existing in the developing economies. Grossman and Helpman (1990, p. 91) have stated that:

the less developed countries *potentially* stand the most to gain from their international relationships, since in principle these countries can draw upon the large stock of knowledge capital already accumulated in the industrialized world.

In short, education alone is not enough for long-run growth, and may not be productive if development policy is not accommodated by an efficient trade policy. Based on the results, it could be inferred that economic growth in Malaysia is a learning-by-doing process brought about by international trade.

Finally, in an era of rapid globalization, it is not appropriate to conduct TFP analysis within the confines of a closed system. Doing so can bias TFP growth downwards. As demonstrated by the Malaysian experience, when the analysis was reworked to incorporate the global environment, TFP growth was found to be higher.

NOTES

[1] The estimations of TFP growth for Malaysia will cover the period 1963–98 instead of 1963–2003. This is partly due to inconsistencies in the data between the earlier and later years (particularly from 2000 onwards). There is also the need to isolate or quarantine four major events: the lagged effects of the 1997 financial crisis, September 11, the Severe Acute Respiratory Syndrome (SARS) epidemic, and the Iraq War. They all have contributed to a downturn in economic activities in Malaysia. In addition, the findings in Chapters 6 and 7 indicated that the period 1999–2003 had biased the capital coefficients downward. When the period 1999–2003 was isolated from the regression analyses, the capital coefficients were found to be significantly higher. This suggests that the four events may have accumulative effects on the production process and investment activities in the Malaysian economy during the 1999–2003 period.

These four events may also have a negative impact on the TFP growth of the Malaysian economy. In order to provide an insight into the effects of the four events on Malaysia's TFP growth, a simple test is conducted. The standard neoclassical growth model (equations 9.1 to 9.4) together with an α value of 0.55 (see Table 9.5) is used to estimate Malaysia's TFP growth for three periods: (1) 1963–2003; (2) 1963–98; and (3) 1999–2003. Period (2) looks at the TFP growth prior to the four events, and period (3) estimates TFP while the four events were taking place. TFP during 1963–2003 averaged 1 per cent per year. During the 1963–98 period, TFP averaged 2.5 per cent per year, which was significantly higher than that in period (1). TFP growth in the period 1999–2003 was found to be –1.5. This is significantly lower than that of periods (1) and (2), suggesting that the four events have impacted upon the productivity of Malaysia.

[2] This is also the case for many of the international comparison of TFP studies (Kim and Lau, 1994; World Bank, 1993; Kawai, 1994; Drysdale and Huang, 1995; Bosworth, 1996; Chen, 1997; Dowling and Summers, 1998).

[3] Furthermore, the results in Chapter 7 suggest that trade played a significant role in the productivity growth of the manufacturing sector.

[4]   The aim is to estimate the value of α based on empirical evidence rather than a predetermined value. The importance of economic theory being closely related to empirical results had been strongly argued by Kaldor. He once said:

> When I talk about the importance of empirical research, I do not want to underestimate the value of economic theory. But what I do think very strongly is that theory must be far more closely related to the results of empirical research. Far too much economic theory is based on trivial *a priori* assumptions which cannot be proved right or wrong, yet strong theoretical conclusions are derived from the models. (Kaldor in Filippini et al., 1996, p 101)

[5]   This is evident by the amount of expenditure allocated to education in order to increase access to primary, secondary and tertiary education. Between 1975 and 2003, public expenditure for education ranged between 19.4 to 25.2 per cent of total government expenditure, with an average increase of approximately 13 per cent per year in real terms over this period.

[6]   The screening hypothesis also goes under various other labels such as credentialism, educational filtering, pig-skin effect, signalling. The original contributors to this particular literature include Arrow (1973), Spence (1974), Stiglitz (1975) and Riley (1976).

[7]   For instance, when pursuing the NEP objectives, the government increased employment opportunities for Malay university graduates at the management levels in the public sector. This resulted in many 'paper-qualified' bureaucrats in the federal government doing the same type of work as those carried out by some clerks at the state and district levels (Azmeer, 1983; Osman Rani and Salleh, 1994).

[8]   The low quality of tertiary education has been acknowledged by the Malaysian authorities. In addressing this concern, the Malaysian authorities have initiated various reforms to upgrade the quality of its higher education system (as discussed in Chapter 8). In addition to the financial commitment, the Malaysian higher education system has undergone significant changes, and the core of these reforms centre around the liberalization of the education system. Since the early 1990s, the Malaysian government has moved from allowing foreign institutions to offer educational programmes in Malaysia in collaboration with local bodies to actually allowing them to establish higher educational institutions within the country.

[9]   In 1992, the share of high-technology products in Malaysian manufacturing exceeded that of Japan, Korea or Taiwan (Narayanan and Lai, 2000). According to the World Bank (1999), high-technology products constituted 67 per cent of Malaysia's total manufacturing exports in 1996. In terms of the 1997 proportion of high-tech exports as a percentage of manufacturing exports, China contributed 21 per cent, Hong Kong 29 per cent, Japan 38 per cent, Korea 39 per cent, the US 44 per cent and Malaysia 67 per cent.

[10] According to Jones (1995), the number of scientists and engineers engaged in R&D in the US has grown from less than 200 000 to almost 1 million. Japan experienced an increase from 120 000 in 1965 to over 400 000 in 1987.

[11] From Robert M. Solow, *Growth Theory: An Exposition*, 2000 Oxford University Press, New York. By permission of Oxford University Press, Inc.

12 An increase in capital investment from k^* to k^*_1, as depicted in Figure 2.1 in Chapter 2 will shift the $sf(k)$ curve upwards to $s_1f(k)$, which in the process raises output y.

13 A large part of productivity growth generated by international trade is facilitated by domestic absorptive capacity made possible by higher levels of human capital.

14 During 1989–98, exports averaged more than 85 per cent of GDP.

15 This does not imply that the neoclassical growth model is no longer suitable to analyse economic growth. On the country, this approach, if specified correctly, still provides a valuable insight into the growth process. As pointed out by Crafts (1997, p. 68): 'improved by new ideas ... it may be possible to refine and extend the estimates of the growth accounting pioneers'.

16 Detailed analysis for this Keynesian approach is found in Solow (1960) and Gapinski (1982, 1998).

17 The model will not incorporate a measurement of R&D (Romer, 1986, 1990) because the resources devoted to domestic R&D sector were limited prior to 1990, and as such would not provide a meaningful analysis.

18 Nehru and Dhareshwar (1993) set a depreciation rate at 0.04. An annual depreciation rate of 0.05 is used, based on the investment decisions and accounting practices of Malaysian firms.

19 The coefficients of ECM (– 1) measure short-run deviation of economic growth from the long-run equilibrium level.

20 If this is the case, it raises new doubts on the high returns to tertiary education that are enjoyed by the Malaysian society. Labour productivity did not appear to be derived from the expansion in the tertiary education. The results suggest that the vast resources devoted to tertiary education may not have been allocated in the most efficient manner. In fact, several authors have questioned the quality of higher-level education and the affirmative education policy in Malaysia (Mehmet and Hoong, 1986; Osman Rani and Salleh, 1994; Snodgrass, 1998).

21 Another possible reason for the insignificant results on tertiary education (despite the high rates of return) is that more than 80 per cent of graduates from local tertiary institutions were employed in the public sector, which on the whole did not contribute directly to manufacturing output.

22 This could be the reason why growth analysis tends to favour primary and secondary education over higher education as a proxy for human capital (Mankiw et al., 1992; World Bank, 1993; Barro, 1997).

23 This is also consistent with many other countries including the member countries of the OECD in their early stages of economic development.

10. Summary of findings and discussions

This concluding chapter summarizes the main findings of the book and highlights some issues for future research. Firstly, initial conditions were found to be important to economic growth. This is because they not only allow economic agents to perform their economic function efficiently, but also because the state of the system today can profoundly impact on how the system will behave in the future. The Malaysian experience demonstrates that initial conditions, in the form of political instability, can have a significant impact on the initial stages of economic development. Briefly, during the initial stages of Malaysia's economic development, the inherited complex social and political conditions hampered the pace of development. The arguments presented in Chapter 4 emphasized that political instability must first be minimized prior to economic 'take-off'. Political stability is achieved through the initiatives put in place by the state as found in the various Five-Year Plans (Chapters 4 and 5). For instance, poverty, which was believed to be a source of ethnic tension and therefore political instability (Chapter 4), was initially addressed through the expansion of the agricultural sector. However, the decline in commodity prices (particularly rubber and tin) meant that the state had to seek an alternative route to minimize ethnic conflicts. The Malaysian government subsequently embarked on the expansion of the manufacturing sector (Chapter 5). Despite the success of the New Economic Policy (NEP) in achieving political stability through poverty eradication and inter-ethnic redistribution (Rasiah and Shari, 2001), there have been many criticisms of the large amount of public expenditure allocated to achieve the NEP's main objectives (Jomo, 1990, 1994; Gomez and Jomo, 1997). In addition, there is also the issue that the key policy instrument used by the Malaysian government to reduce interracial economic differences (Chapters 4 and 5) is the discriminatory allocation of public expenditure in favour of the Malays (Lim, 1973; Jomo, 1990).

On the one hand, by taking efficiency as the main criterion to judge the allocation of public expenditure on restructuring the Malaysian society, the ethnic-based distribution policies can be considered to be a failure (Jomo, 1994; Gomez and Jomo, 1997). On the other hand, as political stability forms the basis for efficient economic production (Galbraith, 1983; Mauro, 1995; Barro, 1997; Keefer and Knack, 1998; Darity and Nembhard, 2000; Yi Feng, 2001), and given that initial conditions and shocks matter (Keynes, 1936; Kaldor, 1972; Nelson, 1996; Crafts, 1997; Setterfield, 1998), then the amount of expenditure (which averaged about RM2.2 billion per year or approximately 2 per cent of total government expenditure, during the 1971–90 period) allocated to establish stability was a small price to pay in return for rapid economic growth.

Perhaps the African experiences strengthen further the case for the maintenance of political stability during the initial stages of economic development. As argued by several authors (Easterly and Levine, 1997; Collier and Gunning, 1998; Ndulu and O'Connell, 1999), the reason Africa is poor is that it is politically unstable.

With reference to the Solow–Swan growth model, political instability can affect the savings variable. When a political regime is unstable, consumers reduce savings and investors decrease investment. With reference to the endogenous growth models, political instability can have a negative impact on human capital accumulation by hindering and disrupting education and physical capital investment. A decline in physical capital investment would mean a decline in learning-by-doing activities as suggested by Kaldor (1960), Arrow (1962) and Romer (1986, 1990). Hence, further research is warranted on the extension of the causal relationship between political democracy and economic growth (Lipset, 1959; Friedman, 1962; Barro, 1997), particularly one that traces the impact of political stability on the evolution of technological progress. The findings in Chapter 9 show that human capital and international trade have had an impact on the growth rates of TFP, and if political instability acts as a deterrent to investment, then it would be expected to have some impact on the evolution of technological progress.

It has been shown that Malaysia's economic growth is driven by the evolution of its production structures toward activities that are associated with increasing returns. Kaldor (1966), as discussed in Chapters 3, 6 and 7, stipulated manufacturing as an engine of growth as it exhibits increasing returns, while the agricultural sector is subject to decreasing returns. This enquiry confirms Kaldor's propositions in that Malaysia's growth was positively related to the expansion of its manufacturing sector. The results suggest that as the Malaysian economy shifted towards higher levels of productivity, the usage of labour declined with a given level of output. This pattern of output growth tends to be associated with labour-saving production techniques. The declining elasticity of employment in relation to output suggests that as the Malaysian economy matures, the capital stock shifts or transforms from a stock which is appropriate for labour-intensive production into one appropriate for less labour-intensive production.

A profound implication of adopting a labour-saving method of production lies with the expansion of capital investment, resulting in the rapid expansion of the manufacturing sector in Malaysia. Capital expansion is an important source of technological progress (Chapter 3). According to the assimilation school of thought (Chapter 2), technological progress is embodied in new capital and cannot be separated from the expansion of capital inputs. Even replacement capital is associated with technical progress (Kaldor and Mirrlees, 1962; Salter, 1966; Singh, 1998). In Kaldor's technical progress function (Chapters 3 and 6), labour-saving production techniques are associated with the evolution of technological progress. Furthermore, capital investment increases Arrow's learning-by-doing activities, which in the process raises technological progress, leading to higher growth rates of output. Hence, the declining coefficient of employment in the manufacturing sector can be explained by the proposition that switching towards a labour-saving production technique will lead to the expansion of capital investment. Through the process of learning-by-doing (Arrow, 1962; Romer, 1986, 1990), labour is able to harness the new technology that is embodied in new capital equipment and, in the process, increase labour productivity and therefore output growth. Following this type of technological progress, a higher K/L ratio will not necessarily lead to a decline in employment, as predicted under a neoclassical framework. The findings in Chapter 6 show that the Malaysian growth experience is consistent with this type of growth dynamics.

Chapter 7 provides empirical evidence that Malaysia's economic growth is an endogenous process. The reported estimates of Kaldor's coefficient show Malaysia's capacity to undertake structural changes that are associated with increasing returns. The significance of the manufacturing sector in the generation of the nation's economic growth and employment is confirmed for Malaysia. Overall productivity growth in the Malaysian economy was found to be positively correlated with employment growth in the manufacturing sector, and negatively correlated with employment growth outside the manufacturing sector. The results also suggest that the growth of Malaysia's manufacturing sector was not constrained by a shortage in labour. The declining labour coefficient in the agricultural sector suggests that excess labour had been transferred to other sectors of the economy without causing a decline in the output of the agricultural sector.

The continuous supply of labour was made possible by the rural–urban migration of workers and a rise in female participation rates (Chapters 4, 5 and 6). The Malaysian experience suggests that a higher utilization of female labour could accelerate the change in the sector's share of labour input and therefore its output shares. From a policy perspective, the key role assigned to the manufacturing sector through a series of industrial plans initiated by the Malaysian government, particularly from the early 1980s onwards, has been crucial to the development of its manufacturing sector. An important lesson that could be learnt from Malaysia's experience is that a developing country that neglects its manufacturing sector is more likely to experience a slower growth rate. Thus, the growing polarization of the world between the rich and poor countries can be explained by the differences in the production structures between increasing returns activities (mainly manufacturing) and diminishing returns activities (mainly agricultural).

Human capital accumulation played an important role in Malaysia's economic growth. Chapter 8 argued the positive contribution of education to the evolution of the nation's production structures. The wide earning differentials, of about three times, between secondary- and tertiary-educated workers give an indication of the productivity of Malaysian labour. This productivity gain is also reflected in both the private and social rates of return to higher education. This is consistent with the findings in Chapters 5, 6 and 7, in that the shifts in production structure and employment patterns reflect the rise in wages. From a policy perspective, Malaysia's education policy provided an avenue by which skills could be constantly upgraded in accordance with the structural transformation of the economy as well as the absorption of new technology in the production process.

However, the results in Chapter 9 suggest that the productivity of labour cannot be entirely due to the variation in wages between the lower and higher educated workforce. Chapter 9 found higher education to be of limited significance. It was largely the lower-educated proportion of the labour force (primary educated), which propelled the growth of the manufacturing sector, suggesting a learning-by-doing growth process which, in turn, is driven by international trade. Technological progress as captured by TFP growth contributed an average of 3.3 per cent to economic growth during the period 1963–98. The findings in Chapter 9 suggest an important policy consideration. A weak R&D or knowledge base does not necessarily mean lower economic growth as postulated by the R&D models of Romer (1986, 1990). The dominant perception that only R&D could propel productivity growth may not be as clear-cut as was once thought according to several authors (Solow, 1994, 2000; Archibugi and Michie, 1995; Jones, 1995) and the results of this book. Instead, the Malaysian experience demonstrates that opening the economy up to the global communities accelerated Malaysia's TFP growth by increasing learning-by-doing activities. It follows that technological progress in Malaysia during the period 1963–98 is consistent with the types proposed by Young (1928), Myrdal (1957), Kaldor (1960), Arrow (1962), Kaldor and Mirrlees (1962), Salter (1966) and Grossman and Helpman (1991).

FURTHER RESEARCH

Economic growth is a complex and dynamic process. It is not entirely confined to the achievement of technological progress as propagated by the neoclassical and endogenous growth frameworks. There are many other factors which could affect the growth process. Based on the findings, further research is needed in the following areas:

1. The role of history in economic growth. This is important because the growth trajectory is a historical process (Robinson, 1962; Kaldor and Mirrlees, 1962; Salter, 1966; Kaldor, 1970, 1972, 1985; Nelson, 1996, 1997; Crafts, 1997; Setterfield, 1998). Extending both the neoclassical and endogenous growth models to incorporate the cumulative effects on growth will contribute to a better understanding of long-run growth.

2. Economic growth is often constructed as an equilibrium process. This is fine if full employment exists, and the growth trend is linear. But this is rarely the case. As pointed out by Harcourt (1988, p. 161):

> to pose economic questions in the usual way of whether there is an equilibrium (or several) and, if so, whether, it is (they are) stable was to place our thinking in a straightjacket.

According to Solow:

> the basic neoclassical model usually has a unique steady state, and all equilibrium paths converge to a steady state ... That is not an airtight statement ... clinging to steady states fosters bad intellectual habits. The main one is the feeling that a causal factor that does not affect the steady-state growth is somewhat uninteresting or trivial. So one invents formulations that will do the trick, even if they have little else to recommend them. (2000, pp. 181–2, *Growth Theory: An Exposition*. By permission of Oxford University Press, Inc)

Nelson (1997, p. 33) pointed out that to 'conform to a general equilibrium model may restrict what we know about how economies grow rather than expand our knowledge'. Hence, by opening up growth analysis to disequilibrium states, a broader and deeper understanding of growth is possible. Further research is warranted on issues which could affect growth trajectories.

3. Better proxies are needed for the estimation of total factor productivity growth. The findings in Chapter 9 highlighted the sensitivity of total factor productivity estimates to the value of α. This may explain why enormous effort has been devoted to the achievement of accuracy in estimating α. However, much of the recent research centred around the labour variable. As α or the capital share is the main determining factor in total factor productivity growth, research on the construction of capital share is long overdue. As pointed out by Crafts (1997, p. 68): 'improved by new ideas ... it may be possible to refine and extend the estimates of the growth accounting pioneers'.

4. The role of aggregate demand in driving productivity growth. One criticism so far of the models used in this book is that they are exclusively focused on the supply side, based on the allocation of resources between present and future consumption. This form of

analysis is unsatisfactory because the decision to allocate resources
between present and future consumption cannot be made or explained
independently of the growth of effective demand (Casaratto, 1999).
Above all, growth of effective demand stimulates innovation. Brouwer
and Kleinknecht (1999) reported that demand growth in a firm's sector
of principal activity has a positive influence on changes in a firm's
R&D effort. Their findings are consistent with Schmockler's (1969)
propositions. Thus, further research on the relationship between aggregate
demand and innovations could shed new light on technological progress.
Fluctuations in aggregate demand will not only have effects on short-run
production and employment, but they can also enhance or hamper
innovation. An area in which more research is warranted is how
recessions can have permanent hysteresis effects on long-run growth
because they retard R&D and learning-by-doing. The importance of
aggregate demand is also acknowledged by Solow:

> So why should it be important to incorporate a serious demand side in
> models of economic growth, apart from analytical tidiness? For one thing,
> observed growth paths are not smooth. They are punctuated by recessions,
> large and small, and by periods of excess demand. How do these
> macroeconomic fluctuations affect the growth path itself? There are obvious
> ways: Rates of investment, and therefore the evolution of capital stocks, are
> affected by short-run fluctuations. (2000, p. 184, *Growth Theory: An
> Exposition.* By permission of Oxford University Press, Inc)

Hence, further research should be devoted to trace the path of potential
output. As Krugman (1998, pp. 156–8) observed:

> one developing country after another has experienced a recession that at
> least temporarily undoes years of economic progress, and finds that the
> conventional policy responses only make things worse. Once again, the
> question of how to keep demand adequate to make use of the economy's
> capacity has become crucial ... If we want to see more economic miracles,
> more nations making the transition from abject poverty to the hope of a
> decent life, we had better find answers to the newly intractable problems of
> depression economics.

A final remark by Young (1928) sums up the pivotal role of aggregate
demand on economic growth:

> It is dangerous to assign to any single factor the leading role in that
> continuing economic revolution which has taken the modern world so far
> away from the world of a few hundred years ago. But is there any other
> factor which has a better claim to that role than the persistent search for

markets? No other hypothesis so well unites economic history and economic theory. (p. 536)

Finally, the issues covered in this book represent only a small constituent of what is thought to be driving output growth, and it is hoped that its findings will provide the basis for rich future developments.

Appendices

Appendix 7.1 Kaldor's three propositions: empirical evidence

Kaldor's First Proposition

There is a strong correlation in all advanced economies between the growth of manufacturing output, g_m, and rate of growth of GDP, g_{GDP}.

$$g_{GDP} = 1.153 + 0.614\, g_m \quad r^2 = 0.959 \tag{A7.1}$$
$$(0.040)$$

(standard error in parenthesis)

To reinforce the above relationship, Kaldor (1966) added an extra assumption of a strong correlation between non-manufacturing output growth, g_{nm}, and manufacturing output:

$$g_{nm} = \alpha + \beta g_m \tag{A7.2}$$

$$g_{nm} = 1.142 + 0.550 g_m \quad r^2 = 0.824 \tag{A7.3}$$
$$(0.080)$$

Kaldor's Second Proposition

Growth of labour productivity in the manufacturing sector, p_m, is positively related to growth of manufacturing output, g_m. Kaldor (1966) also assumed that growth rate of manufacturing output is equal to the sum of productivity growth, p_m, and employment growth, e_m, which can be expressed as:

$$g_m = p_m + e_m \tag{A7.4}$$
where
$$p_m = \alpha + \beta\, g_m \tag{A7.5}$$
$$e_m = -\alpha + (1 - \beta) g_m \tag{A7.6}$$

Only if equations (A7.5) and (A7.6) are equal will the estimates be the same. Sum of the constants of equations (A7.5) and (A7.6) should be zero, and sum of the regression coefficients be unity, irrespective of the correlations involved (Kaldor, 1966).

$$p_m = 1.035 + 0.484\, g_m \quad r^2 = 0.826 \tag{A7.7}$$
$$(0.070)$$

$$e_m = -1.028 + 0.516\, g_m \quad r^2 = 0.844 \tag{A7.8}$$
$$(0.070)$$

Kaldor's Third Proposition

Kaldor's (1966) estimates also showed that overall productivity growth, p_{GDP}, is positively correlated with employment growth in the manufacturing sector, e_m, and negatively related with growth of employment in the non-manufacturing sector, e_{nm}:

$$p_{GDP} = 2.899 + 0.821e_m - 1.183e_{nm} \qquad r^2 = 0.842 \qquad \text{(A7.9)}$$
$$(0.367).$$

Appendix 9.1

Table A 9.1 ARDL estimates of the standard production function

Regressor	Coefficient	Standard error	T-ratio (Prob)
LY (−1)	1.0442	0.17347	6.0194 (0.000)
LY (−2)	−0.27847	0.16838	−1.6538 (0.109)
LK	0.76768	0.076832	9.9917 (0.000)
LK (−1)	−0.97749	0.16869	−5.7945 (0.000)
LK (−2)	0.339	0.14594	2.3229 (0.027)
Constant	0.33346	0.15862	2.1022 (0.044)
Time	0.0043433	0.0047729	0.91000 (0.370)
R-Squared	0.99509	R-Bar-Squared	0.99407
S.E. of Regression	0.058166	F-stat. $F(6, 29)$	979.2319 (0.000)
Mean of Dependent Variable	4.3544	S.D. of Dependent Variable	0.75548
Residual Sum of Squares	0.098116	Equation Log-likelihood	55.2104
Akaike Information Criterion	48.2104	Schwarz Bayesian Criterion	42.6681
DW-statistic	2.0345		

Diagnostic tests		
Test statistics	LM version	F version
Serial Correlation	CHSQ (1) = 0.84145 (0.772)	$F(1, 28) = 0.065599$ (0.800)
Functional Form	CHSQ (1) = 4.8033 (0.028)	$F(1, 28) = 4.3111$ (0.047)
Normality	CHSQ (2) = 1.9531 (0.377)	Not applicable
Heteroscedasticity	CHSQ (1) = 1.0198 (0.313)	$F(1, 34) = 0.99123$ (0.326)

Notes: Autoregressive Distributed Lag Estimates ARDL (2, 2) selected based on Akaike Information Criterion. Dependent variable is LY. 36 observations used for estimation from 1963 to 1998.

Appendix 9.2

Table A9.2   ECM equation of the standard production function

Regressor	Coefficient	Standard error	T-ratio (Prob)
dLY1	0.27847	0.16838	1.6538 (.109)
dLK	0.76768	0.076832	9.9917 (.000)
dLK1	− 0.33900	0.14594	− 2.3229 (.027)
dConstant	0.33346	0.15862	2.1022 (.044)
dTime	0.0043433	0.0047729	0.91000 (.370)
ecm (− 1)	− 0.23426	0.099576	− 2.3526 (.025)

Notes: Error correction representation for the selected ARDL model ARDL (2,2) selected based on Akaike information criterion. Dependent variable is dLY. 36 observations used for estimation from 1963 to 1998.

Appendix 9.3

Table A9.3 ARDL estimates of the standard production function with human capital

Regressor	Coefficient		Standard error	T-ratio (Prob)
LY (– 1)	0.65137		0.10181	6.3978(.000)
LK	0.7598		0.074699	10.1715 (.000)
LK (– 1)	– 0.62099		0.081637	– 7.6067 (.000)
e1	0.51446		0.21659	2.3752 (.024)
Constant	0.80945		0.20177	4.0117 (.000)
Time	0.020074		0.0056721	3.5391 (.001)
R-Squared	0.99504		R-Bar-Squared	0.99421
S.E. of Regression	0.057492		F-stat. F(5, 30)	1202.8 (0.000)
Mean of Dependent Variable	4.3544		S.D. of Dependent Variable	0.75548
Residual Sum of Squares	0.099159		Equation Log-likelihood	55.0202
Akaike Information Criterion	49.0202		Schwarz Bayesian Criterion	44.2696
DW-statistic	1.5828			

Diagnostic tests		
Test statistics	LM version	F version
Serial Correlation	CHSQ (1) = 1.7390 (0.187)	F(1, 29) = 0.4720 (0.235))
Functional Form	CHSQ (1) = 0.70077 (0.403)	F(1, 29) = 0.57572 (0.454)
Normality	CHSQ (2) = 7.2914 (0.026))	Not applicable
Heteroscedasticity	CHSQ (1) = 0.33246 (0.564)	F(1, 34) = 0.31691 (0.577)

Notes: Autoregressive Distribution Lag Estimates ARDL (1,1,0) selected based on Akaike Information Criterion. Dependent variable is LY. 36 observations used for estimation from 1963 to 1998.

Appendix 9.4

Table A9.4   ECM equation with human capital

Regressor	Coefficient	Standard error	T-ratio (Prob)
dLK	0.75980	0.074699	10.1715 (.000)
dE_1	0.51446	21659	2.3752 (.024)
dConstant	80945	20177	4.0117 (.000)
dTime	0.020074	0.0056721	3.5391 (.001)
ecm (-1)	-0.34863	.10181	-3.4242 (.002)

Notes: Error correction representation for the selected ARDL model ARDL (1,1,0) selected based on Akaike information criterion Dependent variable is dLY. 36 observations used for estimation from 1963 to 1998.

Appendix 9.5

Table A9.5   ARDL estimates of the standard production function with openness

Regressor	Coefficient	Standard error	T-ratio (Prob)
LY (– 1)	0.96082	0.18552	5.1790 (0.000)
LY (– 2)	– 0.3672	0.17434	– 2.1063 (0.045)
LK	0.70957	0.078589	9.0289 (0.000)
LK (– 1)	– 0.89716	0.17823	– 5.0338 (0.000)
LK (– 2)	0.35995	0.14594	2.4664 (0.021)
O	0.094169	0.073276	1.2851 (0.210)
O (– 1)	– 0.17076	0.15944	– 1.0710 (0.294)
O (– 2)	0.31454	0.15608	2.0153 (0.054)
Constant	0.826	0.3052	2.7064 (0.012)
Time	0.0070987	0.0047907	1.4818 (0.150)

R-Squared	0.99602	R-Bar-Squared	0.99464
S.E. of Regression	0.055293	F-stat. $F(9, 26)$	723.1178 (0.000)
Mean of Dependent Variable	4.3544	S.D. of Dependent Variable	0.75548
Residual Sum of Squares	0.079489	Equation Log-likelihood	58.9999
Akaike Information. Criterion	48.9999	Schwarz Bayesian Criterion	41.0823
DW-statistic	2.0473		

Diagnostic tests		
Test statistics	LM version	F version
Serial Correlation	CHSQ (1) = 0.13271 (0.716)	$F(1, 25) = 0.092502$ (0.764)
Functional Form	CHSQ (1) = 1.3561 (0.244)	$F(1, 25) = 0.97861$ (0.332)
Normality	CHSQ (2) = 1.0203 (0.600)	Not applicable
Heteroscedasticity	CHSQ (1) = 0.040873 (0.840)	$F(1, 34) = 0.038646$ (0.845)

Notes: Autoregressive Distributed Lag Estimates ARDL (2, 2, 2) selected based on Akaike Information Criterion. Dependent variable is LY. 36 observations used for estimation from 1963 to 1998.

Appendix 9.6

Table A9.6　ECM equation with openness

Regressor	Coefficient	Standard error	T-ratio (Prob)
dLY1	0.36720	0.17434	2.1063(.044)
dLK	0.70957	0.078589	9.0289 (.000)
dLK1	− 0.35995	0.14594	− 2.4664 (.020)
dO	0.094169	0.073276	1.2851 (.209)
dO1	− 0.31454	0.15608	− 2.0153 (0.54)
dConstant	0.82600	0.30520	2.7064 (.011)
dTime	0.0070987	0.0047907	1.4818 (.150)
ecm (− 1)	− 0.40638	0.13873	− 2.9294 (.007)

Notes:　Error correction representation for the selected ARDL model ARDL (2,2,2) selected based on Akaike information criterion. Dependent variable is dLY. 36 observations used for estimation from 1963 to 1998.

Appendix 9.7

Table A9.7   ARDL estimates of α in the standard production function with openness and human capital

Regressor	Coefficient	Standard error	T-ratio (Prob)
LY (– 1)	0.79271	0.18948	4.1837 (0.000)
LY (– 2)	– 0.32925	0.16374	– 2.0108 (0.055)
LK	0.73988	0.074689	9.9061 (0.000)
LK (– 1)	– 0.77454	0.1756	– 4.4109 (0.000)
LK (– 2)	0.26736	0.1427	1.8736 (0.073)
e₁	0.46745	0.21321	2.1925 (0.038)
O	0.11451	0.069063	1.6580 (0.110)
O (– 1)	– 0.1779	0.14894	– 1.1944 (0.244)
O (– 2)	0.32768	0.14589	2.2460 (0.034)
Constant	1.2392	0.3417	3.6265 (0.001)
Time	0.017616	0.0065598	2.6855 (0.013)

R-Squared	0.99666	R-Bar-Squared	0.99533
S.E. of Regression	0.051641	F-stat $F(10, 25)$	746.5811 (0.000)
Mean of Dependent Variable	4.3544	S.D. of Dependent Variable	0.75548
Residual Sum of Squares	0.06667	Equation Log-likelihood	62.1656
Akaike Information. Criterion	51.1656	Schwarz Bayesian Criterion	42.4562
DW-statistic	2.1419		

Diagnostic tests		
Test statistics	LM version	F version
Serial Correlation	CHSQ (1) = 1.0741 (0.300)	F(1, 24) = 0.73811 (0.399)
Functional Form	CHSQ (1) = 0.22023 (0.639)	F(1, 24) = 0.14772 (0.704)
Normality	CHSQ (2) = 1.4780 (0.478)	Not applicable
Heteroscedasticity	CHSQ (1) = 0.11732 (0.732)	F(1, 34) = 0.11117 (0.741)

Notes: Autoregressive Distributed Lag Estimates ARDL (2, 2, 0, 2) selected based on Akaike Information Criterion. Dependent variable is LY. 36 observations used for estimation from 1963 to 1998.

Appendix 9.8

Table A9.8   ECM equation with openness and human capital

Regressor	Coefficient	Standard Error	T-Ratio (Prob)
dLY1	0.32925	0.16374	2.0108 (.054)
dLK	0.73988	0.074689	9.9061 (.000)
dLK1	− 0.26736	0.14270	− 1.8736 (.072)
dE1	0.46745	0.21321	2.1925 (.037)
dO	0.11451	0.069063	1.6580 (.109)
dO1	− 0.32768	0.14589	− 2.2460 (.033)
dConstant	1.2392	0.34170	3.6265 (.001)
dTime	0.017616	0.0065598	2.6855 (.012)
ecm (− 1)	− 0.53654	0.14252	− 3.7647 (.001)

Notes: Error correction representation for the selected ARDL model ARDL (2,2,0,2) selected based on Akaike information criterion. Dependent variable is dLY. 36 observations used for estimation from 1963 to 1998.

References

Abramovitz, M. (1986), 'Catching-up, forging ahead, and falling behind', *Journal of Economic History*, 36, 385–406.

Aghion, P. and P. Howitt (1992), 'A model of growth through creative destruction', *Econometrica*, 60, 325–51.

Aghion, P. and P. Howitt (1998), *Endogenous Growth Theory*, MIT Press, Cambridge, MA.

Aghion, P. and J.G. Williamson (1998), *Growth, Inequality and Globalization: Theory, History and Policy*, Cambridge University Press, Cambridge.

Alavi, R. (1996), *Industrialisation in Malaysia: Import Substitution and Infant Industry Performance*, Routledge, London.

Ali, A. (1992), *Malaysia Industrialization The Quest for Technology*, Oxford University Press, Singapore.

Anand, S. (1983), *Inequality and Poverty in Malaysia: Measurement and Decomposition*, Oxford University Press, Oxford.

Archibugi, D. and J. Michie, (1995), 'The globalisation of technology: a new taxonomy', *Cambridge Journal of Economics*, 19 (1), 121–40.

Ariffin, J. (1992), *Women and Development in Malaysia*, Pelanduk Publications, Petaling Jaya.

Arrow, K. (1962), 'The economic implications of learning by doing', *Review of Economic Studies*, 29, 155–73.

Arrow, K. (1973), 'Higher education as a filter', *Journal of Public Economics*, 2 (3), 193–216.

Arunatilake, N., S. Jayasuriya and S. Kelegama (2001), 'The economic cost of the war in Sri Lanka', *World Development*, 29 (9), 1483–500.

Aschauer, D.A. (1989), 'Is public expenditure productive?' *Journal of Monetary Economics*, 23 (2), 177–200.

Asian Development Bank (1993), *Asian Development Outlook*, Oxford University Press, Manila.

Asian Development Bank (1997), *Emerging Asia: Changes and Challenges*, Oxford University Press, Manila.

Asian Development Bank (1998), *Asian Development Outlook*, Oxford University Press, Manila.

Azmeer, R. (1983), 'The optimization of human resources management toward achieving greater productivity', paper presented at the National Seminar on Public Sector Accounting, Malaysian Association of Public Accounting, Kuala Lumpur.

Bank Negara Malaysia, *Annual Report,* (various years 1982–2004), Percetakan Nasional Malaysia Berhad, Kuala Lumpur.

Bank Negara Malaysia (1994), *Money and Banking in Malaysia*, Percetakan Nasional Malaysia Berhad, Kuala Lumpur.

Barker, B. and A. Goto (1998), 'Technological systems, innovation and transfer', in G. Thompson (ed.), *Economic Dynamism in the Asia-Pacific*, Routledge, London, pp. 250–71.

Barro, R.J. (1989), *Economic Growth in a Cross Section of Countries*, National Bureau of Economic Research Working Paper 2855.

Barro, R.J. (1990), 'Government spending in a simple model of endogenous growth', *Journal of Political Economy*, 98 (5/Part II) s103–s125.

Barro, R.J. (1991), 'Economic growth in a cross-section of countries', *Quarterly Journal of Economics*, 105 (2), 407–43.

Barro, R.J. (1997), *Determinants of Economic Growth: A Cross-Country Empirical Study*, MIT Press, Cambridge, MA.

Barro, R.J. (1999), 'Determinants of democracy', *Journal of Political Economy*, 107 (6/Pt 2), s158–s183.

Barro, R.J. and J.W. Lee (1993), 'International comparisons of educational attainment', *Journal of Monetary Economics*, 32 (3), 363–94.

Barro, R.J. and X. Sala-i-Martin (1991), 'Convergence across states and regions', *Brookings Papers on Economic Activity*, 1, 107–82.

Barro, R.J. and X. Sala-i-Martin (1992), 'Convergence', *Journal of Political Economy*, 100 (2), 223–51.

Barro, R.J. and X. Sala-i-Martin (1995), *Economic Growth*, McGraw-Hill, New York.

Baumol, W. (1986), 'Productivity growth, convergence, and welfare: what the long-run data show', *American Economic Review*, 76 (5), 1072–085.

Beaudry, P. and D. Green (1998), *What is Driving US and Canadian Wages: Exogenous Technical Change or Endogenous Choice of Technique?* National Bureau of Economic Research Working Paper 6853.

Benhabib, J. and M.M. Spiegel (1994), 'The role of human capital in economic development: evidence from aggregate cross-country data', *Journal of Monetary Economics*, 34 (2), 143–73.

Bernate, G.A. (1996), 'Does manufacturing matter? A spatial econometric view of Kaldor's Laws', *Journal of Regional Science*, 36, 463–77.

Bils, M. and P.J. Klenow (2000), 'Does schooling cause growth?' *American Economic Review*, 90 (5), 1160–83.

Blaug, M. (1972), *The Correlation Between Education and Earnings: What Does it Signify?* New York University Press, New York.

Blaug, M. (1976), 'The empirical status of human capital theory: a slightly jaundiced view', *Journal of Economic Literature*, 14 (3), 827–55.

Blaug, M. (1992), *The Methodology of Economics: Or How Economists Explain*, Cambridge University Press, Cambridge.

Bosworth, B.P. (1996), 'Economic growth in East Asia: accumulation versus assimilation: comment', *Brookings Papers on Economic Activity*, 2, 197.

Bowie, A. (1988), 'Redistribution with growth? The dilemmas of state-sponsored economic development in Malaysia', *Journal of Developing Societies*, 4, 52–66.

Bowie, A. (1991), *Crossing the Industrial Divide: State, Society, and the Politics of Economic Transformation in Malaysia*, Columbia University Press, New York.

Boyer, R. and P. Petit (1981), 'Employment and productivity growth in the EEC', *Cambridge Journal of Economics*, 5 (1), 47–58.

Brouwer, E. and A. Kleinknecht (1999), 'Keynes-Plus? Effective demand and changes in firm-level R&D: an empirical note', *Cambridge Journal of Economics*, 23 (3), 385–91.

Campos, E.J. and H. Root (1996), *The Key to the Asian Miracle: Making Shared Growth Credible*, Brookings Institution, Washington, DC.

Carvalho, F. (1983), 'On the concept of time in Shacklean and Sraffian economies', *Journal of Post Keynesian Economics*, 6 (2), 265–80.

Casaratto, S. (1999), 'Savings and economic growth in neoclassical theory', *Cambridge Journal of Economics*, 23, 771–93.

Caselli, F., G. Esquivel and F. Lefort (1996), 'Reopening the convergence debate: a new look at crosscountry growth empirics', *Journal of Economic Growth*, 1, 363–89.

Casillas, L.R. (1993), 'Kaldor versus Prebisch on employment and industrialization', *Journal of Post Keynesian Economics*, 16 (2), 268–88.

Caves, R.E. and L.B. Krause (1984), *The Australian Economy: A View From the North*, Brookings Institute, Washington, DC.

Chan, G. (1996), 'The graduate and skills labour markets: dimensions of manpower management', in C.Y. Lim (ed.), *Economic Policy Management in Singapore*, Addison-Wesley, Singapore, pp. 83–103.

Chang, H.J. (1998), *The Initial Conditions of Economic Development: Comparing the East Asian and the Sub-Saharan African Experiences*, Report prepared for the UNCTAD Trade and Development Report, UNSTAD, Geneva.

Chen, E.K.Y. (1979), *Hyper-Growth in Asian Economies: A Comparative Study of Hong Kong, Japan, Korea, Singapore and Taiwan*, Macmillan, London.

Chen, E.K.Y. (1997), 'The total factor productivity debate: determinants of economic growth in East Asia', *Asian-Pacific Economic Literature*, 18–38.

Chenery, H.B. and L. Taylor (1968), 'Development patterns among countries and over time', *Review of Economics and Statistics*, 50 (4), 391–416.

Cheong, K.C. and K.C. Lim (1981), 'Implications of the transfer of technology and primary ancillary linkages: a case study of the electronics and electrical industries in Malaysia', *Jurnal Ekonomi Malaysia*, 3&4, 119-146.

Chiang, A.C. (1992), *Elements of Dynamic Optimization*, McGraw-Hill, New York.

Christensen, L.R., D. Cummings and D.W. Jorgensen (1995), 'Economic growth, 1947–1973: an international comparison', in D.W. Jorgensen (ed.), *Productivity vol.2: International Comparisons of Economic Growth*, MIT Press, Cambridge, MA, pp. 203-54.

Clague, C., P. Keefer, S. Knack and M. Olson, (1996), 'Property and contract rights in autocracies and democracies', *Journal of Economic Growth*, 1 (2), 243–76.

Collier, P. and W.J. Gunning (1998), 'Explaining African economic performance, *Journal of Economic Literature*, 37 (1), 64–111.

Collins, S.M. and B.P. Bosworth (1996), 'Economic growth in East Asia: accumulation versus assimilation', *Brookings Papers on Economic Activity*, 2, 135–203.

Cornwall, J. (1976), 'Diffusion, convergence and Kaldor's Laws, *Economic Journal*, 86 (342), 307–14.

Cornwall, J. and W. Cornwall (1992), *Structural Change and the Productivity Slowdown*, Department of Economics, Dalhousie University, Working Paper no. 92-04.

Cornwall, J. and W. Cornwall (1994), 'Growth theory and economic structure', *Economica*, 61, 237–51.

Crabtree, D. and A.P. Thirlwall (eds) (1993), *Keynes and the Role of the State*, Macmillan, London.

Crafts, N.F.R. (1997), 'Endogenous growth: lessons for and from economic history', in M.D. Kreps and K.F. Wallis (eds), *Advances in Economics and Econometrics: Theory and Applications, Seventh World Congress*, vol. 2, Cambridge University Press, Cambridge, pp. 38–78.

Cripps, T.F. and R.J. Tarling (1973), *Growth in Advanced Capitalist Economies 1950–1970*, Cambridge University Press, Cambridge.

Darity, W., Jr and J.G. Nembhard (2000), 'Racial and ethnic economic inequality: the international record', *American Economic Review*, 90 (2), 308–11.

Das, D.K. (1998), 'The dynamic growth of the electronics industry in Asia', *Journal of Asian Business*, 14 (4), 67–99.

De Long, J.B. (1988), 'Productivity growth, convergence, and welfare: comment', *American Economic Review*, 78 (5), 1138–54.

De Long, J.B. and L.H. Summers (1991), 'Equipment investment and economic growth', *Quarterly Journal of Economics*, 106, 445–502.

Denison, E.F. (1962), *Sources of Growth in the United States and the Alternatives before Us*, Supplement Paper 13, Committee for Economic Development, New York.

Denison, E.F. (1964), 'Measuring the contribution of education to economic growth', *In the Residual Factor and Economic Growth*, OECD, Paris, pp. 13–55.

Denison, E.F. (1967), *Why Growth Rates Differ*, Brookings Institution, Washington, DC.

Denison, E.F. (1974), *Accounting for United States Economic Growth, 1929–1969*, Brookings Institution, Washington, DC.

Department of Statistics, Malaysia, *Census of Manufacturing Industries*, (various years, 1963–73), Percetakan Nasional Malaysia Berhad, Kuala Lumpur.

Department of Statistics, Malaysia, *Yearbook of Statistics,* (various years, 1965–2004), Percetakan Nasional Malaysia Berhad, Kuala Lumpur.

Doraisami, A. (1996), 'The Malaysian economic miracle and Australia's place in Asia: what do Malaysian economists think?', *Economic Papers*, 14 (4), 29–36.

Dougherty, C. (1991), 'A comparison of productivity and economic growth in G-7 countries', PhD dissertation, Harvard University, Massachusetts.

Dowling, M. and P.M. Summers (1998), 'Total factor productivity and economic growth: issues for Asia', *Economic Record*, 74 (225), 170–85.

Dowrick, S. (1991), *Technological Catch Up and Diverging Incomes: Patterns of Economic Growth 1960–88*, Discussion Paper No. 259, Australian National University, Canberra.

Dowrick, S. and D.T. Nguyen (1989), 'OECD comparative economic growth 1950–85: catch-up and convergence', *American Economic Review*, 79 (5), 1010–30.

Drabble, J.H. (2000), *An Economic History of Malaysia, c. 1800–1990: The Transition to Modern Economic Growth*, MacMillian Press, London.

Drysdale, P. and Y. Huang (1995), 'Technological catch-up and economic growth in East Asia', *Economic Record*, 73 (222), 201–11.

Durlauf, S. and P. Johnson (1995), 'Multiple regimes and cross-country growth behaviour', *Journal of Applied Econometrics*, 10, 365–84.

Easterly, R. and S. Fischer (1995), 'The Soviet economic decline', *World Bank Economic Review*, 9 (3), 341–71.

Easterly, W., R. King, R. Levine and S. Rebelo (1991), *How Do National Policies Affect Long-Run Growth? A Research Agenda*, World Bank Paper No. 794, World Bank, Washington.

Easterly, W.R. and R. Levine (1997), 'Africa's growth tragedy: policies and ethnic divisions', *Quarterly Journal of Economics*, 122 (4), 1203–50.

Edwards, S. (1993), 'Openness, trade liberalization and growth in developing countries', *Journal of Economic Literature*, 31 (3), 1358–93.

Einarsson, T. and M.H. Marquis (1999), 'Formal training, on-the-job training and the allocation of time', *Journal of Macroeconomics*, 21 (3), 423–42.

Elias, V. (1990), *Sources of Growth: A Study of Seven Latin American Economies*, ICS Press, San Francisco.

Elmslie, B. and W. Milberg (1996), 'The productivity convergence debate: a theoretical and methodological reconsideration', *Cambridge Journal of Economics*, 20 (2), 153–82.

Elson, D. and R. Pearson (1981), 'The subordination of women and the internationalisation of factory production', in K. Young, C. Wolkowitz and R. McCullagh (eds.), *Of Marriage and the Market: Women's Subordination in International Perspective*, CSE Books, London, pp. 144-66.

Evans, P. (1996), 'Using crosscountry variances to evaluate growth theories', *Journal of Economic Dynamics and Control*, 20, 1027–49.

Federation of Malaya (1950), *Draft Development Plan (1950–1955)*, Government Printer, Kuala Lumpur.

Federation of Malaya (1961), *Second Five Year Plan, 1961–1965*, Government Printing Office, Kuala Lumpur.

Feinstein, C. (1999), 'Structural change in the developed countries during the twentieth century', *Oxford Review of Economic Policy*, 15 (4), 35–55.

Felipe, J. (1998), 'The role of the manufacturing sector in Southeast Asian development: a test of Kaldor's First Law', *Journal of Post Keynesian Economics*, 20 (3), 463–85.

Filippini, C., F. Targetti and A.P. Thirlwall (1996), *Nicholas Kaldor: Causes of Growth and Stagnation in the World Economy*, Cambridge University Press, Milano.

Fingleton, B. and J.S.L. McCombie (1998), 'Increasing returns and economic growth: some evidence for manufacturing from the European Union regions', *Oxford Economic Papers*, 50, 89–105.

Fishlow, A. (1990), 'The Latin American state', *Journal of Economic Perspectives*, 4 (3) 61–74.

Fisk, E.K. and H. Osman Rani (1982), *The Political Economy of Malaysia*, Oxford University Press, Kuala Lumpur.

Frankel, M. (1962), 'The production function in allocation and growth: a synthesis', *American Economic Review*, 52, 995–1002.

Friedman, M. (1962), *Capitalism and Freedom*, University of Chicago Press, Chicago.

Fuentes, A. and B. Ehrenreich (1982), *Women in the Global Factory*, Institute for New Communications, New York.

Galbraith, J.K. (1983), *The Voice of the Poor: Essays in Economic and Political Persuasion*, Harvard University Press, Cambridge, MA.

Galbraith, J.K. (1994), *The World Economy Since the Wars: A Personal View*, Sinclair-Stevenson, London.

Galton, F. (1886), 'Regression towards mediocrity in hereditary stature', *Journal of the Anthropological Institute of Great Britain and Ireland*, 15, 246–363.

Gan K. P. (1995), 'Human capital formation: a public policy approach', *Singapore Economic Review*, 40 (2), 159–83.

Gapinski, J. (1982), *Macro Economic Theory: Statics, Dynamic and Policy*, McGraw-Hill, New York.

Gapinski, J. (1997), 'A tigers' tale of two cities', *Asia Pacific Journal of Economics and Business*, 1, 79–94.

Gapinski, J. (1998), 'Economic growth in the Asia Pacific region', *Asia Pacific Journal of Economics and Business*, 2 (1), 68–91.

Garegnani, P. (1970), 'Heterogeneous capital, the production function and the theory of distribution', *Review of Economic Studies*, 37, 407–36.

Gerschenkron, A. (1962), *Economic Backwardness in Historical Perspective, A Book Essays*, Belknap Press of Harvard University Press, Cambridge, MA.

Gills, M., D.H. Perkins, M. Roemer and D.H. Snodgrass (1996) *Economics of Development*, W.W. Norton & Company, New York.

Glomm, G. and B. Ravikumar (1994), 'Public investment in infrastructure in a simple growth model', *Journal of Economic Dynamics and Control*, 18 (6), 1173–87.

Goh, P.C. (1999), 'The semiconductor industry in Malaysia', in K.S. Jomo, G. Felker and R. Rasiah (eds), *Industrial Technology Development in Malaysia: Industry and Firm Studies*, Routledge, London, pp.125–49.

Gomez, E.T. and K.S. Jomo (1997), *Malaysia's Political Economy: Politics, Patronage and Profits*, Cambridge University Press, Cambridge.

Grace, E. (1990), *Shortcircuiting Labour: Unionising Electronic Workers in Malaysia*, INSAN, Kuala Lumpur.

Grammy, A.P. and D. Assane (1996), 'New evidence on the effect of human capital on economic growth', *Applied Economics Letters*, 4, 121–4.

Granger, C.W.J. (1997), 'On modeling the long run in applied economics', *Economic Journal*, 107, 169–77.

Greenwald, B.C. and J.E. Stiglitz (1986), 'Externalities in economies with imperfect information and incomplete markets', *Quarterly Journal of Economics*, 101 (2), 229–64.

Grossman, G. and E. Helpman (1990), 'Trade innovation and growth', *American Economic Review*, 80 (2), 86–91.

Grossman, G. and E. Helpman (1991), *Innovation and Growth in the Global Economy*, MIT Press, Cambridge, MA.

Grossman, G. and E. Helpman (1994), 'Endogenous innovation in the theory of growth', *Journal of Economic Perspectives*, 8 (1), 23–44.

Guyton, L.E. (1994), *Japanese FDI and the Transfer of Japanese Consumers Electronics Production to Malaysia*, United Nations Development Programme, Kuala Lumpur.

Hahn, F.H. (1989), 'Kaldor on growth', *Cambridge Journal of Economics*, 13 (1), 47–57.

Hahn, F.H. and R.C.O. Matthews (1964), 'The theory of economic growth: a survey', *Economic Journal*, 74, 779–902.

Harberger, A.C. (1996), 'Reflections on economic growth in Asia and the Pacific', *Journal of Asian Economics*, 7 (3), 365–92.

Harcourt, G.C. (1963), 'A critique of Mr Kaldor's model of income distribution and economic growth', *Australian Economic Papers*, 2 (1), 20–36.

Harcourt, G.C. (1972), *Some Cambridge Controversies in the Theory of Capital*, Cambridge University Press, Cambridge.

Harcourt, G.C. (1976), 'The Cambridge controversy: old ways and new horizons – or dead end?', *Oxford Economic Papers*, 28 (1), 25–65.

Harcourt, G.C. (1982), 'Capital theory much ado about something', in P. Kerr (ed.), *The Social Science Imperialists Selected Essays*, Routledge and Kegan Paul, London.

Harcourt, G.C. (1988), 'Nicholas Kaldor 12 May 1908 – 30 September 1986', *Economica*, 55 (218), 159–70.

Harcourt, G.C. (2001), *50 Years a Keynesian and Other Essays*, Palgrave, New York.

Harrison, A. (1996), 'Openness and growth: a time-series, cross-country analysis from developing countries', *Journal of Development Economics*, 48 (2), 419–47.

Hart, P.E. (1995), 'Galtonian regression across countries and the convergence of productivity', *Oxford Bulletin of Economics and Statistics*, 57 (3), 287–93.

Helpman, E. and A. Rangel (1999), 'Adjusting to a new technology: experience and training', *Journal of Economic Growth*, 4, 359–83.

Hirschman, A. (1958), *Strategy of Economic Development*, Yale University Press, New Haven, CT.

Hirschman, C. (2001), *Hirschman on Drabble: An Economic History of Malaysia c1800–1990*, online: http://eh.net/bookreviews/library, accessed 12 July 2001.

Hobday, M. (1995), 'East Asian latecomer firms: learning the technology of electronics', *World Development*, 23 (7), 1171–93.

Hoffmann, L. and S.E. Tan (1980), *Industrial Growth, Employment, and Foreign Investment in Peninsular Malaysia*, Oxford University Press, Oxford.

Hoerr, O.D. (1975), 'Education, income, and equity in Malaysia', in D. Lim (ed.), *Readings on Malaysian Economic Development*, Oxford University Press, Kuala Lumpur.

Huang, F.M. (1996), *Population and the Asian Economic Miracle: Education and Earning in Taiwan*, Discussion paper no. 9716, Institute of Economics, Academia Sinica, Taiwan.

Hunt, E.K. (1979), *History of Economic Thought: A Critical Perspective*, Wadsworth Publishing Company, Belmont, CA.

Huq, A. (1994), *Malaysia's Economic Success*, Pelanduk Publications, Kuala Lumpur.

Immigration Department Malaysia, online, http://www.imi.gov.my/frameeng.html, accessed 15 July 2000.

Inada, I.K. (1963), 'On a two-sector model of economic growth: comments and a generalization', *Review of Economic Studies*, 30 (June), 119–27.

Institute of South East Asian Studies (1997), *Regional Outlook: Southeast Asia 1997–98*, Singapore.

Institute of South East Asian Studies (1998), *Regional Outlook: Southeast Asia 1998–99*, Singapore.

International Bank of Reconstruction and Development – IBRD (1955), *The Economic Development of Malaya*, Johns Hopkins Press, Baltimore, MD.

International Labour Organization (1970), *Towards Full Employment*, International Labor Organization, Geneva.

International Monetary Fund (1986), *International Financial Statistic Yearbook*, Washington, DC.

International Monetary Fund (1998), *International Financial Statistic Yearbook*, Washington, DC.

Jesudason, J.V. (1989), *Ethnicity and the Economy: The State, Chinese Business and Multi-Nationals in Malaysia*, Oxford University Press, Singapore.

Jomo, K.S. (1990), *Growth and Structural Change in the Malaysian Economy*, Macmillan, London.

Jomo, K.S. (1991), 'Wither Malaysia's new economic policy?' *Pacific Affairs*, 63 (4), 469–99.

Jomo, K.S. (ed.) (1993), *Industrialising Malaysia: Policy, Performance, Prospects*, Routledge, London.

Jomo, K.S. (1994), *U-Turn? Malaysian Economic Development Policy after 1990*, James Cook University of North Queensland, Townsville.

Jomo, K.S. and C. Edwards (1993), 'Malaysian industrialisation in historical perspective', in K.S. Jomo (ed.), *Industrialising Malaysia: Policy, Performance, Prospects*, Routledge, London, pp. 14–39

Jomo, K.S. and P. Todd (1994), *Trade Unions and the State in Peninsular Malaysia*, Oxford University Press, New York.

Jones, C.I. (1995), 'Time series tests of endogenous growth models', *Quarterly Journal of Economics*, 110, 495–525.

Jones, C.I. (1997), 'On the evolution of the world income distribution', *Journal of Economic Perspectives*, 11 (3), 19–36.

Jorgenson, D.W. (1988), 'Productivity and postwar US economic growth', *Journal of Economic Perspective*, 2, 23–42.

Jorgenson, D.W. and Z. Griliches (1967), 'The explanation of productivity growth', *Review of Economic Studies*, 34, 249–83.

Kaldor, N. (1957), 'A model of economic growth', *Economic Journal*, 67, 259–300.

Kaldor, N. Kaldor, N. (1960), *Essays on Economic Stability and Growth*, Gerald Duckworth & Co., London.

Kaldor, N. (1966), *Causes of the Slow Rate of Economic Growth of the United Kingdom*, University of Cambridge Press, Cambridge.

Kaldor, N. (1967), *Strategic Factors in Economic Development*, Cornell University Press, New York State School of Industrial and Labor Relations, Ithaca, NY.

Kaldor, N. (1968), 'Productivity and growth in manufacturing industry: a reply', *Economica*, 35 (140), 385–91.

Kaldor, N. (1970), 'Some fallacies in the interpretation of Kaldor', *Review of Economic Studies*, 37, 1–7.

Kaldor, N. (1972), *Advanced Technology in a Strategy for Development: Some Lessons from Britain's Experience in Automation and Developing Countries*, ILO, Geneva.

Kaldor, N. (1985), *Economics without Equilibrium*, M.E. Sharpe, Armonk, NY.

Kaldor, N. and J.A. Mirrlees (1962), 'A new model of economic growth', *Review of Economic Studies*, 29, 174–92.

Kasper, W. (1974), *Malaysia: A Study in Successful Economic Development*, American Enterprise Institute for Public Policy Research, Washington, DC.

Kawai, H. (1994), 'International comparative analysis of economic growth: trade liberalization and productivity', *Developing Economics*, 32 (4), 373–97.

Keefer, P. and S. Knack (1998), 'Political stability and economic stagnation', in S. Borner and M. Paldam (eds), *The Political Dimension of Economic Growth: Proceedings of the IEA Conference Held in San Jose, Costa Rica*, St Martin's Press, New York.

Kendrick, J.W. (1961), *Productivity Trends in the United States*, Princeton University Press, Princeton, NJ.

Kendrick, J.W. (1973), *Postwar Productivity Trends in the United States, 1948–1969*, NBER, Columbia University Press, New York.

Kenny, C. and D. Williams (2001), 'What do we know about economic growth? Or, why don't we know very much?', *World Development*, 29 (1), 1–22.

Keynes, J.M. (1936), *The General Theory of Employment, Interest, and Money*, Macmillan, London.

Khan, M.S. and M.S. Kumar (1997), 'Public and private investment and the growth process in developing countries', *Oxford Bulletin of Economics and Statistics*, 59 (1), 69–88.

Khong, H.L. (1991), 'Service sector in Malaysia: structure and change', PhD thesis, University of Cambridge, Cambridge.

Khoo, B.T. (1994), 'Mahathir Mohamad: a critical study of ideology, biography and society in Malaysian politics', PhD thesis, Flinders University, Adelaide.

Khor, K.P. (1983), *Recession and the Malaysian Economy*, Institut Masyarakat, Kuala Lumpur.

Kim, J.L. and L.J. Lau (1994), 'The sources of economic growth of the East Asian newly industrialized countries', *Journal of the Japanese and International Economies*, 8, 235–71.

Kim, J.L. and L.J. Lau (1995), 'The role of human capital in the economic growth of the East Asian newly industrialized countries', *Asia Pacific Economic Review*, 1 (3), 3–22.

King, J.E. (ed.) (1994), *Economic Growth in Theory and Practice*, Edward Elgar Publishing Aldershot, UK. and Brookfield, US.

Knack, S. and D. Keefer (1995), 'Institutions and economic performance: cross-country tests using alternative institutional measures', *Economics and Politics*, 7 (3), 207–27.

Krugman, P. (1994), 'The myth of Asia's miracle', *Foreign Affairs*, December, 62–78.

Krugman, P. (1997), *The Age of Diminished Expectations*, MIT Press, Cambridge, MA.

Krugman, P. (1998), *The Return of Depression Economics*, Penguin Press, London.

Kuznets, S. (1957), 'Quantitative aspects of economic growth of nations: II. Industrial distribution of national product and labor force', *Economic Development and Cultural Change*, 5, Supplement.

Landes, D. (1969), *The Unbound Prometheus: Technological Change and Industrial Development in Western Europe from 1750 to the Present*, Cambridge University Press, Cambridge.

Lang, K. and D. Kropp (1986), 'Human capital versus sorting: the effects of compulsory attendance laws', *Quarterly Journal of Economics*, 101, 609–24.

Lau, L.J., D.T. Jamison and F.F. Louat (1991), *Education and Productivity in Developing Countries: An Aggregate Production Function Approach*, Working

Paper, no. 612, Policy, Research and External Affairs, World Bank, Washington, DC.

Layard, R. and G. Psacharopolous (1974), 'The screening hypothesis and the returns to education', *Journal of Political Economy*, 82 (5), 985–98.

Lee, H.L. (1978), *Public Policies and Economic Diversification in West Malaysia, 1957–1970*, University of Malaya Press, Kuala Lumpur.

Levine, R. and D. Renelt (1991), *Crosscountry Studies of Growth and Policy: Methodological, Conceptual and Statistical Problems*, World Bank Policy Research Working Paper, No. 608.

Levine, R. and D. Renelt (1992), 'A sensitivity analysis of cross-country growth regressions', *American Economic Review*, 82 (4), 942–63.

Levine, R. and S. Zervos (1993), 'What we have learned about policy growth from cross-country regressions', *American Economic Review*, 83(2), 426–30.

Lim, D. (1973), *Economic Growth and Development in West Malaysia, 1947–1970*, Oxford University Press, Kuala Lumpur.

Lim, D. (ed.) (1975), *Readings on Malaysian Economic Development*, Oxford University Press, Kuala Lumpur.

Lim, D. (1983), *Further Readings on Malaysian Economic Development*, Oxford University Press, Kuala Lumpur.

Lipset, S.M. (1959), 'Some social prerequisites of democracy: economic development and political legitimacy', *American Political Science Review*, 53, 69–105.

Lucas, R.E., Jr (1988), 'On the mechanics of economic development', *Journal of Monetary Economics*, 22 (1), 3–42.

Lucas, R.E., Jr (2000), 'Some macroeconomics for the 21st century', *Journal of Economic Perspectives*, 14 (1), 159–68.

Maddison, A. (1982), *Phases of Capitalist Development*, Oxford University Press, Oxford.

Maddison, A (1983), 'A comparison of levels of GDP per capita in developed and developing countries, 1700–1980', *Journal of Economic History*, 43, 27–41.

Maddison, A (1987), 'Growth and slowdown in advanced capitalist economies: techniques of quantitative assessment', *Journal of Economic Literature*, 25, 649–98.

Maddison, A (1991), *Dynamic Forces in Capitalist Development: A Long-Run Comparative View*, Oxford University Press, Oxford.

Maddison, A (1993), *Explaining the Economic Performance of Nation 1829–1989*, Working Paper No. 174, Department of Economics, Australian National University, Canberra.

Mahathir, M. (1970), *The Malay Dilemma*, Times Books International, Singapore.

Malaysia (1965), *First Malaysia Plan 1966–1970*, Government Press, Kuala Lumpur.

Malaysia (1971), *Second Malaysia Plan 1971–1975*, Government Press, Kuala Lumpur.

Malaysia (1976), *Third Malaysia Plan 1976–1980*, Government Press, Kuala Lumpur.

Malaysia (1981) *Fourth Malaysia Plan 1981–1985*, Government Press, Kuala Lumpur.

Malaysia (1986), *Fifth Malaysia Plan 1986–1990*, Government Press, Kuala Lumpur.

Malaysia (1991), *Sixth Malaysia Plan 1991–1995*, Government Press, Kuala Lumpur.

Malaysia (1996), *Seventh Malaysia Plan 1996–2000*, Government Press, Kuala Lumpur.

Malaysia (2001), *Eighth Malaysia Plan 2001–2005*, Government Press, Kuala Lumpur.

Mankiw, N.G., D. Romer and D.N. Weil (1992), 'A contribution to the empirics of economic growth', *Quarterly Journal of Economics*, 107, 407–37.

Marshall, A. (1922), *Principles of Economics*, (8th edn), Macmillan, London.

Martin, W. and D. Mitra (2001), 'Productivity growth in agriculture versus manufacturing', *Economic Development and Cultural Change*, 49 (2), 403–22.

Maurer, R. (1994), *International Trade and Economic Growth: A Survey of Empirical Studies*. Kiel Working Paper, no. 660.

Mauro, P. (1995), 'Corruption and growth', *Quarterly Journal of Economics*, 110, 681–712.

Mayer, T. (1992), *Truth Versus Precision in Economics*, Edward Elgar, Aldershot, UK and Brookfield, US.

McCallum, B.T. (1969), 'The instability of Kaldorian models', *Oxford Economic Papers*, New Series, 21, 56–65.

McCombie, J.S.L. (1998), 'In defense of Kaldor: A comment on Casillas's "Kaldor versus Prebisch on employment and industrialization"', *Journal of Post Keynesian Economics*, 21 (2), 353–61.

McCombie, J.S.L. and J. de Ridder (1983), 'Increasing returns, productivity, and output growth: the case of the United States', *Journal of Post Keynesian Economics*, 5 (3), 373–87.

Means, G.P. (1991), *Malaysian Politics: The Second Generation*, Oxford University Press, Singapore.

Mehmet, O. and Y.Y. Hoong (1986), *Human Capital Formation in Malaysian University: A Socio-Economic Profile of the 1983 Graduates*, Institute of Advanced Studies, University of Malaya, Kuala Lumpur.

Minami, R. (1986), *The Economic Development of Japan: A Quantitative Study*, St Martin, New York.

Ministry of Finance, Malaysia, *Economic Report*, (various years 1982–2005), Percetakan Nasional Malaysia Berhad, Kuala Lumpur.

Munnell, A.H. (1992), 'Infrastructure investment and economic growth', *Journal of Economic Perspective*, 64 (4), 189–98.

Myrdal, G. (1957), *Economic Theory and Underdeveloped Regions*, Duckworth, London.

Narayanan, S. and Y.W. Lai (1993), 'Human resources constraints on technology transfer: an empirical analysis of the electronics and electrical sector in Penang, Malaysia', *Singapore Economic Review*, 38 (2), 155–65.

Narayanan, S. and Y.W. Lai (2000), 'Technological maturity and development without research: the challenge for Malaysian manufacturing', *Development and Change*, 31 (2), 435–57.

Nayagam, J. (1991), 'Labour issues in the plantation sector', paper presented at the National Seminar on Agricultural Primary Commodities, June, Kuala Lumpur.

Ndulu, B.J. and S.A. O'Connell (1999), 'Governance and growth in Sub-Saharan Africa', *Journal of Economic Perspective*, 13 (3), 41–66.

Nehru, V. and A. Dhareshwar (1993), 'A new database on physical capital stock: sources, methodology and results', *Rivista de Analisis Economico*, 8 (1), 37–59.

Nelson, R.R. (1996), *The Sources of Economic Growth*, Harvard University Press, Cambridge, MA.

Nelson, R.R. (1997), 'How new is new growth theory', *Challenge*, 40 (5), 29–58.

Nelson, R.R. and H. Pack (1999), 'The Asian miracle and modern growth theory', *Economic Journal*, 109, 416–36.

Nelson, R.R. and E. Phelps (1966), 'Investment in humans, technological diffusion, and economic growth', *American Economic Review*, 56 (2), 69–75.

Nelson, R.R. and S. Winter (1982), *An Evolutionary Theory of Economic Change*, Harvard University Press, Cambridge, MA.

Obstfeld, M. and K. Rogoff (1996), *Foundations of International Macroeconomic*, MIT Press, Cambridge, MA.

Okun, A.M. (1962), 'Potential GNP: its measurement and significance', in *Proceedings of the Business and Economics Statistics Section, American Statistical Association*, American Statistical Association, Washington, DC, pp. 98–103.

Onn, F.G. (1989), *The Malaysian Economic Challenge in the 1990s: Transformation for Growth*, Longman, Singapore.

Pack, H. (1994), 'Endogenous growth: intellectual appeal and empirical shortcomings', *Journal of Economic Perspectives*, 8, 55–72.

Palley, T.I. (1996), 'Growth theory in a Keynesian mode: some Keynesian foundations for new endogenous growth theory', *Journal of Post Keynesian Economics*, 19 (1), 113–35.

Pencavel, J. (1993), 'Higher education, economic growth, and earnings', in W.E. Becker and D.R. Lewis (eds.), *American Higher Education and Economic Growth*, Kluwer Academic Publishers, MA, pp.51–85.

Pesaran, M.H. and B. Pesaran (1997), *Microfit 4.0*, Oxford University Press, Oxford.

Pesaran, M.H., Y. Shin and R.J. Smith (1996), *Testing for the Existence of a Long Run Relationship*, Department of Applied Economics Working Paper no. 9622, University of Cambridge, Cambridge.

Pillai, P. (1992), *People On the Move: An Overview of Recent Immigration and Emigration in Malaysia*, Institute of Strategic and International Studies, Kuala Lumpur.

Pollard, S. (1981), *Peaceful Conquest: The Industrialisation of Europe 1760–1970*, Oxford University Press, Oxford.

Pritchett, L. (1997), 'Divergence, big time', *Journal of Economic Perspective*, 11 (3), 3–17.

Pritchett, L. (1998), *Patterns of Economic Growth: Hills, Plateaus, Mountains and Plains*, World Bank Policy Research Working Paper, No. 1947.

Psacharopoulos, G. (1973), *Returns to Education: An International Comparison*, Elsevier, San Francisco, CA.

Psacharopoulos, G. (1975), *Earnings and Education in OECD Countries*, OECD, Paris.

Psacharopoulos, G. (1981), 'Returns to education: an updated international comparison', *Comparative Education*, 17, 321–41.

Psacharopoulos, G. (1985), 'Returns to education: a further international update and implications', *Journal of Human Resources*, 20, 583–604.

Psacharopoulos, G. (1994), 'Returns to investment in education: a global update', *World Development*, 22 (9), 1325–43.

Puthucheary, J.J. (1960), *Ownership and Control in the Malayan Economy*, Eastern Universities Press, Singapore.

Quah, D.T. (1993), 'Galton's fallacy and tests of the convergence hypothesis', in T.M. Andersen and K.O. Moene (eds), *Endogenous Growth*, Blackwell, Oxford, pp. 37–54.

Quah, D.T. (1995), *Empirics for Economic Growth and Convergence*, Discussion Paper No. 253, Centre for Economic Performance, London.

Quah, D.T. (1996a), 'Empirics for economic growth and convergence', *European Economic Review*, 40 (6), 1353–75.

Quah, D.T. (1996b), 'Twin peaks: growth and convergence in models of distribution dynamics', *Economic Journal*, 106 (437), 1045–055.

Quah, D.T. (1997), 'Empirics for growth and distribution: stratification, polarization, and convergence clubs', *Journal of Economic Growth*, 2 (1), 27–59.

Osman Rani, H. and I.M. Salleh (1994), 'The public sector', in K.S. Jomo (ed.), *Malaysia's Economy in the Nineties*, Pelanduk Publications, Petaling Jaya, pp. 195–232.

Ranis, G., F. Stewart and A. Ramirez (2000), 'Economic growth and human development', *World Development*, 28 (2), 197–219.

Rao, V.V.B. (1980), *Malaysia: Development Pattern and Policy 1947–1971*, Singapore University Press, Singapore.

Rao, V.V.B. and C. Lee (1995), 'Sources of growth in the Singapore economy and its manufacturing and service sectors', *Singapore Economic Review*, 40 (1), 83–115.

Rasiah, R. (1988), 'the Semiconductor Industry in Penang: Implication for the New International Division of Labour Theories', *Journal of Contemporary Asia*, 18 (1), 24-46.

Rasiah, R. and I. Shari (2001), 'Market, government and Malaysia's new economic policy', *Cambridge Journal of Economics*, 25 (1), 57–78.

Rebelo, S. (1991), 'Long-run policy analysis and long run growth', *Journal of Political Economy*, 99 (3), 500–521.

Riley, J.G. (1976), 'Information, screening and human capital', *American Economic Review*, 66, 227–52.

Riley, J.G. (1978), 'Testing the educational screening hypothesis', *Journal of Political Economy*, 8 (5/Pt 2), s227–s252.

Robinson, J. (1953), 'The Production Function and the Theory of Capital', *Review of Economic Studies*, vol. 21, 81-106.

Robinson, J. (1956), *The Accumulation of Capital*, MacMillan, London.

Robinson, J. (1962), *Essays in the Theory of Economic Growth*, MacMillan, London.

Robinson, J. (1965), 'Solow on the rate of return', in J. Robinson (ed.), *Collected Economic Papers*, vol. 3, Blackwell, London.

Robinson, J. (1978), *Contribution to Modern Economics*, Basil Blackwell, Oxford.

Robinson, J. (1980), 'Time in economic theory', *Kyklos*, 33 (2), 219–29.

Rodrik, D. (1998), 'Why do more open economies have bigger governments?' *Journal of Political Economy*, 106, 997–1032.

Rodriguez, F. and D. Rodrik (1999), *Trade Policy and Economic Growth: A Skeptics Guide to the Cross-National Evidence*, working paper, University of Maryland, College Park, MD.

Romer, D. (1996), *Advanced Macroeconomics*, McGraw-Hill, New York.

Romer, P.M. (1986), 'Increasing returns and long run growth', *Journal of Political Economy*, 94, 1002–37.

Romer, P.M. (1987), 'Crazy explanations for the productivity slow-down', *NBER Macro-economics Annual*, MIT Press, Cambridge, MA.

Romer, P.M. (1990), 'Endogenous technical change', *Journal of Political Economy*, 98, s71–s102.

Romer, P.M. (1993), 'Idea gaps and object gaps in economic development', *Journal of Monetary Economics*, 33, 543–73.

Romer, P.M. (1994), 'The origins of endogenous growth', *Journal of Economic Perspectives*, 8, 3–22.

Rosenberg, N. (1994), *Exploring the Black Box: Technology, Economics, and History*, Cambridge University Press, Cambridge.

Rothschild, K.W. (1959), 'The limitations of economic growth models: critical remarks on some aspects of Mr. Kaldor's model', *Kyklos*, 12 (4), 567–86.

Rowan, H. (ed.) (1998), *Behind East Asian Growth: The Political and Social Foundations of Prosperity*, Routledge, London.

Rowthorn, R.E. (1975), 'What remains of Kaldor's Law?' *Economic Journal*, 85, 10–19.

Ruggles, R. (1979), *Employment and Unemployment Statistics as Indexes of Economic Activity and Capacity Utilization*, Background Paper No. 28, National Commission on Employment and Unemployment Statistics, Washington, DC.

Sala-i-Martin, X. (1996), 'The classical approach to convergence analysis', *Economic Journal*, 106, 1019–36.

Salter, W.E.G. (1962), 'Marginal labour and investment coefficients of Australian manufacturing industry', *Economic Record*, 38 (82), 137–56.

Salter, W.E.G. (1966), with addendum by W.B. Reddaway, *Productivity and Technical Change*, Cambridge University Press, Cambridge.

Sarel, M. (1994), *On the Dynamics of Economic Growth*, IMF Working Paper 94/138, International Monetary Fund, Washington.

Sarel, M. (1996), 'Growth in East Asia: what we can and what we cannot infer from it', *Economic Issues 1*, International Monetary Fund, Washington.

Sarel, M. (1997), *Growth and Productivity in ASEAN Countries*, IMF Working Paper WP/97/97, International Monetary Fund, Washington.

Sato, K. (1966), 'On the adjustment time in neoclassical growth models', *Review of Economic Studies*, 33, 263–8.

Schmockler, J. (1969), *Innovation and Economic Growth*, Harvard University Press, Cambridge, MA.

Schultz, T.W. (1961), 'Investments in human capital', *American Economic Review*, 51 (1), 1–17.

Schultz, T.W. (1975), 'The value of the ability to deal with disequilibria', *Journal of Economic Literature*, 13, 827–42

Schumpeter, J.A. (1934), *The Theory of Economic Development*, Harvard University Press, Cambridge, MA.

Schwarz, G. (1992), 'Democracy and market-oriented reform: a love–hate relationship', *Journal of Political Economy*, 96, 652–62.

Scott, M.F.G. (1993), 'Explaining economic growth', *American Economic Review*, 83 (2), 421–5.

Setterfield, M. (1998), '"History versus equilibrium" and the theory of economic growth', *Cambridge Journal of Economics*, 21 (3), 365–78.

Shah, R.K. (1991), 'Fallibility in human organization and political systems', *Journal of Economic Perspectives*, 5, 67–88.

Shaikh, A. (1974), 'Laws of Production and Laws of Algebra: The Humbug Production Function', *Review of Economics and Statistics*, 56 (1), 115–20.

Sharma, B. (1996), *International Relations in ASEAN: A Comparative Study*, International Law Book Services, Kuala Lumpur.

Shell, K. (1969), 'Applications of Pontryagin's maximum principle to economics', in H.W. Kuhn and G.P. Szego (eds), *Mathematical Systems Theory and Economics*, vol. 1, Springer-Verlag, Berlin, pp. 241–92.

Singh, A. (1994), 'Openness and the market friendly approach to development: learning the right lessons from development experience', *World Development*, 22 (12), 1811–23.

Singh, A. (1998), 'Growth: its sources and consequences', in G. Thompson (ed.), *Economic Dynamism in the Asia-Pacific*, Routledge, London, pp. 55–82.

Smith, A. (1776), *An Inquiry into the Nature and Causes of the Wealth of Nations*, Strahan & Caddell, London.

Smolny, W. (2000), 'Post-war growth, productivity convergence and reconstruction', *Oxford Bulletin of Economics and Statistics*, 65 (5), pp. 589–606.

Snodgrass, D.R. (1975a), 'The fiscal system as an income redistributor in West Malaysia', in D. Lim (ed.), *Readings on Malaysian Economic Development*, Oxford University Press, Kuala Lumpur, pp. 269–91.

Snodgrass, D.R. D.R. (1975b), 'Trends and patterns in Malaysian income distribution, 1957–70', in D. Lim. (ed.), *Readings on Malaysian Economic Development*, Oxford University Press, Kuala Lumpur, pp. 251–68.

Snodgrass, D.R. D.R. (1980), *Inequality and Economic Development in Malaysia*, Oxford University Press, Kuala Lumpur.

Snodgrass, D.R. (1998), 'Education in Korea and Malaysia', in H. Rowan (ed.), *Behind East Asian Growth: The Political and Social Foundations of Prosperity*, Routledge, London, pp.165–84.

Solow, R.M. (1956), 'A contribution to the theory of economic growth', *Quarterly Journal of Economics*, 70, 65–94.

Solow, R.M. (1957), 'Technical change and the aggregate production function', *Review of Economics and Statistics*, 39, 312–20.

Solow, R.M. (1960), 'Investment and technical progress', in K.J. Arrow, S. Karlin and P. Suppes (eds), *Mathematical Methods in the Social Sciences 1959*, Stanford University Press, Stanford, CA, pp.89-104.

Solow, R.M. (1994), 'Perspective on growth theory', *Journal of Economic Perspectives*, 8 (1), 45–54.

Solow, R.M. (2000), *Growth Theory: An Exposition*, Oxford University Press, New York.

Spence, A.M. (1974), *Market Signalling: Information Transfer in Hiring and Related Processes*, Harvard University Press, Cambridge, MA.

Spinanger, D. (1986), *Industrialization Policies and Regional Economic Development in Malaysia*, Singapore, Oxford University Press.

Sraffa, P. (1960), *Production of Commodities by Means of Commodities: Prelude to a Critique of Economic Theory*, Cambridge University Press, Cambridge.

Srinivasan, T.N. (1985), 'Neoclassical political economy, the state, and economic development' *Asian Development Review*, 3, 93–110.

Stern, N. (1991a), 'Public policy and the economics of development', *European Economic Review*, 35, 241–71.

Stern, N. (1991b), 'The determinants of growth', *Economic Journal*, 101, 122–33.

Stiglitz, J.E. (ed.) (1966), *The Collected Scientific Papers of Paul A. Samuelson*, 2 vols, MIT Press, Cambridge, MA.

Stiglitz, J.E. (1975), 'The theory of screening, education and the distribution of income', *American Economic Review*, 65, 283–300.

Stiglitz, J.E. (1986), The new development economics', *World Development*, 14, 257–65.

Swan, T.W. (1956), 'Economic Growth and Capital Accumulation', Economic Record, vol.32 (2), pp.334–61.

Targetti, F. and A. Foti (1997), 'Growth and productivity: a model of cumulative growth and catching up', *Cambridge Journal of Economics*, 21 (1), 27–43.

Taubman, P. and T. Wales (1973), 'Higher education, mental ability and screening', *Journal of Political Economy*, 81, 28–36.

Taylor, R.J. (2004), 'Can labour-savings, capital-intensive production techniques reduce unemployment rates in developing countries? Evidence from Malaysia', *Australian Journal of Labour Economics*, 7 (4), 513–23.

Temple, J.R.W. (1998), 'Equipment investment and the Solow model', *Oxford Economic Papers*, 50, 39–62.

Tham, S.Y. (1995), 'Productivity, growth and development in Malaysia', *Singapore Economic Review*, 40 (1), 41–63.

Thirlwall, A.P. (1983), 'A plain man's guide to Kaldor's growth laws', *Journal of Post Keynesian Economics*, 5 (3), 345–58.

Thirlwall, A.P. (1999), *Growth and Development with Special Reference to Developing Economies*, 6th edn, Macmillan, London.

Thomas, V. and Y. Wang (1992), 'Government policies and productivity growth: is East Asia an exception?' presented at World Bank Workshop on The Role of Government and Asian Success, East-West Center, Hawaii.

Thompson, G. (ed.) (1998), *Economic Dynamism in the Asia-Pacific: The Growth of Integration and Competitiveness*, Routledge, London.

Thorburn, T. (1977), *Primary Commodity Exports and Economic Development: Theory, Evidence and a Study of Malaysia*, John Wiley, London.

Toh, K.W. and K.S. Jomo (1983), 'The nature of the Malaysian State and Its implications for development planning', in K.S. Jomo and J.R. Wells (eds), *The Fourth Malaysian Plan: Economic Perspectives*, Malaysian Economic Association, Kuala Lumpur, pp. 22–44.

Turner, M.S. (1993), *Nicholas Kaldor and the Real World*, M.E. Sharpe, New York.

Turnham, D. and I. Jaeger (1971), *The Employment Problem in Less Developed Countries: A Review of Evidence*, OECD Development Center, Paris.

United Nations (1997), *Trade and Development Report: Globalization, Distribution and Growth*, United Nations, New York.

Valdés, B. (1999), *Economic Growth: Theory, Empirics and Policy*, Edward Elgar, Cheltenham, UK and Northampton, MA, USA.

Verdoorn, P.J. (1949), 'Fattori che regolano lo sviluppo della produttivita del lavoro', *L'Industria*, 1, pp. 3–10.

Von Neumann, J. (1945), 'A model of general equilibrium', *Review of Economic Studies*, 13 (1), 1–9.

Wilson, P. (2000), 'The dilemma of a more advanced developing country: conflicting views on the development strategy of Singapore', *Developing Economies*, 38 (1), 105–34.

World Bank (1983), *Accelerated Development in Sub-Saharan Africa: An Agenda for Action*, World Bank, Washington, DC.

World Bank (1993), *The East Asian Miracle: Economic Growth and Public Policy*, Oxford University Press, Oxford.

World Bank (1997), *World Development Report 1997: The State in a Changing World*, Oxford University Press, Oxford.

World Bank (1999), *World Development Report: Knowledge for Development*, Oxford University Press, Oxford.

World Bank (2000), *World Development Report 2000–01*, Oxford University Press, Oxford.

World Bank (2002), *Global Economic Prospects and the Developing Countries*, Washington, DC.

Yi Feng (2001), 'Political freedom, political instability, and policy uncertainty: a study of political institutions and private investment in developing countries', *International Studies Quarterly*, 45 (2), 271–94.

You, J.I. (1994), 'Macroeconomic structure, endogenous technical change and growth', *Cambridge Journal of Economics*, 18, 213–33.

Young, A.A. (1928), 'Increasing returns and economic progress', *Economic Journal*, December, 527–8.

Young, A. (1992), 'A tale of two cities: factor accumulation and technical change in Hong Kong and Singapore', in Olivier J. Blanchard and Stanley Fisher (eds), *NBER Macroeconomics Annual 1992*, MIT Press, Cambridge, MA, pp. 13–54.

Young, A. (1994), 'Lessons from the East Asian NICs: a contrarian view', *European Economic Review*, 38 (3/4), 964–73.

Young, A. (1995), 'The tyranny of numbers: confronting the statistical realities of the East Asian growth experience', *Quarterly Journal of Economics*, 110 (3), 641–80.

Yuan, T. (1983), 'Growth and productivity in Singapore: a supply side analysis', PhD dissertation, Harvard University, MA.

Young, A. (1985), 'Growth without productivity', *Journal of Development Economics*, 18, 25–38.

Index

Abramovitz, M. 146
accumulation of factor inputs 27–9
  and East Asian economic growth
    29–31
age and labour force participation,
  Malaysia 121–2
aggregate demand and productivity
  growth 209–11
aggregate production function, Solow-
  Swan model 10–11
  criticism of 13–16
Aghion, P. 43–4, 96, 162, 187
agricultural sector, Malaysia
  employment 124–5, 126
  exports 111
  value added 110
  wages 170–71
Alavi, R. 35
Alliance coalition, Malaysia 69–70
Anand, S. 66
ARDL *see* Autoregressive-Distributed
  Lag
Arrow, K. 49–50
Aschauer, D.A. 33
assimilation of factor inputs 27–9
assimilation theories 31–6
Autoregressive-Distributed Lag (ARDL)
  190–92
  standard production function 214
  standard production function with
    human capital 216
  standard production function with
    openness 218
  standard production function with
    openness and human capital 220

Barro, R.J. 21, 24, 42, 60, 162
Baumol, W. 21, 22–3
Beaudry, P. 168
Benhabib, J. 162
ß-convergence 20

Bils, M. 162
Blaug, M. 168
Bosworth, B.P. 33, 179
Brouwer, E. 210

Cambridge Controversy 13–16
capital aggregation 188–9
capital controversy 13–16, 188
capital investment
  and economic growth 32–3
  and human capital 187
  and technological progress 180, 206–7
capital-reversing 15
Carvalho, F. 15
case study approach, reasons for 4–7
Casillas, L.R. 159
Chan, G. 168
Chang, H.J. 85
Chen, E.K.Y. 132–3, 195
Chenery, H.B. 107
Chinese community, Malaysia 67, 68
Collier, P. 59
Collins, S.M. 33, 179
conditional convergence 21
convergence 19–27
  arguments against 22–7
  and economic maturity 146
  and production structures 147
  support for 20–22
Cornwall, J. 86, 121, 148
Cornwall, W. 86, 121
Crafts, N.F.R. 5, 55–6, 59, 209
Cripps, T.F. 159
cross-country analysis, limitations 4–6

De Long, J.B. 25, 32
de Ridder, J. 151
Denison, E.F. 162, 168
divergence in growth rates 22–7
Domar growth analysis model 41
double-switching 15

Stern, N. 84, 131
Stiglitz, J.E. 84
Summers, L.H. 32
Summers, P.M. 34, 179, 195
Swan, T.W. 9

Targetti, F. 146
Tarling, R.J. 159
tax incentives for manufacturing,
    Malaysia 99, 101
Taylor, L. 107
technical knowledge, flow of 48–9
technical progress
    and capital investment 180, 206–7
    and economic growth 149
technical progress function (Kaldor) 40,
    41, 45–8, 131–40, 187, 207
    and Malaysia 131–40
technological progress 2
    and economic growth 9–37
    and female labour, Malaysia 130–31
    impact on output and employment
        131–40
    see also total factor productivity
Temple, J.R.W. 4
tertiary education *see* higher education
Tham, S.Y. 35, 179
Thirlwall, A.P. 85
tin exports, Malaysia 74–7
total factor productivity (TFP) 2, 9–10
    criticism of 39
    and economic growth 27–37

estimation 179–80, 188–202
    and human capital 181–6
    Malaysia 35–6, 188–202
    and openness 186–8
trade, effect on economy, Malaysia
    72–6
trade openness, effect on TFP 186–8
Turner, M.S. 131

unemployment, Malaysia 78–9, 139–40
United Nations, income divergence
    report 23
university education *see* higher
    education

Valdés, B. 4
Verdoorn, P.J. 147
Verdoorn's Law 47
Von Neumann, J. 42

Williams, D. 141, 157
Williamson, J.G. 96
women and the labour market, Malaysia
    127–31, 207

Yi Feng 60
You, J.I. 41
Young, A. 27–8, 29, 33
Young, A.A. 42, 210
Yuan, T. 29–30

Zervos, S. 4, 26